MW00773450

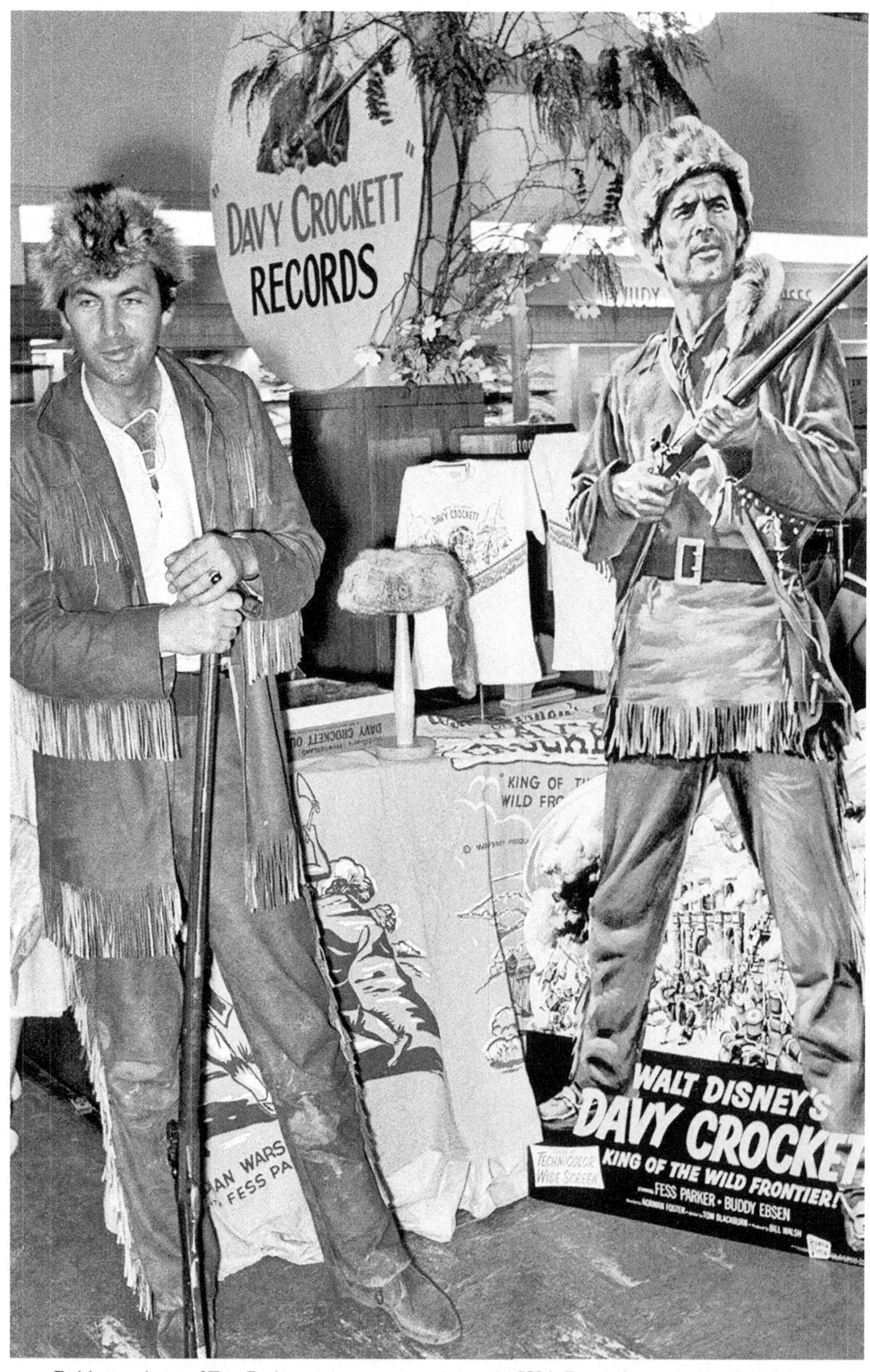


Publicity photo of Fess Parker on a promotional tour for Walt Disney's *Davy Crockett*.

# The Accidental Fame and Lack of Fortune of West Tennessee's David Crockett

**R. Scott Williams**

*I leave this rule,*
*for others when I am dead*
*Be always sure, you*
*are right, then go, a head*

*David Crockett*

Union City, Tennessee

Also by R. Scott Williams

*An Odd Book: How the First Modern Pop Culture Reporter Conquered New York*

*The Forgotten Adventures of Richard Halliburton: A High-Flying Life from Tennessee to Timbuktu*

To my parents

Robert Lafayette Williams
and
Shirley Lovelace Williams

Descendants of the earliest settlers of West Tennessee

The Accidental Fame and Lack of Fortune
of West Tennessee's David Crockett

Book cover design by Tom Martin
TomMartinDesign.com

Illustration by Michelle Williams
based on an 1834 oil painting of
David Crockett by Chester Harding

Edited by Jennifer Wildes

ISBN: 978-0-9986997-4-5

Library of Congress Control Number: 2021910373



Bulk ordering information:
TheRealDavidCrockett.com

"I stood no chance to become great in any other way than by accident."

—David Crockett

"We know not how many ages the fame of this gentleman will last, but he certainly makes a pretty considerable noise in his own time."

—George Pope Morris, *New-York Mirror*, 1834

# Contents

## Prelude

# Also, Who's David Crockett?

In the fifth episode of the twentieth season of the animated series *The Simpsons*, the family arrives at a cabin in the woods to celebrate the Fourth of July. Bart looks at the cabin and says with confidence, "A log cabin? What am I, Davy Crockett?" He then looks at his father, Homer, and adds, "Also, who's Davy Crockett?"

In order to answer that question for Bart, you must first separate the real man from the myth and then the myth from the international entertainment icon he became. The real man, David Crockett, was a Tennessee settler who lived during a pivotal period in American history. He served in the Tennessee state legislature from 1821 to 1824 and in the United States House of Representatives from 1827 to 1831, then from 1833 to 1835. His political career took place during the Jacksonian Era, nestled between the Revolutionary and Civil Wars. Crockett played a role on the main stage as Americans struggled to figure out just who they were going to be, now that that they had fought for and won their independence.

He was both literally and symbolically a "common man," and that was a role that grew more important as governing the country shifted away from the educated eastern elites to regular working-class Americans. Crockett also became the living embodiment of western expansion for people who had only read about what lay beyond the Allegheny Mountains. He literally and symbolically blazed a trail representing an exciting, new type of American that thrilled early media and entertainment consumers. He made them excited about what could be found down the river or just over the next mountain.

As Crockett purposefully crafted a public image of a "poor man's friend," his supporters and opponents discovered his popularity also resulted in votes. Crockett may not have been sent to a fancy boarding school or attended West Point, but he could protect your cabin from Red Sticks, hunt down and kill a dozen bears, and argue a bill on the floor of United States Congress while wealthier, more influential men were still trying to decide which cravat to wear to the office. All the while, Crockett was unknowingly creating a "type" with characteristics that would one day be seen in fictional characters like Jed Clampett, Andy Taylor, and Gomer Pyle. For them, a lack of fancy degrees did not equal a lack of intelligence, and their accent and rural backgrounds did not equate to ignorance. Quite the opposite; like Crockett, underestimate them, and you'll be the fool.

Crockett combined traits of all the men he had worked, played, and hunted with through the years. The image he created for the public was a combination of the longhunters, flatboat pilots, soldiers, and settlers of Tennessee he had known his entire life. He took their language, culture, and humor and projected it to the public.

Crockett became a muse in every sense of the word. In Greek mythology, the Muses were daughters of Zeus and included the goddesses of literature, poetry, music, dance, and comedy. Today, the word is used to describe someone who inspires creativity. In Crockett's day, something about the successes and failures of this uneducated frontiersman from Tennessee inspired writers, artists, and performers of all kinds.

Crockett shows up in every channel of artistic expression available to creatives in the early decades of the nineteenth century. These were frequently second- and third-generation Americans who were creating popular culture from scratch. They had a clean slate and wanted the work to be *uniquely*

*American.* They even had the challenge of figuring out exactly what that meant. It was only natural that they would gravitate toward the man who represented both the danger and the thrill of settling the wild frontier.

For Crockett, you could add journalism to the list of goddesses. Today, he would likely be a mere footnote in history without innovations in printing technology and the dramatic increase in the number of people who could both read and afford a newspaper. Reporters found that writing about him—and copying and reprinting what others had written—sold newspapers; so, they wrote more and more about Crockett, and the public ate it up.

Crockett had both friends and enemies in Washington, D.C., then called Washington City. And thanks to his immense charisma, sense of humor, and ability to charm an audience, his friends who were forming the Whig party used him to campaign against his enemies, including the biggest of them all, Andrew Jackson. Crockett's circle of friends and political associates included James K. Polk, Henry Clay, Sam Houston, and other notables of the day who had taken the torch of democracy from the founding fathers and were trying mightily to keep it burning.

After his tragic death at the Alamo in Texas, the commercialization of Crockett's name and likeness that he had begun during his lifetime took on mythical proportions. Through publications filled with "tall tales" like the *Davy Crockett Almanacs* that were published until 1856, he morphed into a nineteenth-century version of Superman. Rather than "leaping over tall buildings in a single bound," this early superhero was able to ride his pet alligator, "Long Mississippi," up Niagara Falls and kill a rattlesnake with his teeth. Superman may have been able to see through walls with his X-ray vision, but Crockett could knock a giant black bear out of a tree with his grin.

There is no shortage of books about David Crockett. As one writer put it, "this nineteenth-century backwoodsman-turned-Congressman conveniently left extensive tracks on printed pages as well as backwoods trails."[1]

It was likely James S. French who wrote the first "unauthorized" biography of Crockett in 1833. Both that and Crockett's autobiography that he wrote later, were considered great successes by the measures of the day. Hundreds of authors would follow, just as inspired by this Tennessee muse as those who had come before. Enter the "library of Crockett," and you'll find academics and historians from the early to mid-twentieth century who explored the man and the myth with the goal of separating the two. Included in that list are Charles and Mary Beard, Vernon Parrington, Joseph Arpad, Richard Dorson, Constance Rourke, Stanley Folmsbee and—the most prolific researcher—James Shackford. His in-depth biography of Crockett was edited by his brother and released posthumously in 1956.

The authors who wrote after 1954 had a different challenge: how to tell the story of someone whose image had been Disneyfied, turned into a caricature, and inspired an entertainment licensing phenomenon. That list of post-Disney writers of books and articles about Crockett includes Catherine L. Albanese, Michael Lofaro, Michael Wallis, Buddy Levy, James R. Boylston, Allen J. Weiner, Mark Derr, Jonathan Kennon Smith, Dan Kilgore, Bill Groneman, William C. Davis, Bob Thompson, Richard Hauk, James E. Crisp, and many others. Using modern research tools and building upon the work that came before, they have added even more depth and breadth to help answer Bart Simpson's question, "Also, who's Davy Crockett?"

This book is not a chronological biography of the life of David Crockett. Those who are seeking that type of book will find many excellent options written by those mentioned earlier. The aim of this book is to explore what fueled Crockett's unlikely rise from uneducated frontiersman to world-famous icon, while also examining the birth of Tennessee during one of the most fascinating periods in American history.

Ultimately, the truth is that Bart's question is impossible to answer. We will never really know for certain the answer to the question, "Who's Davy Crockett?" But hopefully, by reading this book, you'll get to know Colonel David Crockett, settler of the wild frontier, member of Congress from Tennessee, and America's first celebrity, just a little better.

**Prelude Notes**

1. Catherine L. Albanese, "Citizen Crockett: Myth, History, and Nature Religion," *Soundings: An Interdisciplinary Journal* 61, no. 1 (1978): 89.

Dime novels got their nickname because the small, paperback books only cost one dime. Inexpensive to produce, they are among the earliest forms of mass media used to take advantage of popular culture and innovations in printing and distribution. One of the most popular topics for the novels was the "Wild West" and the men and women who conquered it. This dime novel, published in 1873, featured David Crockett who had been dead 37 years but was still one of the individuals most associated with westward expansion.

I never had the opportunity of college learning, like cotton planters' boys. No, I have been raised in the humble walks of life—but I have been taught the glorious privileges of American freedom and independence.

—David Crockett

# Part One

# Tennessee

First published in the 1870s then republished in 1908, *Davy Crockett's Boy Hunter* was a dime novel produced as part of publishers Erastus and Irwin Beadle's Frontier Series. In the story, young readers are introduced to a young Crockett serving as a scout with a group of Tennessee volunteers during the Creek War.

**The image is one thing and the human being is another. It's very hard to live up to an image, put it that way.**

**—Elvis Presley**

## Chapter One

# Northwest

David Crockett had a problem to solve. And as he stood there with his young son, surveying his new property in Northwest Tennessee early in 1822, he hoped this piece of unsettled wilderness might be the answer. The thirty-five-year-old frontiersman with a second wife and blended family had just lost much of his business in a flood back where they had been living in Lawrenceburg about 175 miles east in Middle Tennessee. The flood had destroyed the gristmill, powder mill, and distillery he had built on Shoal Creek to the tune of three thousand dollars—three thousand borrowed dollars, making the loss even more painful. While things looked bad for Crockett in that moment, little did he know that in just a few years, he would be one of the most famous men in the world.

Crockett had recently been elected a state legislator for his home in Lawrence County, Tennessee, so it would seem rebuilding there would have been much easier. But since childhood, Crockett had never liked to stay in one place for too long. It was as though he had been searching for something since childhood. A solution presented itself in this one thousand acres of land in the northwest corner of the state near present-day Rutherford,

Tennessee about forty miles from Kentucky to the north and Missouri to the west. It had been granted to his wife's father, Robert Patton, by the state of North Carolina for his service as a soldier in the Revolutionary War. Patton deeded eight hundred of those acres over to Crockett and his wife, Patton's daughter, Elizabeth, for $1,600. Later, more of the Patton and Crockett extended family would join David and Elizabeth Crockett in Northwest Tennessee, and they would be among the first White settlers to call the region home. They would find taming this wilderness would be far from easy, with getting there being the first challenge. Early Tennessee historian Joseph S. Williams wrote of "its richness of soil, giant forests, impenetrable canebrakes, tare-blanket thickets, grape and bamboo jungles, and the wild pea-vine in spring and summer, so thickly matted—overrunning the undergrowth—as to impede travel on foot and horseback."[1] Much of West Tennessee was covered with forests of giant walnut, oak, poplar, maple, and many other varieties of trees that had grown through their natural lifecycle undisturbed by men for thousands of years. Clearing that land for agriculture would provide the logs needed for the rudimentary cabins built by those early settlers.

Although he was never much of a farmer, the game that was plentiful throughout the region made the challenge of settling down in Northwest Tennessee worth the effort for Crocket. He wrote, "It was a complete wilderness, and full of Indians who were hunting. Game was plenty of almost every kind, which suited me exactly, as I was always fond of hunting."[2] Buffalo, deer, bear, wolves, panthers, and even elk could be found everywhere, and fish were plentiful in the rivers and streams. The sounds of smaller birds like bluebirds, crows, owls, and woodpeckers filled the forests. During certain times of the year, waterfowl like ducks and geese appeared because the rivers and tributaries of West Tennessee were a frequent stop as they made their way from their breeding grounds in Canada and the northern United States to their wintering grounds along the Gulf of Mexico and in Central and South America.

The Chickasaw used this area as a hunting ground, but called it "the land of the shakes." About a decade before Crockett arrived, the area had really lived up to its Native American nickname. Today, it's known the region sits atop what has been named the New Madrid Fault Line, a 150-mile long seismic zone that runs through present-day Illinois, Indiana, Missouri, Arkansas, Kentucky, Tennessee, and Mississippi. Between December 1811 and February 1812, a series of three large earthquakes, accompanied by month of tremors and aftershocks, occurred near New Madrid, Missouri.

Eliza Bryant, a settler living near present-day Hickman, Kentucky, wrote about the morning of December 16, 1811 when she woke up a little after two in the morning and experienced what she described as "a very awful noise resembling loud but distant thunder, but more hoarse and vibrating, which was followed in a few minutes by the complete saturation of the atmosphere with sulphurious vapor." In a letter to her minister, Reverend Lorenzo Dow, she wrote:

> The screams of the inhabitant, the cries of the fowls and beasts of every species, the falling trees, and the roaring of the Mississippi, the current which was retrograde for a few minutes owing, as it is supposed, to an eruption in its bed, formed a scene truly horrible… the surface of the earth was from time to time by these hard shocks covered to various depths by sand and water. In some places, however, a substance resembling coal or impure stone coal was thrown up with the sand.[3]

The much-celebrated naturalist, John James Audubon, who is known for his illustrations of birds of North America, was in Kentucky on a research trip in January 1812 when he experienced one of the tremors. The horse he was riding paused and then, as he described, "placed one foot after another on the ground with as much precaution as if walking on a smooth sheet of ice." As he prepared to dismount to try and figure out the cause of his horse's peculiar behavior, the earth itself answered his question. He wrote, "the ground rose and fell in successive furrows like the ruffled waters of a lake."[4] Tremors continued for months, and Audubon wrote of the behavior waterfowl and other animals. He observed that just before people felt a tremor, birds took to the sky, dogs began barking, and cows bellowed in the fields. Geographer Timothy Flint confirmed the observations of others like Audubon and Bryant. He was on a flatboat during a tremor and wrote of the terror made even more horrible by "the loud screaming of waterfowl on the river."[5]

At least two thousand small tremors occurred along the New Madrid Fault Line during the next year leading up to the biggest on February 7, 1812. That one caused parts of the earth to shift and rise as much as twelve feet, while in other spots, the land opened up and shifted thirty or more feet toward the sky. Remarkably, some portions of the ground that opened up were more than five miles in length. Men navigating flatboats down the river that day later told stories of the Mississippi River suddenly flowing backwards over giant waterfalls created by the shift. Water rushed in to fill the giant fissures that had opened up. The earthquake was so powerful, claims were made that bells rang all the way to Boston. Even President James Madison and his wife, Dolley, said they felt them in the White House. On February 11, Madison wrote to Thomas Jefferson, "The re-iteration of earthquakes continues... There was one here this morning at 5 or 6 minutes after 4 o'clock. It was rather stronger than any preceding one, and lasted several minutes."[6]

A few days after that earthquake, the first steamboat to travel the Mississippi River made its way through thousands of floating trees, wrecked and abandoned boats, and dead animals floating in the water. The captain, inventor Nicholas Roosevelt, was a distant cousin of the presdiential branch of the family tree. He finally came upon an island where he felt comfortable docking. That night, the entire island sunk into the Mississippi River and disappeared forever.

What was left in Northwest Tennessee when the earthquakes stopped was Reelfoot Lake, a shallow lake covering fifteen thousand acres that—Crockett would be among the first to discover—would become a fisherman and hunter's paradise. Cypress trees and stumps could be seen both inside and around the lake that was filled with all types of fish, and the surface was dotted with lily pads, saw grass, moss seed, and even wild rice.

Getting to his new home to explore Reelfoot Lake and the surrounding area was not easy, even for someone like Crockett with experience in the outdoors. He made that initial trip with his fourteen-year-old son, John Wesley Crockett, and another young man named Abram Henry. There were no roads, but if they were lucky, they could find the paths Native Americans had created on their annual trips through the area to hunt. Sometimes Crockett resorted to just hacking through the wilderness, one step at a time, with the tomahawk he carried. The wilderness was thick around them as the men and the horse they brought to carry their tools and supplies slowly made their way west. They had to stay alert, with the possibility of running into dangers of all kinds around every corner.

Crockett knew what he was doing since he had grown up around Tennessee's longhunters, explorers usually from the Virginia settlements, who made months-long expeditions into the wilderness. As a young boy, he heard their stories in his father's tavern as they headed back east with animal skins and meat to sell. The earliest of the longhunters were called the "Overmountain People" because they crossed the Appalachian Mountains to settle small communities that became Tennessee's first settlements. They traveled either singularly or in small groups of two or three because any more would scare away the game and draw the attention of the Native Americans.

Daniel Boone, fifty-two years older than Crockett, is the longhunter at the top of the list of early settlers to show up in history books today, and is frequently mentioned in the same breath as Crockett. Boone made a name for himself after creating a route through the Cumberland Gap and then exploring present-day Kentucky. However, his exploits weren't made known to most Americans of the day until a book about him was published by John Filson. The land west of the Appalachians was seen by the first American politicians as a way to compensate soldiers for their Revolutionary War service. Not surprisingly, many soldiers did not see migrating through the wilderness with their families, while dodging hostile Native Americans, wild animals, and other dangers, as a reward and quickly sold their land. One of the earliest speculators to see potential in buying and reselling the veterans' land around present-day Kentucky and Ohio was Filson, a young schoolteacher from Pennsylvania.

Filson made his way to Kentucky in the fall of 1783 in his mid-thirties. Although he had limited survival skills and knew nothing about hunting or farming, he began working in the region as a teacher as he surveyed the land, ultimately creating the first map of Kentucky.

Along the way, he met Daniel Boone, who had already perfected all the skills Filson had arrived to Kentucky knowing nothing about. As he completed his map and reviewed his notes, Filson knew he had the makings of a good book that would also serve as an advertisement to help sell land grants he had purchased. He made his way back east to Delaware, where early printer James Adams published Filson's map as part of his book, *The Discovery, Settlement and Present State of Kentucke: And An Essay towards the Topography, and Natural History of that important Country*. About one third of the book featured the adventures of Boone, written in the first person, beginning with the sentence, "Curiosity is natural to the soul of man, and interesting objects have a powerful influence on our affections."[7]

Those words that Filson put into Boone's mouth could not have been truer. Boone's exploits thrilled the rest of the country, curious about what they would find over the mountains. Americans were just settling into their new country and already beginning to think about western expansion. Filson provided them with the "interesting object" that certainly had "a powerful influence on their affections." The section Filson wrote in the voice of Boone ended,

> This account of my adventures will inform the reader of the most remarkable events of this country.—I now live in peace and safety, enjoying the sweets of liberty, and the bounties of Providence, with my once fellow-sufferers, in this delightful country, which I have seen purchased with a vast expence of blood and treasure, delighting in the prospect of its being, in a short time, one of the most opulent and powerful states on the continent of North-America; which, with the love and gratitude of my country-men, I esteem a sufficient reward for all my toil and dangers.[8]

The book was a huge hit and editions were printed in America, France, Germany, and London. It inspired some early Americans to cross the mountains and claim for themselves some of those "bounties of Providence" Filson wrote about.

A lesser-known longhunter was Thomas "Bigfoot" Spencer. Considered the first White settler in Middle Tennessee, he planted his first crop there in the spring of 1778. Weighing in at over three hundred pounds, Spencer supposedly got his name when a group of Native Americans came across his footprint in the snow and were so shocked by the size, they were certain they had stumbled upon a giant. According to one story about Spencer, he spent one entire winter living in a hollowed-out sycamore tree. In 1794, Spencer was returning to his home in Middle Tennessee from Virginia when he was ambushed and murdered by Native Americans near the present-day community of Crab Orchard, Tennessee.

Crockett came from men and women like these whose curiosity and desire for a better life for their families drove them west. That day in 1822 when Crockett first arrived in Northwest Tennessee, he referred to a copy of the recent survey that had been conducted of his father-in-law's land grant. He found a section of the property for his family's cabin that would be above the flood plain, yet still close to the Obion River. There, he would clear enough land to build a cabin and plant some corn to supplement the meat from the hunting he knew that he could do to provide food when he returned with his wife and children to their new home in the wilderness.

Crockett no doubt noticed the discrepancies between the survey he had been given and the land he saw before him. Mapping a large territory was difficult. In June 1775, surveyors Colonel James Robertson, Henry Rutherford, and Edward Harris and their crews of four other men for each loaded up flatboats in Nashville and headed down the Cumberland, Ohio and Mississippi Rivers into the Western Territory to begin the first land surveys. Using a compass and chains that were measured out to six feet, they used trees, bodies of water, large rocks, and anything else that could be noted as a marker. To make certain land owners received what they paid for, a "portion of excess" was frequently included. This caused a great deal of confusion—and many lawsuits—among West Tennessee's early settlers.

With the task of selecting a cabin location checked off of his list, Crockett attached leather hobbles to his horse's front legs, let it loose in a nearby pasture, and set off to meet his neighbors, the Owens family. They lived seven miles away and on the other side of Rutherford Fork, a tributary of the Obion River. It was cold, it was wet, and they had no boat to get there.

Considered taller than average for the time at around six feet, Crockett was broad-shouldered, and writers would later describe him as "without surplus flesh" at around two hundred pounds. Years on the frontier had left him in good shape, and this was the type of physical activity for which Crockett was suited. He was ready to rise to the challenge. But in this case, he would nearly sink to it, as the three men spent much of the next few hours pushing forward through the muddy swamp that separated them from the neighbors. Their path took them through freezing water that was sometimes up to Crockett's neck, so he would reach ahead with a large pole checking for gaps and ditches that were difficult to see because of all the mud. When he found one, he would use his tomahawk to cut down a small tree, make a temporary bridge, and help the boys across it. Although the trip was challenging for David and Abram Henry, it was even worse for young John Wesley Crockett, who had to swim much of the way through the freezing water that was over the fourteen-year-old's head.

Finally, they arrived at the neighbor's home who was likely very surprised to see a man and two boys walking out of the swamp toward his cabin. Throughout Crockett's life, he occasionally found himself in the right place at the right time, and this was certainly one of those times. With Crockett's new neighbor were several men who had just made history piloting the first flatboat to make it that far up the Obion River. Not only did this fortunate encounter provide men with whom Crockett could trade game to help him quickly build his cabin, they also traded for staples, including barrels of meal and salt and ten gallons of whiskey that would make his family's first months in Northwest Tennessee much easier. Crockett stored the supplies inside the very basic cabin he and the other men swiftly constructed, loaded up his tools, and headed back to Lawrence County. It's possible that as he looked behind him and surveyed the completed work, he wondered what his wife would think of her new home. He knew this was not what she had bargained for, but he must have hoped that she would see this move as a way for them to pay off their debts and settle in a place where they could make a new life together with their blended family.

David Crockett never used the name "Davy," and he was not, as the exaggerated folk-hero stories would later claim, able to "casually beat enough 'hot ile' out of a bear to thaw the earth's axes so that the sun could rise and shine when he was cold."[9] He did, however, have a sense of restlessness and a determination to beat what seemed like impossible odds. Crockett's optimism manifested itself in an urge to keep moving, always looking for a better situation—and a way to get his debts paid—around the next corner.

Perhaps being one of nine siblings competing for very few resources had something do with it, or it could have been the challenge of having a father like John Crockett, who could never quite get away from the bill collector.

The elder Crockett was a Revolutionary War veteran who fought at the Battle of Kings Mountain in 1780, a major victory for the colonists. He and his wife, Rebecca Hawkins, had settled and raised their children in Greene County, Tennessee where the Limestone Creek joins the Nolichucky River.

When David Crockett was a boy, his father moved the family and opened a tavern on the road for the many settlers who were on the move between Virginia and Tennessee. Later, Crockett looked back on that tavern and called it a place of "hard times, and plenty of 'em."[10] To get away, he spent much of his late childhood and adolescent years either on the road doing odd jobs as a runaway or working for free for those to whom his father owed money. When he briefly returned home to Jefferson County, Tennessee as a young man, he had been away for so long and matured so much, that his own family didn't recognize him as he sat in his father's tavern.

Crockett was anxious for a family of his own and, after a few failed attempts at romance, married his first wife, Polly Finley, in 1806. The young couple settled down in a rented cabin in Elk River, Tennessee in Franklin County long enough to start a family. John Wesley Crockett arrived in 1807, followed by William Finley in 1809 and daughter Margaret in 1812. He later admitted he was better at increasing his family than his fortune.[11] A few years of farming someone else's land made it clear that furthering one's status and financial situation while renting another man's property would prove to be impossible. Like other settlers, Crockett quickly learned that he needed land of his own if he and his family were going to have a chance at improving their lot in life—a sentiment he would draw on throughout his political career.

The treaty between the Cherokee and the United States in early 1806 opened an area of Tennessee, along what is now the Alabama state line, for settlement. In the fall of 1811, Crockett and his family packed what they could carry on a few horses and moved west. For a few years, they made their home on the east branch of Mulberry Creek in Lincoln County, Tennessee. Crockett found the area unacceptable for hunting, so in early 1813, he and his family moved to Franklin County, Tennessee and settled at Bean's Creek on a rented homestead that had already been named "Kentuck."

Crockett's first wife, Polly, died in 1815 at age twenty-seven, leaving him to care for their three small children, ages eight, six, and three. His family stepped in for a while and his brother and sister-in-law moved in to help, but that was only a short-term solution.

The problem of who could help him raise his children—and take care of him—was solved in 1816 when he married Elizabeth Patton, a widow in his Franklin County community whose husband had died fighting the Creeks. She was quite a bit wealthier than her new husband and had two young children of her own, George and Margaret Ann. Crockett noted in his autobiography that Elizabeth was industrious, owned a "snug little farm," and was living very comfortably. He knew a good thing when he saw it and claimed he was "sly as a fox going to rob a hen-roost" by first befriending her children, knowing that if they liked him, he stood a good chance of winning over their mother. His strategy worked. Their blended family quickly grew even larger with the addition of Robert Patton in 1816, Rebecca Elvira in 1818, and Matilda in 1821. Crockett was fortunate to have found an industrious wife with means of her own who, it seems, was willing to accept a husband who was rarely at home and who struggled to settle down in one place. While very little is known about Elizabeth Patton Crockett, it's safe to say, whether she realized it or not at the time, that she had chosen a husband who was destined for a life of adventure. During the next decade, she would watch her second husband rise from being a poor, uneducated widower with few prospects to becoming one of the most well-known and popular men in the country and a possible candidate for president of the United States.

**Chapter One Notes**

1. Joseph S. Williams, *Old Times in West Tennessee* (Memphis: W. G. Cheeney Printer and Publisher, 1873), 37.
2. David Crockett, *Narrative of the Life of David Crockett, of the State of Tennessee* (Philadelphia: E. L. Carey and A. Hart, 1834), 148.
3. Wilson A. Nelson, "Reelfoot—An Earthquake Lake," *National Geographic* (January 1923): 103.
4. James P. Jones. "Audubon and the New Madrid Earthquake." *The Register of the Kentucky Historical Society* 67, no. 3 (1969): 191.
5. Ibid., 195.
6. James Madison, *Letters and Other Writings of James Madison, Volume Two* (Philadelphia: J. B. Lippincott & Co.), 526.
7. John Filson, *The Discovery, Settlement, and Present State of Kentucke* (Delaware: John Adams, 1884), 39.
8. Ibid., 62.
9. Richard M. Dorson, *Davy Crockett, American Legend* (New York: Arno Press, 1977), 9.
10. Crockett, *Narrative*, 22.
11. Ibid., 68.

*Retrieved from the Digital Public Library of America*

Boxing champion Jim Jeffries is pictured here with an unidentified child. Jeffries was the star of *Davy Crockett*," a theatrical performance that opened November 10, 1904, at the Grand Opera House in Seattle. Immediately following was a "boxing exhibition."

**Fame is a vapor, popularity an accident.**

**—Horace Greeley**

## Chapter Two

# Murder

Although they didn't know it then, when David Crockett and others began settling in what would become Lawrence County, Tennessee, about halfway between present-day Memphis and Chattanooga, they were carving out a community near what is thought by some historians today to be the early Chickasaw village, Chicasa. It had been the location of the first encounter between the Chickasaw and explorers from Spain three hundred years earlier.

Hernando de Soto, a Spanish explorer and conquistador, arrived in present-day Tampa, Florida in May 1539 with ten ships carrying seven hundred conquistadors on board. He had played a major role in the Spanish conquests of Central America and Peru and had become rich in the slave trade. The intentions of de Soto and his men were made obvious as they traveled northwest, kidnapping, torturing, and murdering Native Americans and plundering supplies as they searched for the silver and gold de Soto was certain they would find in this exciting new world. It was just a matter of time before they encountered the Chickasaw. While they primarily lived in present-day North Mississippi around Tupelo, the Chickasaw hunted throughout West and Middle Tennessee and parts of Alabama and Kentucky.

During the cold winter of 1540, de Soto and his men took over Chicasa, one of the Chickasaw's abandoned hunting villages. Minkolosa, the Chickasaw leader at the time, reluctantly agreed to meet with de Soto to get to know these strange men better. If he was going to protect his people from these invaders that some thought were gods, he was going to need to first find their weaknesses. For a short while, the Chickasaw and the conquistadors maintained a tense but somewhat peaceful relationship in spite of the explorers' tendency to take whatever they wanted, whenever they wanted it. Finally, de Soto decided it was time to move on, and Minkolosa's worst fears came true as the conquistadors attempted to enslave some of the Chickasaw. De Soto demanded Minkolosa provide men to carry their supplies and women to serve his soldiers' more carnal desires. In March 1541, while the conquistadors slept, the Chickasaw attacked. The half-dressed, unprepared Spaniards attempted to fight, but Minkolosa's plan to lull the soldiers into complacency had worked.

When the sudden ambush was over, the entire village had been burned to the ground, more than a dozen conquistadors were dead, and much of their supplies, including more than fifty horses, had been destroyed. De Soto survived, but he and his men fled the area to continue their search for riches. By May 1541, only around four hundred of de Soto's men were still alive as they arrived, sick and exhausted, south of present-day Memphis to earn the recognition of being the first Europeans to see the Mississippi River.

They built flatboats and crossed in the dark of night to avoid the Native Americans they saw on the giant river, but as it turned out, de Soto's end would not come at the hands of the indigenous warriors. He died of fever in 1542 on the west bank of the Mississippi River, likely near present-day McArthur, Arkansas. Knowing their reputation had preceded them, de Soto's men wrapped his body, along with large stones, and sunk it in the Mississippi River to prevent the Native Americans from finding the body and questioning their deity. The Chickasaw would not encounter another European for more than 150 years.

While this bit of American history was unknown to Crockett and the others settling there in Middle Tennessee in 1817, they were very much aware of the violent battles that had taken place in their own time between White settlers and Native Americans. And for Crockett, it was personal.

When he was a young boy, the family stories he overheard from the adults around him surely included the 1777 murder of his paternal grandparents. When they first migrated over the Appalachian Mountains into what would eventually become Tennessee, they settled in Carter's Valley, one of four communities that had been established in Northeast Tennessee.

Others were settling on the Watauga, the Holston, and the Nolichucky Rivers. As these pop-up settlements began to grow, the frontier entered a new phase, and the possession of land took on a powerful significance. It meant freedom and independence. When the settlers living around what is now Elizabethton, Tennessee were informed that they had crossed the line and were told by the British to relocate north, they refused to leave.

Instead, they formed the Watauga Association. In defiance of the British, the association even negotiated their own deals with the Cherokee that included a ten-year lease of the land on which they had settled. Some members of the tribe were opposed to allowing White settlers on their lands under any condition. A group of renegades called the Chickamauga, led by Cherokee Chief Dragging Canoe, wreaked havoc upon the settlers in spite of the lease agreement. Some, like Crockett's grandparents, ended up paying the ultimate price for seeking land and a better life for their family.

David Crockett's father, John, and his father's brother Robert were away when a band of Creek and Chickamauga—the Cherokee who parted ways with their tribe over treaties with the White settlers—descended on the family cabin near what would later become Rogersville, Tennessee in Hawkins County. Their son Joseph had been shot in the arm, an injury that resulted in the permanent loss of the use of that hand. Although there are no records that prove it, some have speculated that the Crocketts had a son named David Crockett Jr., also killed in the attack, and a daughter who was scalped but survived. Perhaps even more intriguing to young David Crockett was the part of the story that included a kidnapping. When the

Native American warriors rode off, they took with them the Crockett's nineteen-year-old son, James—an act made even more cruel by the fact that James could neither hear nor speak.

When David Crockett was around eight years old, this story from the old days became a current event when, nearly eighteen years after the kidnapping, James Crockett's brothers finally discovered his whereabouts and purchased him from a Native American trader. James Crockett had been a teenager when he was kidnapped from his family but returned a thirty-seven-year-old man. According to family legend, they discovered that while living among the Native Americans, he had accompanied them to gold and silver mines; however, he had been blindfolded during those visits and, being deaf, had no way of knowing where they were. The story that was passed down through the generations was that after James, nicknamed "Dumb Jimmie," returned home, he spent the last years of his life searching the places he had traveled with his captors without ever finding a single mine.

The quest for land and other natural resources of early Tennessee settlers, like the Crockett family, placed them at the beginning of one of the ugliest aspects of early American history. It began when Europeans first arrived in North America to find loosely formed communities made up of an estimated ten million "Indians" speaking nearly three hundred languages in thousands of dialects.

The early Tennessee settlers primarily dealt with the Creek, Chickasaw, and Cherokee tribes. The Creeks lived in North Alabama and Northeast Mississippi along the Tennessee River. The Chickasaws were located in Northern Mississippi and Alabama and claimed all of West Tennessee and a portion of Middle Tennessee as their hunting ground, while the Cherokee claimed Southeastern Tennessee and Northeast Georgia as their homeland. Ultimatley, no matter where they lived, what alliances they made, or how hard they fought, they were doomed.

The first blow came from disease. Native Americans were not immune to many illnesses the settlers brought to the new world including smallpox, measles, pneumonia, and other sicknesses that claimed many lives and decimated the tribes. Then came the treaties that systematically parted the Native American's with their land and pushed them further and further west. Eventually, an end to this chapter came for Crockett's home state in December 1838 when the last group of Cherokee left Red Clay, Tennessee and began marching the one thousand miles to Oklahoma. It was called the Trail of Tears, and more than four thousand never made it and died along the way.

Fast forward to 1900, and only three hundred thousand Native Americans from any tribe remained in America. Those years of betrayal, battles, and bigotry that decimated the indigenous tribes of the country left hundreds of thousands of Native Americans and White settlers dead.

Many Americans felt blameless because of "manifest destiny," the idea that the United States was destined by God to expand its dominion and spread democracy and capitalism across the entire North American continent. Although the actual term wouldn't be coined until much later—appearing in an editorial published in an 1845 issue of *The Democratic Review*—that attitude among most settlers was certainly prevalent right from the beginning.

A pamphlet printed from an address delivered by Colonel John A. Garder in 1876 in Dresden, Tennessee provides a prime example of how many early settlers and their descendants justifed the removal of Native Americans. He said, "The race that preceded us in the occupation of this country were untutored savages, unaccustomed with the arts of husbandry; dependent on the fruits of the chase for both food and raiment."[1]

For many, any blame or guilt was not only sidestepped by noting it was "God's will," they also claimed the "savages" were not using most of the land they claimed to possess anyway, so it was free for the taking. Although the land did eventually end up in the hands of the settlers, they didn't get it without a fight.

**Chapter Two Notes**

1. Gardner, John A. "Early Times in Weakley County: An Address." *The West Tennessee Historical Society Papers* no. 8, (1963): 69.

For years after his death, the publication of a series of almanacs contributed to the spread of humorous "tall tales" and folklore about David Crockett. The outrageous writing and clever woodcut illustrations in the almanacs provide excellent examples of early-American humor and popular culture.

**I always want to say to people who want to be rich and famous, 'try being rich first.' See if that doesn't cover most of it.**

**—Bill Murray**

**Chapter Three**

# War

An ambitious and charismatic Shawnee warrior chief, Tecumseh, created a large community called Prophetstown where the Tippecanoe and the Wabash Rivers come together near present-day Lafayette, Indiana. Living together in the community were Native Americans from different tribes with the ultimate goal of uniting all tribes into one nation in order to retain their land and drive the settlers away for good. Tecumseh traveled the country with his brother, Tenskwatawa or "the Prophet." The two siblings were from a set of triplets, but one of the brothers had died in infancy. They preached that all tribes should maintain autonomy from Europeans, reject their customs, and fight to drive them off Native American land for good. While individuals from many tribes did join forces with the brothers, others were resistant because of the animosity and bad blood that had existed between many of the tribes for generations. Unable to unite, some continued to fight on their own, while some joined forces with the White settlers, the British, or others wanting to have dominion over a piece of North America.

One mythical story about the brothers that has been told for generations intersects with Crockett's life and his eventual move to Northwest Tennessee.

It began when Tecumseh met with a tribe of Creeks near Montgomery, Alabama to persuade them to join his confederacy. As the story was told, the chief declared that they would soon know he was sent by the "great spirit" because after he returned home, he would stomp his feet three times, and they would "feel their houses shake down through the Mississippi." Supposedly, it didn't take long for his declaration to come true, as this was shortly before the first of the New Madrid earthquakes that contributed to the formation of Reelfoot Lake.

Unfortunately for Tecumseh, it would take more than a series of earthquakes for some of the Creeks to stop fighting long enough to join forces with anyone. But that was the least of his worries at the time. On November 7, 1811, Indiana territorial governor William Henry Harrison led around one thousand soldiers in attacking Prophetstown while Tecumseh was away. They burned the village to the ground and destroyed the food the Native Americans had stored for the winter. Although he had been away during that first battle with Harrison, Tecumseh was ultimately killed during the War of 1812 in the Battle of the Thames in which Harrison led American soldiers against Tecumseh's Confederacy and the British.

For decades, a debate occurred in popular culture and politics about who actually killed Tecumseh. In 1836, Kentucky representative Richard Mentor Johnson, one of the many individuals credited with killing the celebrated Shawnee chief, won the vice presidency on the ticket with Martin Van Buren, running with the slogan "Rumpseh dumpseh, Johnson killed Tecumseh." Not to be outdone, during the next presidential election in 1840, William Henry Harrison and his running mate, John Tyler, used the battles to promote their own political campaign with the slogan and popular song "Tippecanoe and Tyler Too."

The biggest threat to Tennessee settlers around the time Harrison was burning down Prophetstown and Johnson either was or was not killing Tecumseh, came from a faction of the Creek called the Red Sticks. Just their name was enough to incite fear, as it came from the two-foot wooden war club they preferred over other weapons. It had a wooden handle, painted red, with a curve at its head that held a small piece of iron, steel, or bone projecting out about two inches. It's not hard to imagine the damage it could—and frequently did—do to the skull of an enemy. The war between the Red Sticks and other Creeks who made treaties with the White settlers took place around the same time as the War of 1812 against Great Britain. British traders in Florida and the Spanish government gave weapons and supplies to the Red Sticks because of their shared interest in preventing the expansion of the United States into the areas over which they had control. Settlers' fury toward the Creeks and fear for their communities had been steadily growing because of violence like the 1812 attack on a small group on the Duck River in Humphreys County, Tennessee. Most of the inhabitants were slaughtered, while one, Martha Crawley, was kidnapped. One sensational account of the attack appeared in the *Tennessee Herald*:

> With savage fury they now forced the door, and commenced a scene of still greater barbarity. They snatched Mrs. Manley's child, only eight days old, from her, scalped it and threw it into the fire place, yelling at a horrid rate. An indiscriminate butchery of the children now took place before their mothers; five children were scalped and murdered, they keeping Mrs. Manley alive as the last victim of their cruelty. After shooting her, they scalped her, and committed unheard of cruelties on her body. They then left the house, taking Mrs. Crawley along as prisoner. [1]

Mrs. Manley survived long enough to share her account but later died of her injuries.

Another vicious attack against the settlers took place on August 30, 1813 when around seven hundred Red Sticks attacked and destroyed an outpost known as Fort Mims about forty miles north of present-day Mobile, Alabama. The Red Sticks were led by William Weatherford, whose Native American name was Red Eagle. They were seeking revenge for a recent ambush by two hundred soldiers on a band of Creeks who were resting and caught unprepared for an attack. The Creeks killed around four hundred of those in the fort including many unarmed men, women, and children, and they captured more than one hundred slaves. According to reports, more than 250 of the victims had been scalped.

A call for help went out, and in September 1813, the Tennessee state legislature passed an act for the defense of Tennessee and what was then called the Mississippi Territory from Red Stick attacks. Crockett, one of the first to sign up, later wrote about his decision to join those Tennesseans answering the call:

> I, for one, had often thought about war, and had often heard it described; and I did verily believe in my own mind, that I couldn't fight in that way at all; but my after experience convinced me that this was all a notion. For when I heard of the mischief which was done at the fort, I instantly felt like going, and I had none of the dread of dying that I expected to feel…The truth is, my dander was up, and nothing but war could bring it right again.[2]

Polly Crockett cared little for whether her husband's dander was up or not, and she begged him not to go. They were living in an area that was new to them, and she had no real support system or protection without her husband. With Crockett away from home, possibly never to return, she would be alone in caring for their two sons who were then ages six and seven and daughter, Margaret Finley. She had been born in November 1812 and named after Polly's mother.

Crockett later wrote he told Polly "that if every man would wait till his wife got willing for him to go to war, there would be no fighting done, until we would all be killed in our own houses."[3] It appears this argument did little to convince her, but she could tell his mind was set. He added, "all she did was to cry a little, and turn about to her work."[4] Crockett left in early October and headed to the rendezvous point in Winchester, Tennessee, where he began what he and the others had been told was either a sixty- or ninety-day enlistment in Captain Francis Jones's company of Tennessee Volunteer Mounted Riflemen in the regiment of Colonel Newton Cannon.

At the top of the chain of command for the army of Tennessee volunteers during the Creek War was Andrew Jackson. He had been commissioned by President James Madison months earlier to defend New Orleans from the British during the War of 1812. Already forty-six years old, Jackson had little military experience, but he was nothing if not ambitious and confident. He was a frequently argumentative, sometimes controversial, and always complicated character prone to dramatic and—at times—violent outbursts when he didn't get his way. Alternatively, he was dedicated to those he thought supported him and showed great loyalty to those he thought were his friends. And he was a man you did not want as an enemy. A successful farmer and lawyer, Jackson had already served in the Tennessee Senate and ran a plantation on thousands of acres of Tennessee land farmed by hundreds of enslaved workers. He also managed a successful whiskey distillery, a cotton gin, and other businesses.

Jackson and his two thousand men, on their way to New Orleans early in the War of 1812, made it as far as Natchez, Mississippi when he received a notice from the War Department that the threat had passed and he should disband his troops. In reality, Major General James Wilkinson, who was nearby with his own troops, did not trust Jackson. Jackson was furious when he was instructed to turn all supplies over to Wilkinson. To make matters even worse, the War Department did not intend to compensate the soldiers or even provide the provisions they needed to make it back to Tennessee.

Jackson assumed the government and Wilkinson conspired to get rid of him and leave his troops with no alternative but to join Wilkinson's force. Jackson had a better idea. He led the men back to Nashville, Tennessee and paid for their food and supplies out of his own pocket. On the trip back to Tennessee, he gave up his horse and walked along with the other soldiers so the sick and wounded could ride rather than walk. It was on the journey back to Nashville that his determination and dedication to support his men earned Jackson the iconic nickname that would stay with him for the rest of his life—"Old Hickory."

Old Hickory had returned to the Hermitage, his home in Nashville, when the news of the massacre at Fort Mims reached him. He saw this as another chance to add "military hero" to his list of accomplishments. It was an opportunity he nearly missed because he was recovering from injuries sustained in another of his many duels and street fights. Jackson had the unfortunate combination of a bad temper and a thin skin. During his life, he attempted to defend perceived insults to his honor, and that of his wife, with what has been estimated to have been as many as one hundred duels.

One had nearly cost him his life seven years earlier. Jackson and long-time rival and fellow racehorse breeder, Charles Dickinson, dueled after Dickinson called Jackson a cheater and publicly referred to his wife, Rachel, as a bigamist. Rachel Donelson Jackson had, in fact, been married before her marriage to Andrew Jackson, and it was true that she and Jackson had unknowingly married before her divorce from her first husband was final. It was a sensitive subject and one that haunted the couple throughout what appears to have been an otherwise happy union.

During the duel on May 30, 1806, Dickinson fired first, sending his bullet right into Jackson's chest. Once again true to his nickname, Old Hickory barely reacted to the blow, took careful aim, and pulled the trigger. His pistol misfired, which meant the duel was over. But rather than walk away, Jackson cocked the gun and pulled the trigger a second time. This bullet hit its mark, mortally wounding Dickinson, who bled to death. While Jackson had gotten his revenge, Dickinson's bullet remained lodged in Jackson's chest for the rest of his life, exacting retribution of its own.

The disagreement that occurred shortly before the Creek War was between Jackson and Tennessee legislator—and Jackson's aide-de-camp—Thomas Hart Benton and his younger brother, Jesse Benton. This one was more barfight than duel. The trouble began when Jackson acted as a "second" for William Carroll, future governor of Tennessee, in a duel against Jesse Benton. Seconds were chosen by the men who were dueling; their job was to ensure that the duel was carried out under "honorable" conditions and with equally-matched, deadly weapons. The duel itself turned out to be more slapstick than violent, with Benton ultimately shot in the seat of his pants. While not life threatening, it was certainly one of the more embarrassing outcomes from a duel in Tennessee history.

Thomas Benton was furious that Jackson had played a role in the shameful affair that made a fool of his younger brother, and he said so publicly, offending Jackson in the process. After an exchange of heated letters, Jackson then made it known that he planned to get his revenge using a horse whip the next time he saw the older brother in person. He got his chance when the Benton brothers arrived in Nashville on business. Jackson and his friend, John Coffee, went to the hotel where the brothers were staying. While the horse whip did little damage in the melee that followed, the guns, swords, and knives that were used that day did. Somehow, no one died, but in the end, Jackson was left with gunshot wounds to his arm and shoulder that did nearly kill him. After losing so much blood that he completely soaked two mattresses at the Nashville Inn where he was taken after the fight, the doctors wanted to amputate. Jackson declined saying, "I'll keep my arm."

The wounds, along with the one from Charles Dickinson back in 1806, never completely healed and Jackson suffered from ailments like chronic headaches, tooth loss, infections, severe abdominal pain, and diarrhea for the rest of his life. Research performed on hair samples from Jackson when the science was available, indicated that many of his symptoms came from lead poisoning caused by those bullets that had remained in his body.

Anyone who saw Jackson at the beginning of the Creek War would have questioned his ability to lead even a small regiment. In a letter to his daughter years later, one soldier wrote of seeing Jackson for the first time:

> He was still suffering pain, and looking pale and emaciated from the wound received in the famous duel with Benton...he was mounted on the old "Duke," the docile brave war horse, that afterward bore his gallant master so proudly on many glorious battlefields. His graceful manly form, usually erect was now bent with pain, and he still carried his arm in a sling. The expression of his countenance was grave and thoughtful and his paled cheek gave evidence of present suffering.[5]

Crockett was initially thrilled with the opportunity of being outdoors and experiencing the grand adventure he assumed war would provide. Of course, he had heard the stories of his father's service during the Revolutionary War, so this was also his chance to prove his own manhood.

His company made it to Beaty's Spring, just past Huntsville, Alabama, where they stopped and waited for a few days to let more soldiers join their growing army of volunteers. Major John H. Gibson of Bedford County, Tennessee arrived and asked Captain Jones for his best scout and rifleman to accompany him across the Tennessee River into Creek territory for a scouting mission. Evidently, Crockett had already made a name for himself and was recommended by the captain. When assigned, Crockett requested that his friend George Russell, another soldier from Franklin County in the volunteer army, be allowed to accompany them.

Russell had quite the Tennessee-frontier pedigree as the son of Major William Russell and the grandson of Revolutionary War hero George Russell. The elder Russell's wife and the younger Russell's grandmother was Elizabeth Bean, a daughter of William Bean, a longhunter and early explorer whose claim to fame included being the first settler in Tennessee. It was in Bean's cabin where the planning began for the formation of the Watauga Association. His son, Russell Bean, was the first White child born in Tennessee. The elder George Russell also made a name for himself by fighting in several significant battles, including the last battle of the Revolutionary War, the Battle at Lookout Mountain in 1782. According to family stories, the elder George Russell was killed in May 1797 while he was on a hunting trip with Daniel Boone. When he didn't return home, the family initiated a search and found their seventy-seven-year-old patriarch dead from an apparent Native American attack. His hunting dog was said to be whimpering at his side.

Although young George Russell was still a teenager when David Crockett requested that he accompany him and Major Gibson on the scouting mission, Crockett knew that Russell, with his experience growing up among Tennessee longhunters, had the skill and experience to accomplish the mission and gave them all the best chance of success. Major Gibson wasn't so sure, and he frustrated Crockett by telling him that he was looking for men and not boys. Crockett was no diplomat and was not intimidated by rank or social status. When his opinions were called into question, he often doubled down and became even more determined to prove his point. He later wrote about the incident:

> I must confess I was a little nettled at this; for I know'd George Russell, and I know'd there was no mistake in him; and I didn't think that courage ought to have been measured by the beard, for fear a goat would have preference over a man. I told the major he was on the wrong scent; that Russell could go as far as he would and I *must* have him along. He saw I was a little wrathy, and said I had the best chance of knowing, and agreed that it should be as I wanted it. He told us to be ready early in the morning for a start; and so we were.[6]

Another time Crockett was disrespected by someone with more authority during the war provides a glimpse into other aspects of his personality. He did not react well when someone thought they were superior to him because of their position, education, or social status. After crossing the Tennessee River at Ditto's Landing near Huntsville, Alabama, Crockett and Gibson decided to separate so they could cover more ground. Crockett took five men, and Gibson took seven. As Crockett and his men explored the area and made contact with friendly Creeks and a couple of escaped slaves, they were told that a large war party of Creeks had been crossing the Coosa River, a tributary of the Alabama River, all day and were headed to where Andrew Jackson and his troops were camped.

Crockett hurried back and reported this news to General Coffee, expecting an immediate reaction and a show of appreciation for this great piece of military intelligence. General Coffee either didn't see the significance or trust the validity of the report coming from Crockett and took no action. Crockett wrote, "I was so mad that I was burning inside like a tar kiln, and I wonder that smoke hadn't been pouring out of me at all points."[7]

When Major Gibson returned the next day and shared the same

information, General Coffee responded quickly. He instructed the soldiers to begin putting up a quarter mile of above-the-ground trenches and sent the report straight to Andrew Jackson. Although it turned out that both men had been intentionally misled, Crockett learned the value of title and rank. "When I made my report, it wasn't believed, because I was no officer," he wrote. "I was no great man, but just a poor soldier. But when the same thing was reported by Major Gibson! why, then it was all as true as preaching, and the colonel believed every word."[8]

The first military victory against the Creeks took place on November 3, 1813 in present-day Calhoun County, Georgia. Coffee took about one thousand soldiers on horses, divided his brigade into two columns, and quietly circled, then attacked, the Creek town of Tallushatchee while the inhabitants were sleeping. He then sent two companies into the center of the circle to draw out the Creeks. His plan worked; when the Creeks realized they were surrounded, they had no other choice but to retreat back into their village where they were trapped. In the attack that followed, around 185 of the Creeks were killed—including women and children—while Coffee lost only five of his soldiers. It was during this battle that Crockett witnessed what he called, "a brutal slaughter," that he would remember for the rest of his life. The murders of his grandparents had been stories, but here, he witnessed human beings being, as he put it, "shot like dogs."[9]

Years later, when Crockett wrote his autobiography, he shared the story of seeing nearly fifty Creek warriors running into a house. When the soldiers, including Crockett, followed them, they stopped when they saw an old woman sitting in the door holding a bow and arrow. Before they could register what was happening, she put her feet against the bow, pressed an arrow into the string, and shot into their group. The arrow hit a lieutenant named Moore who had been standing near Crockett. He wrote that it was the first time he had seen someone killed with a bow and arrow.

The furious solders—already hyped up from fear and adrenaline—attacked, and the Creeks stood no chance. The woman who shot the arrow was torn apart by more than twenty lead balls, used as bullets during that time, and those in the house were burned alive. The next day, Crockett and others returned to the village where the carcasses of the burned Creeks gave what he described as "a very terrible appearance." To make the story even worse, Crockett wrote about the starving soldiers finding potatoes in the cellar of the burned house:

> We found a fine chance of potatoes...and hunger compelled us to eat them, though I had a little rather not, if I could have helped it, for the oil of the Indians we had burned up on the day before had run down on them, and they looked like that had been stewed with fat meat. We then again returned to the army, and remained there for several days almost starving as all our beef was gone.[10]

And this was apparently tame compared to what else he observed. Years later, the publishers of Crockett's autobiography edited out some of the stories from that battle they deemed "too violent."

Another young man, Richard K. Call, had been attending college at Mount Pleasant Academy in Montgomery County, Tennessee when he left school to join the Tennessee militia. Years later, Call would become an early territorial governor of Florida. In his journal, he wrote, "I became restless and excited, nor could any longer confine my thoughts and attention to books. I desired to participate in the glories of war."[11] While Crockett was fighting the Creek warriors at Tallushatchee, Call was with Jackson's regiment that had marched down the west bank of the Coosa River and begun laying out Fort Strother. When word of the victory against the Creeks arrived, a battalion that included Call was immediately sent as reinforcements. Call wrote about the Creeks they found that next morning:

> They fought bravely to the last, none asking or receiving quarter, nor did resistance cease until the last warrior had fallen. Humanity might well have wept over the gory scene before us. We found as many as eight or ten dead bodies in a single cabin, sometimes the dead mother clasped the dead child to her breast, and to add another appalling horror to the bloody catalogue – some of the cabins had

> taken fire, and half consumed human bodies were seen amidst the smoking ruins.[12]

After the battle, an orphaned ten-month-old boy was discovered in the arms of his dead mother. Andrew Jackson had been an orphan himself, and since he and Rachel had no children of their own. They took in and cared for many young people through the years at their plantation, the Hermitage. This included Andrew Jackson Jr., Rachel's nephew, who was five when Jackson was handed the orphaned Creek baby. In what Jackson biographer Jon Meacham called "a combination of charity and condescension,"[13] Jackson decided to keep the infant himself and sent him home to Rachel with a note that explained, "I send on a little Indian boy for Andrew." He instructed that Lyncoya, as they named him, be kept in the house rather than with the slaves. Jackson provided the same education for Lyncoya that he did for Andrew Jr. and later even tried pulling strings to get him an appointment to West Point. When Lyncoya died of tuberculosis at age sixteen, he was working as an apprentice to a saddle maker in Nashville. He was buried at the Hermitage in an unmarked grave.

A few days after the victory against the Creeks at Tallushatchee, Jackson was at Fort Strother when he was informed by a Creek warrior friendly to the soldiers that Fort Leslie, thirty miles to the south, was being attacked by Red Sticks. The warrior had escaped by wrapping himself in the skin of a dead hog and crawling through the woods to safety. Jackson sent two thousand soldiers, including Crockett, to attempt the same style of attack that had worked at Tallushatchee. During the battle, Crockett observed a group of Creek warriors who "were all painted as red as scarlet, and were just as naked as they were born…came rushing forth like a cloud of Egyptian locusts, and screaming like all the young devils had been turned loose, with the old devil of all at their head."[14] Although three companies of militia retreated and allowed about seven hundred Creeks to break free and escape, the battle was considered a success with around three hundred Creeks killed, more than one hundred injured.

Based on things he wrote and some of the actions he took later in his career, it's obvious the "Injun' fighter" aspect of Crockett's public persona was not something he necessarily perpetuated. He was far more interested in hunting for food for his fellow soldiers, who received little, if any, rations or other supplies. Crockett received special permission to spend much of his time hunting to take meat back to the camp. It was clear that was how he preferred to spend his time as a soldier.

And when that time drew to an end, he was ready to go home, as were many of the Tennesseans who had enlisted around the same time as Crockett. Their worn-out clothing provided no protection from the dropping temperatures, their horses were exhausted, and the soldiers themselves were near starving. They had resorted to chewing on boiled beef hides and eating acorns. Many began deserting or leaving quickly as their term of service expired. At one point, a group of soldiers prepared to return home but were stopped by Jackson himself, who threatened to shoot the first soldier who left. They knew he would, too, so they returned to camp.

In his 1833 autobiography, Crockett wrote the story in a much different way in order to position Jackson as weak and ineffective and himself as a hero. He wrote,

> We got ready and moved on till we came near the bridge, where the general's men were all strung along on both sides, just like the office-holders are now, to keep us from getting along to the help of the country and the people. But we all had our flints ready picked, and our guns ready primed, that if we were fired on we might fight our way through, or all die together; just as we are now determined to save the country from ready ruin, or to sink down with it...when we had passed, no further attempt was made to stop us; but the general said, we were "the damned'st volunteers he had ever seen in his life; that we would volunteer and go out and fight, and then at our pleasure would volunteer and go home again, in spite of the devil.[15]

Crockett was likely not even present for any of the soldiers' attempted mutinies against Jackson or attempts to depart as a group. His autobiography also included an embellishment of his service record to include the battles at Emuckfaw and Enotachopco Creek, during which he was already back at "Kentuck" with his family. Crockett had enlisted for ninety days, and according to research of the payroll and muster records done by Crockett biographer, John B. Shackford, it appears that when his ninety days of enlistment was up on December 23, 1813, he returned home.

As he shared stories about his experiences during the Creek War with friends and family members, one encounter Crockett claimed to have overheard from Andrew Jackson made a great story and had a lasting impact. Crockett's company was evidently insubordinate, and their captain took the matter up with Jackson. According to Shackford, Crockett heard Jackson reply, "Don't you make orders on your men without maturing them, and then you execute them no matter what the cost; and that is all I have to say."[16] Crockett humorously summed up the already brief statement to friends by stating, "The old general told the captain to be sure he was right and then go ahead." The amusing story spread through the camp and, after Crockett became famous, several variations of "be sure you are right and then go ahead" became his catchphrase. Whether the origination story was accurate or not, Crockett was later nicknamed the "The Go Ahead Man," and he even sold autographed prints of his portrait with the phrase in his handwriting and with his signature.

On March 27, 1814, Andrew Jackson struck a near fatal blow to the Creek resistance to White settlement once and for all at the Battle of Horseshoe Bend near present-day Central Alabama. That winter, Red Sticks and Creeks who were not loyal to the White settlers gathered in the village of Tohopeka inside a bend of the Tallapoosa River. The number of Creek warriors had been greatly diminished by the previous battles, so the war chief Menawa had no more than one thousand warriors to prepare for a fight. Jackson and Coffee, split up, surrounded the Red Sticks, and began the battle. The Creeks were no match for the seven hundred infantry, six hundred Cherokees and Creeks who allied with the Americans, and two thousand soldiers of the East and West Tennessee militia. The result was a slaughter in which more than eight hundred Red Sticks were killed, while Jackson and Coffee only lost fifty men. The Creeks who remained later signed the Treaty of Fort Jackson that opened up more of the Mississippi Territory for settlement, giving the U.S. government more than twenty million acres, about half of what is present-day Alabama.

Jackson's Creek enemies called him "Mad Dog" and "Sharp Knife" because he wiped out much of their tribe. The soldiers called him "Old Hickory" for reasons already noted, but after his victories, he had a new title. The U.S. War Department officially commissioned him "Major General." Major General Andrew Jackson was put in charge of the Seventh Military District that included Tennessee, Louisiana, and the entire Mississippi Territory. It is unknown how Crockett felt back in Franklin County as he heard the news of the heroics of Andrew Jackson and the West Tennessee volunteers who were victorious at Horseshoe Bend, but something triggered a desire to reenlist in September 1814. It could have been a bit of jealousy over his fellow Tennessean's success while Crockett was home with his family; more likely, he was ready for another adventure.

Crockett was not the type to stay home, and signing up for another term of service provided an opportunity to explore the territory of Florida, a place he had never been. He later blamed his desire to reenlist on wanting a taste of "British fighting." Again, Polly was against his leaving, but just like when he enlisted the first time, her demands carried little weight. He wrote, "Here again the entreaties of my wife were thrown in the way of my going, but all in vain; for I always had a way of just going ahead, at whatever I had a mind to."[17]

In September 1814, Crockett arrived at Camp Blount with about one thousand other volunteers, where he enlisted for six months as one of John Cowan's company of Tennessee Mounted Gunmen, serving as a third sergeant. Again, for much of this term of service, Crockett spent his time hunting. Food was again in short supply, and the soldiers were often starving. Six weeks before his enlistment was set to expire, he returned home on a furlough, then paid another man to finish out his term of service, which was common at that time.

Meanwhile, Andrew Jackson headed south and became a national hero in the Battle of New Orleans. On January 8, 1815, Jackson and a mostly untrained army of around four thousand, made up of volunteers, Native Americans, and New Orleans residents—including a pirate or two—defended the city against a thirty-minute attack by the British, who numbered more than eight thousand. After the smoke cleared, the United States had suffered only sixty casualties while the better trained and experienced British army lost two thousand, including three generals and seven colonels. Although a treaty with the British had actually already been signed, many newspapers wrote articles that positioned Andrew Jackson as a "savior of American freedom." Overnight, he became the most beloved hero in the young country. As one Pennsylvania minister later wrote, "The fame of the hero of New Orleans is imperishable."[18]

Around the same time, things were not going well for David Crockett. It's likely that Polly was not well when he arrived home, although in his autobiography, he wrote about this period without many details or a timeline. He wrote, "I found them all well and doing well; and though I was only a rough sort of a backwoodsman, they seemed mighty glad to see me." He added with a touch of defensiveness, "...however little the quality folks might suppose it. For I do reckon we love as hard in the backwood country, as any people in the whole creation."[19]

Crockett had reason to be defensive when he wrote that years later. Polly Crockett died June 7, 1815, likely from lingering illness after the birth of her daughter or from one of the sicknesses like malaria, tuberculosis, cholera, or influenza that settlers died from with great frequency during that time. Polly's death left Crockett, a husband and father who spent very little time at home, a widower with no money, three small children to care for, and very few prospects for the future.

## Chapter Three Notes

1. Tom Kanon, "The Kidnapping of Martha Crawley and Settler-Indian Relations Prior to the War of 1812." *Tennessee Historical Quarterly* 64, no. 1 (2005): 4.
2. Crockett, *Narrative*, 72.
3. Ibid., 73.
4. Ibid.
5. Caroline Mays Brevard, "Richard Keith Call," *The Florida Historical Society Quarterly*, Volumes 1 & 2 (April 1908): 6.
6. Crockett, *Narrative*, 75.
7. Ibid., 75.
8. Ibid., 82.
9. Ibid., 88.
10. Ibid., 89-90.
11. Brevard, "Richard Keith Call," 5.
12. Richard K. Call, "The Journal of Governor Richard K. Call," State Library and Archives of Florida, 20.
13. Jon Meacham, *American Lion, Andrew Jackson in the White House* (New York: Random House New York, 2008), 34.
14. Crockett, *Narrative*, 92.
15. Ibid., 95.
16. James Atkins Shackford, *David Crockett, The Man and the Legend* (Chapel Hill: The University of North Carolina Press, 1956), 26.
17. Crockett, *Narrative*, 101.
18. B. M. Dusenbery, *Monument to the Memory of General Andrew Jackson* (Philadelphia: Walker & Gillis, 1846), 338.
19. Crockett, *Narrative*, 123.

*Library of Congress*

Growing up, future president Theodore Roosevelt Jr. read stories about David Crockett and developed an appreciation for the frontiersman's love of hunting. In September 1883, Roosevelt made his first trip to the American West, after which he began a lifelong passion for nature and conservation. In this photo, taken by George Grantham Bain in 1885, Roosevelt is seen in the buckskin, moccasins, and animal fur cap that became so closely associated with Crockett.

**Fame is a fickle food upon a shifting plate.**
**—Emily Dickinson**

**Chapter Four**

# Treaties

Issues relating to West Tennessee land and Native Americans were interwoven throughout the lives and careers of both David Crockett and his nemesis, Andrew Jackson. While Jackson worked hard to part the Native Americans from all their land as quickly as possible, Crockett's goal was to make sure the poor West Tennessee squatters got to keep what he saw as their fair share of it. Between 1785 and 1830, using negotiation tactics that included threats, coercion, bribery, and blackmail, all that land was slowly ceded to the United States.

One of the first agreements between White settlers and Native Americans was the Treaty of Chickasaw Bluffs. Signed in October 1801, the Chickasaw agreed to accept $700 in goods in exchange for letting the United States widen the Natchez Trace. This natural trail extended from Nashville, Tennessee through Alabama to Natchez, Mississippi and linked three rivers: the Cumberland, the Tennessee, and the Mississippi. It was first used by bison and other animals to travel back and forth between salt licks near what would become Nashville and the grasslands along the Mississippi River. It was also a path frequently taken by Native Americans making their way to hunting grounds and was later used by explorers and settlers. The Treaty of Chickasaw Bluffs gave the United States Army permission, under Chickasaw supervision, to make the trail wide enough from one end to the other for wagons, and it gave the Chickasaw exclusive rights to build inns, trading posts, and ferries along the route. While the arrangement did provide a brief period of economic gain for those Chickasaws who were in a position to take advantage of the opportunity, it also opened the door for more settlers to notice potential in the fertile Chickasaw land for farming.

A second treaty was signed in 1805 at Chokkilissa', the primary village of the Chickasaw. This marked the first time that the tribe ceded land to the United States government. They were given $20,000 in cash, and the government paid off $20,000 of debt that members of the tribe had accumulated at trading posts. In exchange, the United States received more than two million acres of Native American hunting ground in present-day Kentucky, central Tennessee, and northern Alabama. Settlers poured into the region during the next decade, buying land and then clearing the timber to farm. Of course, boundaries set in the treaties were not adhered to by the settlers, who usually didn't even know where they were. Squatters—settlers who lived on a piece of land without owning it—made some of the Chickasaw land their own by simply moving onto it, building a cabin, and clearing the land for farms. For many settlers, the Native American's lack of "improving" the land was proof they didn't own it. To them, it was up for grabs, and treaties were not even necessary.

Andrew Jackson felt the same way, but saw treaties as the simplest way to get what he and many of the American people wanted while preventing more bloodshed. As a result of his legal background, temperament, and experience with Native Americans, he got very good at seperating them from their land. From 1814 to 1824, Jackson led or was part of nine out of eleven treaties with Native American tribes on behalf of the United States.

Early on, he and others negotiating on behalf of the country discovered that the best way to get what they wanted was to deal primarily with the Native Americans who were "mixed-blood." This typically meant that their mothers were Native American, and their fathers were White.

This was the case with George Colbert, who was the second oldest of five sons of his father, Scottish trader James Logan Colbert, and one of the three Chickasaw women with whom the elder Colbert established different homes, families, and trading posts. James Colbert made his home along the Tombigbee River and established himself as a friend to the Chickasaw during the mid-1700s, when they and the British fought with the French and the Choctaw. His son, George Colbert, along with George's brothers, Levi and William, became influential because of their familiarity with the English language and their business experience from working with their father and his business associates. They were valuable as translators and negotiators for both sides, but the brothers also capitalized on their unique position and did very well for themselves. For example, George Colbert opened a very successful trading post on the Natchez Trace, taking advantage of the agreement in the 1801 treaty that gave the Chickasaw exclusivity.

Andrew Jackson put his negotiation skills to good use after a dispute arose in 1816 between the Creek, the Chickasaw, and the Cherokee about the boundary between tribes in Northwest Alabama. The United States government saw an opportunity and made plans to purchase the land "to keep harmony among the tribes." Jackson and delegates from the United States met with Chickasaw representatives on September 8, 1816 at George Colbert's home, the Chickasaw Council House. The Cherokee delegation was late, and the Creeks didn't even bother attending. By the end of the negotiation, Jackson and the others from his delegation had purchased the disputed land from the Cherokee, whether they actually owned it or not. Jackson noted in his report afterward, "...it was found both well and polite to make a few presents to the chiefs and interpreters."[1] When the Chickasaw leaders continued their fight, claiming the Cherokee had no right to agree to anything on their behalf, another meeting was arranged. This one was held at "Turkey's Town," sometimes called Turkeytown, on the Coosa River, near present-day Cherokee County, Alabama. Jackson wasn't worried; he wrote,

> It was soon found that a favorable result to the negotiation was not to be anticipated unless we addressed ourselves feelingly to the

> predominant and governing passions of all Indian tribes...presents were offered to the influential chiefs amounting to $4,500, to be paid on the success of the negotiations. The measure seemed to produce some sensible effect.[2]

The "presents" worked. The Treaty of Turkeytown, signed by representatives of the Cherokee in 1816, opens with a paragraph, "To perpetuate peace and friendship between the United States and Cherokee tribe, or nation, of Indians, and to remove all future causes of dissension which may arise from indefinite territorial boundaries..." Of course, that treaty did not remove "all future causes of dissension" because what most settlers and land speculators really wanted was all Native Americans moved as far away as possible.

Two years later, the Chickasaw were back at the negotiating table. This time, along with Jackson was Isaac Shelby, a Revolutionary War hero and two-time governor of Kentucky. Those representing the Chickasaw included Chief Tishomingo, Chinubby "the Boy King," and George and Levi Colbert. The Treaty of Old Town, later known as the Jackson Purchase, was negotiated and signed on October 19, 1818.

Although Jackson and Shelby walked away having accomplished their mission, it wasn't without a disagreement between the two men, who were both used to being in charge. A decade after the treaty was signed and a few years after Shelby's death, it was reported in newspapers that he had predicted that Jackson's presidential administration would be "a reign of fury and turbulence." Shelby's prediction was said to be a result of Jackson's actions during the treaty negotiation. The writer claimed that Shelby privately shared with his family that had Jackson's "rash, hot-headed temper" not been restrained, "it would have cost the nation double the sum for the land that was ultimately purchased" and that Jackson had displayed "disinterested patriotism."[3] Jackson would have readied his dueling pistols after reading Shelby's accusation in print, but by the time this second-hand report was shared, Shelby was already in his grave on the grounds of his estate, Traveler's Rest, in Lincoln County, Kentucky.

Someone else who personally witnessed the negotiations with the

Cherokee that was still alive, however, was Jackson's close friend and trusted advisor, William Berkeley Lewis. Born in northern Virginia, Lewis settled in Nashville in 1809, where he worked in one of the Tennessee land offices. Lewis was taller than most other men of his day at more than six feet and was said to have had "shoulders as broad as a door."[4]

Educated, smart, and ambitious, Lewis served as an assistant quartermaster to Jackson in 1812 and earned his trust while recruiting Tennessee volunteers and providing Jackson's army with as many provisions as he could get. He even persuaded the Nashville Bank to loan him money that he used to personally purchase supplies for the soldiers. After Jackson's triumph in New Orleans, it was Lewis who prepared the hero's homecoming celebration in Nashville.

During the early years of their friendship, Lewis earned Jackson's loyalty and trust, and that would pay off in years to come. In addition to succeeding in his professional endeavors, Lewis also made a shrewd choice in his personal life in 1813 when he married Margaret Lewis. She was a daughter of William Terrell Lewis, one of Tennessee's wealthiest land speculators and planters who had died earlier that same year. Not only did the marriage improve Lewis's financial lot in life, it practically made he and Jackson family as Margaret was one of Jackson's wards.

After his marriage, William Lewis was suddenly the owner of many properties, including the Nashville Inn. Considered a social hotspot for the notables of Tennessee at the time, the hotel's guestbook reads like a who's who of government and military leaders. It was there that Jackson was taken after his barfight with Thomas Hart Benton. Tennessee governor Willie Blount hosted a dinner at the Nashville Inn to present Jackson with a sword given by the state of Mississippi after his victory in New Orleans. When he was governor of Tennessee, Sam Houston even called the inn home. And when the leaders of the city, including Jackson, wanted to impress the Marquis de Lafayette during his patriotic tour of America, they held a banquet there.

Through the years, Aaron Burr, James Monroe, Martin Van Buren, and King Louis Philippe of France all spent at least an evening or two under its roof.[5]

Thanks to his bride, Lewis was also now the owner of a 150-acre estate with a mansion called Fairfield that was so large, it later became Nashville's St. Margaret's Hospital. Fairfield was located on the road between Nashville and Jackson's home, the Hermitage, so Jackson was a frequent houseguest.

According to a letter from Lewis published in the *Argus of Western America* on July 12, 1828, the comments against Jackson attributed to Shelby couldn't have been further from the truth. According to Lewis's account, it was actually Shelby whose temper got the best of him during the negotiations with the Chickasaw. Lewis wrote that he, too, was serving as an agent for the United States and that Jackson and Shelby had agreed in advance to pay no more than $300,000 for the land.

Toward the end of the negotiation, after they had agreed verbally to $280,000 at $20,000 per year for fourteen years, Levi Colbert asked for "one cent" to be added to the deal. Colbert noted, "the American nation is as strong as iron—great, rich and strong, and one cent is nothing to it." Jackson replied that if the addition of one solitary additional cent would satisfy them, then "the younger brother must satisfy the older brother," and they shook hands. Later that evening, Jackson discovered from the interpreter that there had been a "misunderstanding" and that he had shaken hands on an additional *year* of payment—another $20,000—not an additional cent. When the Chickasaws arrived to sign the treaty, they were informed of the misunderstanding, and it appeared the entire deal was at risk of falling apart. According to Lewis's version, Shelby was adamant that they not budge from the agreed-upon fourteen years of payments, but Jackson was eager to close the deal, so he was willing to give the Chickasaw what they wanted.

As Jackson pointed out to Shelby, they had agreed to go as high as $300,000, and that is where they had ended up. Frustrated, Shelby then responded that he had actually intended that amount to include the expenses of holding the negotiations.

In order to get the treaty signed, Lewis proposed to Shelby that if the fifteenth payment of $20,000 was the only thing keeping him from moving forward, Lewis himself would put up a personal bond of $20,000 in case the government was unwilling to include the fifteenth year (an unlikely scenario). Jackson and Lewis would then find buyers who were interested in purchasing West Tennessee land. Shelby finally agreed, and the treaty was signed, adding two thousand square miles to the state of Kentucky, now referred to as the Jackson Purchase, and six thousand square miles to Tennessee, filling out the western portion of the state.

In a letter to the secretary of war, John C. Calhoun, signed by Jackson and Shelby, they were clearly proud of their accomplishment and wrote, "We trust you will see in our procedure all our genius and efforts used to obtain the object of our mission and the means used by which we obtained success, we hope [it] will be approved by the President."[6]

Afterward, according to Lewis, Shelby apparently had a change of heart. He wrote, "Governor Shelby, when he reflected on the part he had acted at the treaty, became convinced, no doubt, that his conduct had been hasty, if not rash. This may be inferred from the circumstance of his directing Col. Butler to destroy the bond he had taken for the last annuity, before he reached Nashville on his return."[7]

What Lewis neglected to include in his letter to the editors of the newspaper was that he had a little secret deal of his own happening under the table. Thanks to his late father-in-law, he owned thousands of acres of valuable land claims in West Tennessee, and once the cession was finalized, they would become even more valuable. He also had his eye on a natural salt lick next to the Big Sandy River, slightly northwest of present-day Henry County, Tennessee, that was in Cherokee territory. Supposedly, without the knowledge of Jackson or Shelby, Lewis had arrived at the negotiation with an agreement already in place with one of his business partners, Robert P. Currin, to establish a salt works at the lick once Lewis obtained rights to the property. Privately, Lewis made a deal with the Cherokee representatives that if they ask to be allowed to keep four square miles around the salt lick, they could lease it back to Lewis for 199 years in exchange for 750 bushels of salt or $750 each year. When it was proposed, Jackson saw no harm in allowing the Cherokees their request and including it in the treaty.

Lewis and the Cherokees signed a lease in secret the day after the treaty was signed. Eventually, Lewis's scheme was uncovered, and although Jackson was exonerated of any guilt, it became political fodder that was used against him for the rest of his political career. The embarrassing fiasco did little to impact Jackson's appreciation for Lewis. As one historian wrote, "Next to bold defiance the old General liked best complete subserviency." He added that Lewis remained a "loyal lieutenant, confidential agent, ghost writer, party fixer, conspirator, and 'kitchen' Machiavelli."[8]

All the trouble Lewis went through to get a little extra for himself was ultimately for nothing. After the mining of the salt lick began at great expense in 1821, rather than reservoirs of the valuable mineral, all they found were artesian wells filled with sulphur water. After spending $50,000, Lewis abandoned the salt lick and left behind ten thousand gallons per hour of steaming hot water gushing out of the ground.

While Lewis's salt lick was a bust, his scheme was a boom for early West Tennessee tourism when the area became a bustling resort catering to those who believed the water had medicinal value. A large, two-story hotel offering spa treatments became a popular destination that included a baseball field, bowling alley, and picnic grounds. The area was later intentionally flooded by the Tennessee Valley Authority and the water that now covers it can be seen from the Big Sandy Peninsula between the Big Sandy and Tennessee Rivers. Visitors to the museum at the Tennessee National Wildlife Refuge located there will find a marker that tells the story of the area. Those who look closely will even notice a photograph of David Crockett's second great-granddaughter, Mildred Tharpe, enjoying the sulphur water at the resort in the 1920s.

Men like Isaac Shelby, William Lewis, and Andrew Jackson began their careers with ambitious goals of obtaining positions that would give them professional power and personal wealth. Because their early years included education and connections to support their ambition, their ascent to prominent roles was not so surprising. The same cannot be said for David Crockett, who had no education, little money, and only a vague awareness of politics. This makes his rise to fame in the next few years even more remarkable.

## Chapter Four Notes

1. Guy B. Braden, "The Colberts and the Chickasaw Nation." *Tennessee Historical Quarterly* 17, no. 3 (1958): 244.
2. Ibid., 244.
3. "General Jackson and Governor Shelby," *Argus of Western America* (July 30, 1828): 1.
4. Marquis James, *The Life of Andrew Jackson* (Indianapolis: The Bobbs-Merrill Company, 1938), 345.
5. Gates P. Thruston, "The Nashville Inn," *The American Historical Magazine and Tennessee Historical Society* Quarterly 7, no. 2 (1902): 176.
6. Correspondence from Isaac Shelby and Andrew Jackson to John C. Calhoun, October 30, 1818, MS-001 Moses Dawson Correspondence, University Archives and Special Collections, Xavier University Library, Cincinnati, Ohio.
7. "Jackson and Shelby," *Argus of Western America,* 1.
8. Louis R. Harlan, "Public Career of William Berkeley Lewis," *Tennessee Historical Quarterly* 7, no. 1 (1948): 4.

*Museum of the City of New York*

*Ballet Ballads*, the first collaboration of composer Jerome Moross and lyricist John Latouche, premiered in 1948 in New York City and was considered a breakthrough in dance. The musical combined elements of American theater, dance, and heritage into a contemporary musical. One of the four acts in the ballet, "The Eccentricities of Davy Crockett," was loosely based on Crockett's life. Pictured are a group of dancers performing a segment inspired by Crockett's association with bear hunting.

**Sometimes you want to go / Where everybody knows your name / And they're always glad you came / You want to be where you can see / Our troubles are all the same / You want to be where everybody knows your name.**

**—Gary Portnoy and Judy Hart Angelo, "Cheers Theme"**

## Chapter Five

# Politics

If you dropped in on David Crockett in the fall of 1817, you would find a respected thirty-one-year-old military veteran who is admired by friends and family for his hunting skills, marksmanship, and ability to thrive outdoors in situations that others wouldn't dare attempt.

And he was a newlywed for the second time. Elizabeth Patton was, by what few accounts there are, a strong woman and a good match for Crockett. She was from a prominent North Carolina family that had some wealth, especially compared to Crockett. With his finances in much better shape thanks to her, he headed east with the blended family that then included five children. They settled 160 acres on Shoal Creek in an area that would soon become Lawrence County, Tennessee.

Crockett's move would lead to numerous life-changing events for him and his growing family. While they would experience the first of many financial setbacks while there, the move also introduced Crockett to the world of politics. It was there he launched his career as a public servant representing West Tennessee and began a fascinating political journey that ended with him being considered as a possible candidate for president of the United States.

Crockett frequently made a good first impression, and shortly after his move to town, he was selected to join four others in laying out the boundaries of the new county, choose a name, and find a good location for the county seat. For the name, they agreed to honor James Lawrence, an American naval officer who became a hero during the War of 1812. Today, Lawrence is most remembered for his final words to those in his command, "Don't give up the ship." As it turned out, naming the town after a man who gave a final command to not give up in a fight was fitting for Crockett, both as a Lawrence County commissioner and for the rest of the political career that lay before him. He was nothing if not tenacious. Crockett and another commissioner wanted the location for the county seat, Lawrenceburg, to be closer to Shoal Creek. The other three men wanted it closer to Jackson's Military Road, which was under construction at the time. Named, of course, in honor of Andrew Jackson after his heroism and contribution to ending the War of 1812, the road would take travelers from Nashville, Tennessee to New Orleans. The location Crockett favored for the county seat had been recommended by the Tennessee General Assembly. Of course, it would also help Crockett personally, as it was near the location of his new gristmill operation. The stalemate over the location of the county seat lasted for years, and by the time the decision was finally made in 1823 to put it near Jackson's Military Road, it no longer really mattered to him. Crockett's business venture on Shoal Creek had been destroyed in a flood, and he had moved his family up to Northwest Tennessee.

While the disagreement raged on, Crockett's role in local government continued to grow. When he first arrived in Lawrence County, he did not believe the absence of someone to maintain "law and order" would be a problem. He quickly came to appreciate the importance of legal structure even in a small community:

> We remained here some two or three years, without any law at all; and so many bad characters began to flock in upon us, that we found it necessary to set up a sort of temporary government of our own...

> we lived in the back-woods, and didn't profess to know much, and no doubt used many wrong words. But we met, and appointed magistrates and constables to keep order. We didn't fix any laws for them, tho'; for we supposed they would know law enough, whoever they might be; and so we left it to themselves to fix the laws.[1]

Crockett was appointed the role of esquire judge or, using a more contemporary term, justice of the peace. These judges met four times a year and administered the legal affairs of the county. They were responsible for dealing with citizens who violated the agreed-upon standards of morality and behavior including adultery, drunkenness, and disorderly conduct. They also heard civil cases and functioned as a grand jury does today. Although Crockett had almost no formal education or experience in many of these areas, he reflected later that he made decisions based on common sense and honesty. He wrote, "I gave my decisions on the principles of common justice and honesty between man and man, and relied on natural born sense, and not on law learning to guide me; for I had never read a page in a law book in all my life."[2]

What inspired Crockett as he began a career of public service is somewhat of a mystery. In his autobiography, he wrote very little about his family, with the exception of several stories about his father, John Crockett, with whom it seems he had a complicated relationship. In one of the stories, Crockett possibly indicates a desire for approval from a father figure was at least part of his motivation in the years to come.

It was common practice at that time for children to work off the debts of their fathers. This was the case when Crockett went to work off the thirty-six dollars that John Crockett owed a man named Abraham Wilson. Crockett noted that he left in six months, as soon as the debt was worked off, although Wilson wanted him to stick around "mighty bad." After six months of working in an environment where, as he described it, "a heap of bad company met to drink and gamble," Crockett was ready to work for his own money and under better conditions. He went to the home of John Kennedy, "an honest, old Quaker," and offered his services. Kennedy agreed to a one-week trial, and at the end of the week, he was so impressed by young Crockett's work ethic that he was eager to offer him a job. Unfortunately, there was one catch. It turned out that Crockett's father also owed Kennedy money, but he gave the younger Crockett the option of paying off his father's forty-dollar debt by working the next six months with no pay. He took Kennedy up on the offer, and although his family was living fifteen miles away from Kennedy's farm, Crockett never once visited them until he could return with the note paid in full. He wrote,

> Some time after I got there, I pulled out the note and handed it to my father, who supposed Mr. Kennedy had sent it for collection. The old man looked mighty sorry, and said to me he had not the money to pay it, and didn't know what he should do. I then told him I had paid it for him, and it was then his own; that it was not presented for collection, but as a present from me. At this, he shed a heap of tears; and as soon as he got a little over it, he said he was sorry he couldn't give me any thing, but he was not able, he was too poor.[3]

This story was written by Crockett when he was working in Washington, surrounded by men who had come from notable families of status and, often, great wealth. While it was likely included to emphasize for potential voters his work ethic and humble beginnings from one of Tennessee's poorest families, it may also reveal some of the motivation for the rest of his unusual career. In the coming years, he worked to help other poor Tennesseans obtain, at a fair price, the land they had already settled and been living on.

During his political career, Crockett would often be underestimated and misunderstood. A story in his autobiography about how he came to be "Colonel Crockett" offers a nice example of the way he responded to perceived injustice. One of Crockett's neighbors, Captain Daniel Matthews, came to him with a proposition. Matthews was a successful farmer and was going to run for the office of colonel of the local regiment. He suggested that Crockett also run in that election but for the position of first major. Like other Tennessee counties, Lawrence County was required to have at least one military regiment with elected officers who had specific roles and responsibilities. Groups of armed citizens that were trained to serve as soldiers when needed had been a big part of the American Revolution, and it was also put into place in Tennessee by these early settlers. It stands to reason that people carving out a home in the wilderness would appreciate an organized system of armed protection and, even better, if those leading the military regiments had actual experience in battle, like Crockett.

Crockett wrote that he first declined Matthews's offer to run because he had seen enough fighting and "wanted nothing to do with the military appointments."[4] Eventually, Matthews convinced Crockett, and he agreed to run. On the day before the election, Crockett, along with many of his and Elizabeth's extended family members who had followed them to the area, arrived at a corn shuckin' that Matthews was hosting. Once a farmer's corn had been picked from the stalks and piled in the yard or the corn crib, friends and neighbors gathered together to shuck the corn by removing the silk and the husk. Many of the men competed on teams to determine who could husk the most corn with the greatest speed, while women typically brought the refreshments. The work was certainly appreciated by those hosting the event, so liquor was usually plentiful. It was the perfect opportunity for political speeches, especially if the host, like Matthews, was planning to announce a run for office himself.

Crockett had been told by Matthews that the event would kick off their mutual campaigns, but he would soon discover that either Matthews' loyalty had shifted, or the man was more conniving than Crockett knew. According to Crockett, while he was at the party, a friend took him aside and whispered the news that Matthews's own son was planning to announce that he was going to be running against Crockett. Did Matthews assume his son could easily beat him? Confused and angry, he confronted Matthews and asked if this new information was true. Possibly in an attempt to avoid any sort of physical confrontation, Matthews tried to flatter Crockett by saying that his son hated running against Crockett more than anyone else in the county.

Whether it was a spur-of-the-moment decision or if he had anticipated it in advance is unknown, but at that point, Crockett let Matthews know that his son had nothing to worry about because Crockett now intended to run for colonel against Matthews himself. Crockett later wrote about what happened next:

> He then made a speech, and informed the people that I was his opponent. I mounted up for a speech too. I told the people the cause of my opposing him, remarking that as I had the whole family to run against any way, I was determined to levy on the head of the mess. When the time for the election came, his son was opposed by another man for major; and he and his daddy were both badly beaten.[5]

While this was written by Crockett many years after it occurred, it shows his approach to campaigning and how he handled those early elections. First, he was usually underestimated by an opponent with more financial success or education. They often were short on ethics and looking out more for themselves than the people they were elected to serve. An abundance of charisma also played a part in his popularity. Years later, one newspaper editor wrote, "David Crockett is neither grammatical nor graceful—we cannot say that he possesses eloquence; but verily there is something, a certain *je ne sais quoi* in the man, that makes people attentive whenever he opens his mouth."[6] In a style that would combine humility, humor, and common sense, Crockett connected with "regular folk" as one of them and asked for their vote.

And he frequently got it, as was the case in his campaign against Matthews. Crockett had experienced his first taste of victory in an election—made even sweeter by defeating someone who thought he was Crockett's superior. Crockett was commissioned lieutenant colonel commandant of the Fifty-seventh Regiment of Militia on March 27, 1818. "Colonel Crockett," rather than the perjorative "Davy," would be the name most frequently used for the rest of his life. This was his first surprising win, but it wouldn't be his last.

He appears to have enjoyed the notoriety and validation that came from his position in the community. In 1821, Crockett decided to try his hand at state government with a run for the General Assembly, the lower house of the Tennessee state legislature. There is no record of how Elizabeth felt about his pursuit of yet another endeavor that would keep him away from home and require the family to spend more money. Like other women of the day, she had little input into her husband's actions, and she had absolutely no power.

With such a large family of small children, she was extremely vulnerable, and his frequent absences were likely not appreciated. Rebecca Elvira Crockett, his and Elizabeth's second child and first daughter together, was born on December 15, 1818. She joined a household that then consisted of Elizabeth's two children: George Patton, age eight, and Margaret Ann Patton, age six; Crockett's three children with his late wife: John Wesley, age eleven, William, age ten, and Margaret, age six; and David and Elizabeth Crockett's first son together: Robert Patton, age two. Their daughter Matilda would be born in August 1821. With seven children to care for, each time her husband left home for another extended period, Elizabeth Crockett must have reflected back to the time early in their marriage when he left and nearly didn't return.

In the fall of 1816, Crockett, along with a few other men, set off to explore what would become central Alabama. Along the way, he became deathly ill with a case of malaria. As he lay incoherent in a stranger's cabin just twenty miles from home, his traveling companions returned to Elizabeth Crockett and informed her that her husband had disappeared and was likely dead.

She hired a man to trace her husband's steps to try and find out for certain if he had died and to find out what had happened to his money and belongings if he was no longer living. The man was still out looking for him when Crockett showed up emaciated, exhausted, and barely alive. Although not funny at the time, he could laugh about it later. Crockett wrote that when Elizabeth told him she had been told he was dead, he "know'd this was a whapper of a lie, as soon as I heard it."[7] Crockett would periodically suffer from the aftereffects of that bout with malaria for the rest of his life.

After that close call and with a house full of little mouths to feed, the thought of him on the road campaigning for office must have been difficult for her, but he would need all the practice he could get for what lay ahead. He wrote that the thought of making a speech at first terrified him, and he choked up as though his mouth was "jam'd and cram'd chock full of dry mush."[8]

As Crockett campaigned at community events like squirrel shoots, dances, corn shuckin's, and parties, he honed his style and discovered that the people of West Tennessee he intended to serve didn't actually want to listen to polished politicians speak for hours about the "judiciary." More times than not, they preferred to be entertained.

Historian and biographer Van Wyck Brooks eloquently described Crockett's style on the campaign trail. He wrote, "He had a tongue of his own...the language of the canebrake, a mixture of fantasy, poetry and backwoods wit, and he won election to Congress with this by telling a few good stories, after letting the other candidates wear out the crowd with oratory."[9]

Crockett kept his speeches short, focused on telling stories, and made sure there was plenty of whiskey to go around. He was not a wealthy son of the aristocracy or owner of a large amount of land, and he owned few if any enslaved people at the time. He was an ordinary, poor farmer and hunter, just like the people he was hoping to represent—frontier settlers with the courage to carve out a life in a dangerous wilderness. Pointing that out seemed to go a long way. Crockett won his campaign to state legislature representing the Tennessee counties of Lawrence and Hickman and attended his first session on September 17, 1821.

A story he told about the first time he met James K. Polk, after Crockett had won his first election, is a good example of how he later positioned those early years in politics. Polk, a Tennessean who would eventually become the eleventh president of the United States, was the clerk of the Tennessee State Senate during Crockett's first term. As Crockett told the story, there was a large group of people standing around talking, and Polk—a young man himself at just thirty-two years old at the time—looked directly at Crockett and said, "Well Colonel, I suppose we shall have a radical change of the judiciary at the next session of the legislature." Although he responded that there certainly would be, he backed out of the group and left as quickly as he could. He wrote, "I was afraid some one would ask me what the judiciary was; and if I knowed I wish I may be shot. I don't indeed believe I had ever before heard that there was any such thing in all nature; but still I was not willing that the people there should know how ignorant I was about it."[10]

In writing about Crockett claiming ignorance of the meaning of the word judiciary, biographer James Shackford didn't buy it:

> The reader can judge for himself whether or not a man who had been around the judiciary for four years as a justice of the peace, court referee, and town commissioner, being daily in the courts, and signing official records, having been elected to several political positions of military rank and now to the state legislature, would be unfamiliar with the word "Judiciary" in the summer of 1821, at thirty-five years of age.[11]

While he was focused on the "regular folk" of his West Tennessee district, his personal fortunes took a dramatic turn for the worse when that flood destroyed the gristmill he and his wife had built. By the time his term ended, he had moved his family up to Northwest Tennessee and put politics behind him—or so he thought.

Early in 1823, Crockett had collected a large number of animal skins while hunting around his new home near Reelfoot Lake. He and his son, John Wesley, loaded them on a horse and took them about forty miles southeast to Jackson, Tennessee, the closest town of any size. He sold the skins and purchased items needed on the frontier that couldn't be grown in the ground or hunted in the woods—like coffee, sugar, gunpowder, and salt. Afterward, he stopped by a local tavern and shared a few drinks with friends from his military days who introduced him to Dr. William Butler and a few others. Butler was planning a run for the state legislature representing five new Tennessee counties that would include the newly formed Carroll County near where Crockett had settled.

As Butler and the others joked with Crockett about running again for the state legislature, Crockett let them know that he was done with politics and wanted nothing to do with it. It was a good thing, too, because it seemed like Crockett wouldn't stand a chance running against a man like Butler anyway. Butler received his medical degree from the University of Pennsylvania, then opened a practice in Murfreesboro, Tennessee in 1813.

He was well connected, having served under Andrew Jackson as a surgeon during the War of 1812. Butler and Jackson even became family when Butler married one of Jackson's nieces, Martha Thompson Hays. In 1820, Jackson and his business partners hired Butler as one of the first land agents for the sale of lots in the new town of Memphis. While in Memphis, Butler quickly determined that life in a river city was not for him. The connection was yet to be drawn, but he saw firsthand the results of yellow fever and malaria that came with living so close to a large body of water, the perfect breeding ground for mosquitoes. The streets, if you could call them that, were filled with mud, and in the summer, the heat and humidity was nearly unbearable.

One newspaper editorial from the small town of Randolph, Tennessee, about thirty miles north of Memphis, shared with readers the fate in store for the flatboat pilots who might fall ill while on the river and stop in Memphis:

> ...low and damp, partly inundated with floods two or three months in each year, leaving ponds and pools of dead stagnant water scattered along the river's valley for a thousand miles, with vegetation luxuriant beyond bounds and a sun at fever heat, filling the atmosphere with a miasma of the most poisonous type, and in a climate whose citizens even flee from the ravages of its deadly maladies, half of the time where the call for a Physician cannot be heard or the healing influence of medicine sought, among strangers hardened in scenes of death, cold and friendless, no mother or sister to soothe and soften with their anxious and watchful presence, the pains of a lingering and a painful sickness, you die, unknown and unwept, and in thoughtless silence buried upon the bank of the river, perhaps without a shroud or coffin, a tree or stick for a tomb-stone, a little hill of mud swelling over your body, and the

> first heaving of the mighty river sweeping all away into the recesses of its turgid bowels.[12]

Butler decided that a little further east was more to his liking. He purchased and donated the land to establish the town of Jackson, Tennessee, about eighty-five miles east of Memphis, and he became one of the new town's first commissioners. This would make him an excellent candidate for the state legislature.

The men continued to push Crockett to throw his hat in the ring. He continued to decline, pointing out that his cabin was far from any "White settlements." Imagine his surprise when several weeks later he heard that his name had been submitted to the *Jackson Gazette* as a candidate. He assumed this was an attempt by Butler and those who had been at the tavern that night to have a little fun at his expense. It was at best, a joke, and at worst, an insult. Unlike Jackson, Crockett wasn't one to defend his honor by pulling out dueling pistols. Instead, he jumped into the race, taking to heart the saying "success is the best revenge." They ran a clean and mostly friendly campaign. Those running for office traveled and made appearances together, as was often the case then, making the same speeches at each stop. Crockett preferred going last, and usually drew the event to a close with a few funny stories and an attempt to connect with the audience using humor. At one stop, Butler was happy to concede to Crockett's request to go first for a change. But Butler surely shook his head in wide-eyed disbelief as Crockett began; he had memorized Butler's entire speech and delivered it word for word.

The other candidates backed out to give Butler a better chance of winning against Crockett, and the two men continued the campaign. Crockett later referred to Butler as the most talented man he had ever run against. Crockett's approach during the campaign shifted to focus on Butler's wealth, and he accused him of being out of touch with common men. According to one story, Butler invited Crockett to dine at his magnificent home. Although not as opulent as the "Little Hermitage" that Butler would build at the intersection of Chester and Royal Streets in Jackson in the years to come, it was one of the finest cabins in West Tennessee at the time. Some family portraits that were painted in Europe and valuable steel engravings may have already been hanging on his walls. Crockett noticed an intricately woven rug and, as a joke, began "hopping like a toad to keep from stepping on the beautiful flowers."[13] At that time, most voters had wood or dirt floors, possibly covered by a dried animal skins or fur, if anything, so a woven rug was considered a luxury few could afford. Crockett made sure to begin including reference to Butler's fancy carpet in his speeches.

While campaigning, Crockett also wrote that he wanted to be certain to leave people no worse off than when he found them. To illustrate, he told Butler in front of a large crowd that he was having a buckskin hunting shirt made with two pockets. He was going to keep a bottle of liquor in one pocket and stash a wad of tobacco in the other. If a man spit out his tobacco to take a drink when offered, Crockett could give him "another chaw" before he left, leaving the voter happy.

West Tennesseans discovered that this down-to-earth backwoodsman was clearly one of them, and they felt they could trust him. After the votes were counted, Crockett beat Butler by 247 votes and began his second term in the state legislature, representing those living in the counties of Carroll, Humphreys, Perry, Henderson, and Madison.

This was Butler's one and only political campaign, and although "the father of Jackson," as he came to be called, would be very successful in business and civic matters until his death in 1882 at age 92, his loss to Crockett became an unfortunate part of his legacy. A 1958 reference to Butler in *The Jackson Sun*, 135 years after the election, noted that he was a "founder of the City of Jackson, distinguished soldier and civilian, even though he was defeated by famous Indian fighter and backwoodsman David Crockett for the first seat from the district in the state legislature in 1823 because 'he had rich carpets on the floor.'"[14]

Another early example of Crockett using his sense of humor to deflect an attempt to insult him because of his humble beginnings came from an encounter with James Coffield Mitchell. A fashionable lawyer originally from Staunton, Virginia, Mitchell settled in Athens, Tennessee and represented the state's third district. After Crockett finished speaking about a matter on the floor of the chamber, Mitchell responded and condescendingly referred to Crockett as the "gentleman from the cane," which no doubt caused those in the chamber to snicker.

Although nearly vanished from the landscape today, early settlers, primarily in the Southeast, encountered vast thickets of cane, the only bamboo native to the United States. Settlers called these thickets canebrakes. The cane could grow up to thirty feet tall, especially around the levees of the Mississippi River floodplain, near where Crockett was living. In a barely disguised display of passive aggression, Mitchell was attempting to negate Crockett's point by implying that he was unsophisticated and ignorant—basically, "from the sticks." When Crockett angrily approached him later, Mitchell feigned surprise that Crockett took offense and claimed he was simply using that term as a literal description of the region Crockett represented.

After considering whether to ignore Mitchell's insult or exact the kind of revenge they preferred back home in the "cane," Crockett decided to let it slide for the moment. As luck would have it, he then found a piece of plaited lace like Mitchell and other fashionable men of the day used to embellish their suits, and it gave him an idea. The next time Mitchell delivered a speech, Crockett fastened the piece of lace to his shirt front and stood to give a rebuttal.

He proudly puffed up his adorned chest as he spoke, much to the delight of the other legislators in the room. Crockett discovered that using humor to disarm those who insulted him was much more effective than Jackson's duels and allowed him to fight back without the risk of having to murder his opponents or worse, end up in the grave himself.

Crockett was certainly in the right place at the right time to experience first-hand the evolution to a new kind of American government and a citizenry with expectations that were changing just as rapidly. Around the time Crockett was beginning his political career, the Panic of 1819 resulted in social and economic unrest tearing through the United States and contributing to a shift in Tennessee politics that would ultimately help pave Crockett's way to Washington.

Beginning in January 1819, the growth in trade that followed the War of 1812 halted, unemployment grew, banks failed, mortgages were foreclosed on, and agricultural prices fell by more than 50 percent in some cases. As investment in land collapsed, farmers and speculators found their West Tennessee land values dropping by up to 75 percent. In addition to impacting the price of land and ruining many speculators, the panic served to remind poor Tennessee farmers just how vulnerable they actually were when all the power was left in the hands of a few wealthy, elite politicians. It was an early step in the transition of power to "regular folk" from the educated elite that had been running both federal and state politics. Historian Charles Grier Sellers pointed out the long-term impact on Tennessee of the recession that followed:

> The results were threefold: (1) a vigorous demand for state relief; (2) a political awakening, which swept the state government out of the hands of the small clique of well-to-do men who had previously controlled Tennessee politics; and (3) a deep-seated hostility to the private banking system and the special opportunities it conferred on a favored few to become wealthy at the expense of the community at large.[15]

In the early years of the country, most of those in political power had been born into wealthy, land-owning families. They believed that as educated aristocrats, they were better suited to know what was best for the country than the poor they served. Frederick Jackson Turner, an early twentieth-century historian who argued that democracy itself was formed by those on the frontier, could have been writing about Crockett's approach to politics when he addressed the expectations of the "intrinsic excellence of the common man":

> When the backwoodsmen crossed the Alleghanies they put between themselves and the Atlantic Coast a barrier which seemed to

> separate them from a region already too much like the Europe they had left...here by the thirties Jacksonian democracy flourished, strong in the faith of intrinsic excellence of the common man, in his right to his own place in the world and in his capacity to share in government. But while Jacksonian democracy demanded these rights it was also loyal to leadership as the very name implies.[16]

As he frequently said and wrote himself, Crockett was "the poor man's friend." While representing his Tennessee counties in both state and federal government, his voting record makes clear that those weren't just empty promises. His loyalties lay with the poor, even when it was unpopular with other Tennessee leaders who demanded unquestionable loyalty to the party. One writer noted that Crockett's terms as a state legislator "were worthy of commendation":

> He consistently spoke and acted in behalf of the economic, educational, and social progress of his constituency, both in public and private matters, and he won the admiration of his colleagues by his moral courage and patriotism. He was handicapped by his lack of formal education, but he was quick to learn and he acquired on his own initiative much essential knowledge...he was able to capitalize on his lack of schooling in the development of his appeal as a representative of the lower class and of the frontier.[17]

During his time in the state legislature, Crockett's emphasis on West Tennessee land and protecting the rights of squatters became quickly evident, and most of his work was focused on that issue, with a few exceptions. One now-forgotten connection between Crockett and a moment in American history came when he presented a bill inspired by a return visit to the United States of a Revolutionary War hero.

In 1777, then nineteen-year-old Marquis de Lafayette left France to join the colonies in fighting the British. Serving on the staff of George Washington with the rank of major general, he played a part in several key moments in the war and, after returning to France, considered America to be his "adopted country." His doors were said to always be open to visiting Americans. In 1824, the sixty-seven-year-old Marquis returned for a tour as a guest of President James Monroe. In one hundred days, he covered five thousand miles visiting fifteen states, electrifying the country along the way.

In a show of patriotic pride and a celebration of freedom from British rule, every place he stopped hosted parades, dinners, and magnificent parties. While in Washington, Lafayette boarded at the same house as Andrew Jackson, serving then as a Tennessee senator. Jackson wrote, "I am delighted by him. All the attentions, all the parties he goes to, never appear to have any effect on him...he has a happy talent of knowing those he has once seen."[18] Lafayette was so impressed by Jackson that he included a visit to Nashville on his tour of the country. After Lafayette returned to France, the impact of his visit would continue with American parks, towns, restaurants—and even babies—named in his honor. Crockett entered a bill to create a new Tennessee county to memorialize the visit, and the General Assembly passed the act that created Fayette County.

For a while at least, Crockett's loyalty to the common man was rewarded with the votes of his constituents. In total, he would win two terms in the Tennessee General Assembly (1821-1823 and 1823-1825) and three terms in the U.S. House of Representatives: the twentieth (1827-1829), twenty-first (1829-1831), and twenty-third (1833-1835).

Crockett wrote that he would rather "keep a good conscience with an empty purse, than to get a bad opinion of myself, with a full one."[19] Campaigns were expensive, as it took money to print the "circulars" and place advertisements in newspapers that voters back home would read to find out what was happening in Washington. And buying all that whiskey for one pocket and tobacco for the other that he wrote about cost money he didn't have. Crockett never ceased coming up with new schemes and business ventures to fund his campaigns. And although one of them left him naked in the middle of the Mississippi River, it also introduced him to someone who would provide friendship, financial support, and political connections during a time he needed them most.

## Chapter Five Notes

1. Crockett, *Narrative*, 133.
2. Ibid., 133.
3. Ibid., 46-47
4. Ibid., 137.
5. Ibid., 138.
6. George Morris Pope, "David Crockett's Own Book," *The New York Mirror* (February 22, 1834): 266.
7. Crockett, *Narrative*, 132.
8. Crockett, *Narrative*, 141.
9. Van Wyck Brooks, *The World of Washington Irving* (Boston: E. P. Duttong & Company, Inc., 1944), 298.
10. Crockett, *Narrative*, 144.
11. Shackford, "David Crockett," 45.
12. S. L. Latham, *Randolph Recorder*, September 16, 1834, 4.
13. Seale Johnson, "Doctor William Edward Butler, Founder of City of Jackson," *Jackson Sun*, September 17, 1943, 2.
14. Elizabeth B. Lloyd, "Dinner and Costume Ball Will Revert Back to History," *Jackson Sun*, October, 21, 1958, 12.
15. Ibid., 66-67.
16. Frederick Jackson Turner, *The Frontier in American History* (New York: Henry Holt and Company, 1921), 302.
17. Stanley J. Folmsbee and Anna Grace Catron, "The Early Career of David Crockett," *The East Tennessee Historical Society's Publications* 28 (1956): 84.
18. Ann Harwell Wells,"Lafayette in Nashville, 1825," *Tennessee Historical Quarterly* 34, no. 1 (1975): 20.
19. Crockett, *Narrative*, 145.

*David Zucker*

Director, producer, and writer David Zucker is known for successful comedies like *Airplane!*, *Ruthless People*, three *Naked Guns*, *Scary Movie 3 and 4,* and many others. Known to be a big fan of David Crockett, he made a cameo appearance in *The Naked Gun 2½* dressed as the frontiersman. Zucker is also a collector of Crockett artifacts and memorabilia and has called Crockett "the Groucho Marx of his day."

**I feel like, when people label people as famous, they take away a lot of substance that they have as a person.**

**—Harry Styles**

**Chapter Six**

# Memphis

After three sessions in the state legislature, Crockett's career in state politics ended in October 1824, as he declined to run again and set his sights on a seat in the U.S. House of Representatives. He ran against incumbent Colonel Adam Rankin Alexander, a popular West Tennessee settler who was another one of the early leaders of Jackson, Tennessee. Alexander also fought under Andrew Jackson in the War of 1812. In 1820, Alexander was one of four surveyors who established a settlement on thirty acres along the Forked Deer River. His cabin, about two miles west of present-day Jackson, became the primary gathering place for planning and handling of civic and legal matters in the early days of Madison County, Tennessee. As more settlers began pouring into the area, they even began calling the county seat Alexandria in his honor. After discovering another community already using that name in Middle Tennessee, the state legislature voted in August 1822 to name the county seat Jackson in honor of Andrew Jackson.

Although forty-four-year-old Alexander was better connected and had more money to spend on a campaign, Crockett may have entered the race thinking he stood a chance of winning because of Alexander's recent vote on tariffs. For most West Tennessee voters, Alexander had been on the wrong side of the Tariff of 1824, voted into law in May of that year. This tariff was a prime example of the conflicts that were arising between the northern states with interests primarily in manufacturing and the agrarian southern states whose economies were more dependent on agriculture. It was important to the large plantation owners that they be able to export crops like cotton and tobacco at a fair price without government restrictions or taxes.

Speaker of the House, Kentuckian Henry Clay, was among those promoting the idea of an "American System" that would benefit the country as a whole. Eventually becoming the Whig Party, they wanted funds for federal "internal improvements," primarily the development of transportation throughout the country like roads, railroads, and rivers.

There was a massive change going on in politics in Washington, fueled in part around the disagreements around how to fund improvements for the growing nation. The Federalist Party of Alexander Hamilton that favored a strong national government was lessening in popularity, while the Democratic-Republican Party of Thomas Jefferson and James Madison was expanding. They stressed liberty and individual rights that cannot be taken away under any circumstance as central values. This appealed to many building the new country.

After the War of 1812, President James Madison had established the Second Bank of the United States and promoted federally funded improvements to the nation's infrastructure and began putting various tariffs into place. For some, that meant moving further away from giving states the right to govern themselves. Of course, this directly impacted the most divisive issue in early nineteenth-century America—what to do about slavery.

Although Crockett lost the election that year by just a few hundred votes, his showing was impressive considering his background, lack of campaign funds, and limited personal connections. When it came to blowback from his vote on the tariff, luck had also been on Colonel Alexander's side that year. Crockett wrote,

> It was the year that cotton brought twenty-five dollars a hundred; and so Colonel Alexander would get up and tell the people, it was all the good effect of this tariff law; that it had raised the price of their cotton, and that it would raise the price of every thing else they made to sell. I might as well have sung salms over a dead horse, as to try to make the people believe otherwise; for they knowed their cotton had raised, sure enough, and if the colonel hadn't done it, they didn't know what had. So he rather made a mash of me this time.[1]

Crockett returned home to Northwest Tennessee to figure out what to do next. His wife and children had a strong support system, and their community included many other family members. Her sisters Margaret Patton Burgin, Sarah Patton Edmundson, and Ann Catherine Patton McWhorter and their husbands and children all settled nearby. After the death of his wife, Elizabeth's father Robert Patton also moved to the area.

Crockett was certainly content to return to the woods of Northwest Tennessee and do some hunting, but the woods also gave him an idea of how he could raise some much-needed campaign funds for the next election. Throughout the region were thick forests of trees that could be cut down and trimmed into the beveled staves used in the production of barrels. All types of goods around the country were stored and shipped in barrels, as they could be rolled down gangplanks of ships, easily loaded onto wagons or pack animals, and then stored as long as needed to keep the contents protected. Used barrels could also be found throughout the country, sliced in half for all sorts of purposes, from feeding animals to holding sleeping babies.

Crockett hired a few men to cut cypress trees down on his property and trim them into staves, likely using a water-powered sawmill he had built there on the Obion River specifically for that purpose. The crew also got busy building two large boats on the edge of the river. The plan was simple: load the strips of cypress wood onto the boats and then sail down the Obion River, into the Mississippi River, and on down to New Orleans.

There, he would sell the staves and the boats for a nice profit and pay the workers. Using the Mississippi River to transport merchandise of all kinds was a common occurrence during that time before roads were developed. One account noted the various types of cargo that could be found on boats making their way down the river:

> We found numbers of them [flat-boats] along the Ohio, detained by low water; and from St. Louis down to New Orleans, sometimes fifteen, twenty, and thirty together. One of the flat-boats is from the Upper Ohio, laden with pine boards, planks, rye, whiskey, and flour; close to it, another from the Falls of the Ohio, with corn in the ear and bulk, apples, and peaches; a third with hemp, tobacco, and cotton. In the fourth, you may find horses regularly stabled together; in the next, cattle from the mouth of the Missouri; a sixth will have hogs, poultry, turkeys; and in a seventh, you see peeping out of the holes the wooley heads of slaves transported from Virginia and Kentucky to the human flesh mart at New Orleans. They have come thousands of miles, and still have to proceed a thousand more, before they arrive at their place of destination.[2]

Rather than supervise the men too closely or cut wood himself, Crockett spent most of his time on several hunting trips while the work was taking place. Although he returned to the area periodically to check on their progress, the pull of the wilderness and the thrill of hunting was too great.

Whether it was for family, friends, and neighbors, or even strangers in need, Crockett was always willing to take to the woods with his hunting dogs in search of bear and other game. In just seven months during that period, he recorded that he and those with him killed 105 bears. Crockett's stories about bear hunting that can be found in his autobiography provide a rare glimpse for those with an interest in the early culture of the region. The "harricanes" he described were possibly sections of deep ridges from the earthquake, where vegetation would not grow but canebrakes were plentiful.

> The next morning we entered the harricane again, and in little or no time my dogs were in full cry. We pursued them, and soon came to a thick cane brake, in which they had stop'd their bear. We got up close to him, as the cane was so thick that we couldn't see more than a few feet. Here I made my friend hold the cane a little open with his gun till I shot the bear, which was a mighty large one. I killed him dead in his tracks. We got him out and butchered him, and in a little time started another and killed him, which now made ten we had killed; and we know'd we couldn't pack any more home, as we had only five horses along; therefore we returned to the camp and salted up all our meat, to be ready for a start homeward next morning.[3]

By the time the two boats were finished and ready for the trip, the crew had produced thirty thousand barrel staves. In February 1826, the staves were loaded, and the boats pushed off into the frigid waters of the Obion River. Making their way down that smaller body of water was no problem, and the men Crockett had hired seemed to know what they were doing. But when they entered the much larger and more powerful Mississippi River, Crockett quickly discovered he had underestimated the current of the river and overestimated the abilities of his crew. Although they had planned to stop at one of the ports along the river, Crockett nor the others could regain control of the boats, so they had no other choice but to tie the two boats together, continue heading down river, and hope for the best.

In the middle of the night, after a particularly rough patch of river nicknamed the "Devil's Elbow" had lived up to its name, it seemed for a moment that the worst was possibly behind them. Crockett took a break in one of the cabins of the two boats that were still tied together and sat, according to him, "thinking on what a hobble we had got into and how much better bear-hunting was on hard land, than floating along on the water, when a fellow had to go ahead whether he was exactly willing or not."[4] Suddenly, he felt the boat strike something solid, lurch sideways, and begin to fill with the cold, brown water of the Mississippi River. The boats had hit a large pile of trees and other debris that had collected near a group of islands on the river called Paddy's Hen and Chickens. Forty years later, in what is still considered the greatest maritime disaster in U.S. history, a 260-foot-long wooden steamboat named the *Sultana* will explode near that very spot. Eighteen hundred former Union prisoners of war from Confederate prisons on the way back to their homes will lose their lives.

The only way out of the cabin for Crockett at that point was through a small hole in the side of the capsizing boat. With a bit of maneuvering, he was able to get his head and arms through the hole, but the rest of his body was stuck inside the boat that was quickly headed to the bottom of the river. Finally, at the last minute, some of the crew managed to pull him through.

His clothes had been torn off and he had been "skinned like a rabbit." Crockett had no choice but to wait there with the rest of the crew on a section of their boat, now lodged against the timber. The following morning, they waved down a large boat that took them to the nearby town of Memphis, high on the bluffs above the river. Although Crockett's entire stave endeavor obviously resulted in no profit and more debt that he would have to pay off, it wasn't a complete loss. As the rescue boat with Crockett and his crew headed downriver to Memphis, he was about to meet a fascinating man who would become both a friend and an anonymous financial supporter for his next political campaign.

Marcus Brutus Winchester, the oldest son of the fourteen children of James Winchester and his wife, Susan Black Winchester, was born May 28, 1796. The elder Winchester served as a brigadier general in the War of 1812, then increased his fortunes as a land speculator and found success in a variety of business ventures. Evidently, he also appreciated history, as indicated by the names of Marcus Brutus and four of his brothers—Lucilius, Valerius Publicola, George Washington, and Napoleon. There's little doubt who, in the years to come, contributed to the idea of naming Memphis, Tennessee after the ancient capital of Egypt on the Nile River.

By 1802, the Winchester family had settled near Gallatin, Tennessee in Sumner County in a Georgian-style mansion named Cragfont. The two-story home was built with limestone from a nearby quarry by craftsmen that Winchester brought to Tennessee from Maryland. Positioned high on a bluff overlooking a stream, it was said to be the most elegant home on the Tennessee frontier at the time.

Young Winchester was sent away to attend school in Maryland. Then, at just sixteen, he joined his father in battle during the War of 1812. Father and son were captured together by the British in the Battle of River Raisin and spent time as prisoners of war in Quebec. Early Memphis historian James Davis wrote that Marcus Winchester made quite an impression:

> He attracted a great deal of attention, for the remarkable beauty of his features and figure, his gentlemanly and soldierlike bearing, and, above all, his astonishing intelligence, though a beardless boy. He met with many English tourists there, who conceived for him a strong attachment, particularly the female portion of them.[5]

Winchester had impressive mentors as well and was there alongside his father in 1818 as he, Andrew Jackson, and Isaac Shelby negotiated with the Chickasaw and signed the Treaty of Old Town. Once the Chickasaw treaty was signed, Marcus Winchester was immediately sent to survey the tracts of land the men now owned together on the Chickasaw bluff that would soon become the town of Memphis.

With dramatic views overlooking the Mississippi River, Marcus Winchester saw those flatboats headed down the river towards New Orleans and, unlike William Butler, Winchester saw potential and made the community that would become Memphis his permanent home. Like Crockett in Lawrence County, Winchester became one of the first justices of the peace in Shelby County. A man who exemplified an entrepreneurial spirit, by the time he and Crockett met early in 1826, Winchester had already served as ferry operator, land agent, store owner, and postmaster. The city had been incorporated the month before Crockett arrived, and who better than Winchester to have been appointed mayor?

Crockett and Winchester's chance meeting took place during a time when Winchester was beginning to experience negative ramifications from his decision to marry Amirante "Mary" Loiselle just a few years earlier.

Although she was said by many to be one of the most beautiful women in the entire region and had been educated in France, the marriage was considered taboo because Mary, who was from New Orleans, was considered non-White. Although historians have speculated and tried to determine her actual race and backstory, ultimately, very little is known about Mary Loiselle Winchester. She had married into one of the wealthiest and most successful families in Tennessee and was noted for her charity and financial support of numerous religious causes. In spite of all that, she was still ostracized by many of the Whites in the river town throughout her life; and because of an 1822 Tennessee law that forbade interracial marriages, the mayor and his family lived outside the city limits of the town he served.

The early Tennessee historian James Davis, left behind stories of the city of Memphis that otherwise would have been lost. He also had a tendency to add color to his narrative by enhancing the facts with his own creative writing. With no guarantee of historical accuracy, his account of the first meeting between Crockett and Winchester certainly captures the personalities of both men:

> Winchester being among the first to witness his condition, taking an ocular measurement of his person, procured the necessary raiment, hastened down and soon afterward returned, supporting the unfortunate adventurer, whom he conducted to his resident. An hour or two later, by the aid of the kind-hearted Mary, with good fire, stimulants, etc., he appeared at the store door in the finest suit of clothes, it was supposed he had ever worn...Other persons were also liberal to the unfortunates in this affair, for those were liberal days and Crockett and his friends were toasted around to considerable extent; when, warmed up by the few imbibings, he became eloquent, told jokes and laughable stories...and it may be that the misfortune at the head of the Old hen was the starting point for his future importance and notoriety.[6]

Regarding the good financial fortune that resulted from meeting Winchester, Crockett obviously agreed to keep the support and "good word" confidential because he included surprisingly little about the meeting in his autobiography published just eight years later. He wrote, "Here I met with a friend, that I never can forget as long as I am able to go ahead at any thing; it was a Major Winchester, a merchant of that place: he let us all have hats, and shoes, and some little money to go upon, and so we all parted."[7]

Crockett biographer John Shackford believed it was Winchester to whom Crockett refers to many times as a "good friend" who lent him money for his congressional campaign. There are also other historical references to a friendship between the two men, including a letter to Winchester from John Overton chastising him for "continued support" of Crockett after Crockett broke from Andrew Jackson and his followers. Winchester would also be included among the friends that Crockett would stop and visit in Memphis several years later when he departed Tennessee for Texas and the Alamo.

With a renewed sense of enthusiasm and access to funding, Crockett launched his 1827 campaign for a seat on the U.S. House of Representatives. He was up against the incumbent Adam Alexander and General William Arnold, a prominent Madison County, Tennessee lawyer who had also served in the War of 1812. Once again, Crockett was underestimated as Alexander and Arnold mostly campaigned against each other, figuring Crockett's chances were too slim to be any real threat.

On Saturday, September 16, 1826, readers who opened their copy of the *Jackson Gazette*, the newspaper from Jackson, Tennessee, read an announcement from Crockett that was both an indictment against the current representation and the "friend to the poor" theme that he would use throughout his political career:

> To the Republican Voters of the 9th Congressional District of the State of Tennessee.
> Fellow-Citizens:
> From a full conviction of the necessity and importance of having this District represented in the Congress of the United States, I

have again been induced to submit my pretentions to a generous, high minded and magnanimous people. In thus tendering to you my services, I am aware that no man can unite the sentiments of the whole of this great national family, let his talents and acquirements be what they may; for the present suffice it for me to say that my politics are of the republican order; I am opposed to the Administration of this man from the Yankee states, called John Q. Adams; I am opposed to the conduct of the Kentucky orator, H. Clay; I am greatly opposed to our present Representative's vote on the Tariff. If I should be your choice, Fellow Citizens, there is one thing I will promise—that I will not set silently, and permit the interest of my District to be neglected, while I got a tongue to speak and a head to direct it. As an independent man, I have independently offered on my own bottom—deny all combination—ask no favors not grant none, further than civility. I am the rich man's safe-guard and poor man's friend.

I am,

David Crockett.

Gibson County, Sept. 16, 1826.[8]

Crockett put Winchester's financial help and West Tennessee connections to good use and spent his time getting in front of as many voters as he could. It was certainly challenging, as eighteen counties then made up the Tennessee's ninth district. The winner of this election would be representing twenty-two thousand individuals that were making their homes in the counties of Carroll, Dyer, Fayette, Gibson, Hardeman, Hardin, Haywood, Henderson, Henry, Lawrence, Madison, McNairy, Obion, Perry, Shelby, Tipton, Wayne, and Weakley.

As he spoke in front of all those voters, it was natural for Crockett to continue to do what seemed to work. He magnified the fact that he was the opposite of the wealthy, educated politicians with law degrees from eastern colleges and fancy carpets in their mansions. A reporter with the *Jackson Gazette* summarized Crockett's style when he wrote, "All his friends admit that he is somewhat eccentric, and that from a defect in his education his stump speeches are not famous for polish or refinement, yet they are plain, forceable, and generally respectful."[9] This is clearly what the people of West Tennessee wanted to send to Washington.

Guy S. Miles, who studied newspaper reports of Crockett's work specifically in the state legislature, came to the conclusion that Crockett quickly became something of a "grass-roots leader." He wrote, "He tangled with other general questions before the House—banking, internal improvements, imprisonment for debt, and relief measures as well as land laws…His understanding of legal technicalities in each case I cannot determine, but it is clear too that he talked much…he spoke consistently from the point of view of the ordinary settler..."[10]

Unfortunately for Adam Alexander, his luck didn't hold out, and the price of cotton dropped in advance of this election. Suddenly, those tariffs didn't look so appealing to West Tennesseans after all. Crockett surprised everyone, especially Alexander, by winning with a healthy majority of the votes. The "Gentleman from the Cane" had come from behind and triumphed against all odds once again. Crockett had been able to convince voters that he was one of them, had their best interests at heart, and would fight for the things that were important to them. Perhaps the reason he was so convincing was for one simple reason: it was true.

**Chapter Six Notes**

1. Crockett, *Narrative*, 173.
2. Charles Sealsfield, *The Americans as They Are* (London: Hurst, Chance & Co., 1828), 108-109.
3. Crockett, *Narrative*, 193-194.
4. Ibid., 196.
5. James D. Davis, *History of Memphis* (Memphis: Hite, Crumpton & Kelly, 1973), 72.
6. Ibid., 149-150.
7. Crockett, *Narrative*, 199.
8. *Jackson Gazette*, September 16, 1826, 3.
9. *Jackson Gazette*, August 15, 1829, 2.
10. Guy S. Miles "David Crockett Evolves, 1821-1824," *American Quarterly* 8, no. 1 (1956): 55.

Tennessee politican Estes Kefauver is seen here in a press photo distributed one of the two times he was a candidate for the Democratic presidential nomination. In 1948, Memphis politician E. H. "Boss" Crump had compared Kefauver to a "deceitful raccoon." In response, Kefauver began wearing a coonskin cap that eventually became his trademark. Years later, he joked with reporters, "I wish Davy Crockett, my fellow Tennessean, had come to life—he would have made a fine running mate." Kefauver represented Tennessee in the U.S. House of Representatives from 1939 to 1949 and in the Senate from 1949 until his death in 1963.

I am at liberty to vote as my conscience and judgment dictates to be right, without the yoke of any party on me, or the driver at my heels, with his whip in hand, commanding me to ge-wo-haw, just at his pleasure. Look at my arms, you will find no party hand-cuff on them!

—David Crockett

Part Two

# Washington City

MR. FRANK MAYO, AS "DAVY CROCKETT."
SARONY,
680 BROADWAY. N. Y.


*Museum of the City of New York*

Actor Frank Mayo, photographed around 1878 by the Sarony Studio of New York, established the lead role in the popular play *Davy Crockett, or Be Sure You're Right, Then Go Ahead*, written by Frank Murdoch. The play was such a success, Mayo played the frontiersman for a quarter century and struggled with being typecast as Crockett. Later in his career, he found success once again portraying Mark Twain's Pudd'nhead Wilson.

**Fame; I'm gonna live forever; I'm gonna learn how to fly high; I feel it coming together; People will see me and cry.**

**—Michael Gore and Dean Pitchford, "Fame"**

## Chapter Seven

# Junto

David Crockett was forty-one years old in October 1827 when he began his journey to what was then named Washington City after winning a seat in the Twentieth Congress of the United States of America. Joining him for part of the trip was his wife, Elizabeth, and twenty-year-old son, John Wesley. Along the way, they planned to stop for a visit with some of his East Tennessee friends and family, then travel on to her parents' home in Swannanoa, North Carolina. Crockett himself would continue to the nation's capital while his wife and son would return home to Northwest Tennessee. As was frequently the case, land was on Crockett's mind even while packing to leave for Washington, as he had recently purchased around two hundred acres in Weakley County, Tennessee for a new farm he and Elizabeth were planning to establish the following year.

The family's first stop was about 140 miles east at what only fifty years earlier had been Fort Nashborough. It was chartered as the city of Nashville, Tennessee in 1806 and had grown quickly into one of the leading cities in the South because of its prime location on the Cumberland River at the entrance to the Natchez Trace, providing convenient access for trade and commerce by both river and road. By the time Crockett and his family stopped for a visit in 1827, it had also become the social and political center of Tennessee. Timothy Flint's *A Condensed Geography and History of the United States* noted in 1828 that Nashville was "pleasantly situated on the south shore of the Cumberland...it is a place that will be often visited, as a resort for the people of the lower country, during the sultry months." He observed, "scarcely any town in the western country has recently advanced with more rapid strides."[1] Arriving from the woods of Northwest Tennessee to the bustling city must have been jarring for the Crocketts. One visitor wrote, "Coming from the wilderness...Nashville, with its airy salubrious position, and its active bustling population, is quite what an oasis in the desert would be."[2]

It was a fitting place for Crockett's time on the national stage to begin, since the short visit had big political significance, although not because of the city's location or role in the Tennessee government. Crockett was stopping for an informal meeting with John Patton Erwin, a young lawyer with close ties to the growing Whig party and an intense hatred for Andrew Jackson. Crockett knew, and obviously didn't care, that the Tennessee cronies in Jackson's camp would not be pleased. Erwin's father, Colonel Andrew Erwin, was a Bedford County, Tennessee planter and land speculator, and an earlier legal battle between Jackson and him had left the elder Erwin nearly ruined.

At just twenty-two years old, John Erwin had been elected an alderman of Nashville, then just four years later, he served as the growing city's mayor. Shortly before Crockett arrived, Erwin had been appointed postmaster and become the editor—and a secret owner—of the anti-Jackson *Nashville Whig*. Already politically well-connected through his father, the family connection to the Whigs grew tighter when John Erwin's brother, James, married Anne Brown Clay, a daughter of Henry Clay. In 1835, John Erwin's sister, Jane, would marry Tennessean John Bell who, after turning against Jackson in the mid-1830s, would earn the nickname among the Jacksonian Democrats of "the Great Apostate."

Crockett had not yet spent one day in Washington, so a meeting with

John Erwin, a very public anti-Jackson Whig, would send a signal to anyone watching. Crockett later wrote that at the time, he was a "friend and supporter of General Jackson, upon his principles *as he laid them down*, and *as I understood them* before his election as president."[3] Of course, the statements "as he laid them down" and "as I understood them" were meant to explain to voters his eventual break with Jackson and the Tennesseans who Crockett felt had betrayed the poor squatters they were supposed to protect.

Erwin was no doubt anxious to meet the frontiersman who would be representing twenty-two thousand West Tennessee voters to gage where his political loyalties would lie. Crockett had certainly drawn attention from various camps when he won the election against Adam Alexander, since Alexander's family connection as the husband of Jackson's niece should have made him more popular than Crockett among Tennessee voters. How Crockett had pulled off a victory was a mystery that many followers of state politics were still trying to figure out.

During Crockett's stop in Nashville, he made sure that Erwin knew he planned to vote with his conscious rather than align with one political party or another. This was good news to Erwin. The assessment he sent Henry Clay after the meeting acknowledged Crockett's independent streak and his popularity but sounded very much like the arrogant, elite politicians Crockett had dealt with his entire career. He had not yet even left Tennessee, and Crockett was already being judged as unworthy by one of the Washington elite:

> He is not only illiterate but he is rough & uncouth, talks too much & loudly, and is by far, more to his proper place, when hunting a Bear, in a Cane Break, than he will be in the Capital. He is independent and fearless & has a popularity at home that is unaccountable... he is the only man I know in Tennessee who could openly oppose Genl. Jackson in his District & be elected to Congress.[4]

Until 1913, senators were elected by state legislators. The "open opposition" to which Erwin referred was Crockett's 1823 support of John

Williams instead of Andrew Jackson for the United States Senate, back when Crockett was a state legislator.

Williams, a lawyer from Knoxville, Tennessee, was married to Melinda White, the daughter of Knoxville's founder, James White. A nod to the small world that existed in early nineteenth-century Tennessee politics, he was also the brother of John Erwin's wife, Frances "Fannie" Williams Erwin. Just like Crockett answering the call in West Tennessee for volunteers at the beginning of the Creek War, young John Williams had done the same on the other side of the state. Popular, handsome, and having proved himself in the War of 1812, he served as colonel under Jackson at the Battle of Horseshoe Bend.

By coming out in support of Williams instead of Jackson, Crockett knew he was potentially making an enemy of some very powerful men, especially as a Tennessee politican. These men had greatly benefited from their relationship with Jackson in the past and could clearly see how a Jackson presidency could benefit them in the future. Included in the group—which was later nicknamed the "Nashville Junto"—was one of Jackson's oldest friends, John Overton, a banker, land speculator, and judge in the Tennessee Superior Court. Joining Overton was John Eaton, a Franklin, Tennessee attorney and aide to Jackson in the War of 1812 who, at twenty-eight years old, was the youngest man to serve in the U.S. Senate. There was also Sam Houston, a soldier who served under Jackson and impressed him with his bravery. Jackson would see this young protégé eventually serve as governor of Tennessee and Texas and president of the Republic of Texas. Others in the Nashville Junto included Felix Grundy, a Nashville attorney and member of the House of Representatives who helped settle a dispute over the state line between Kentucky and Tennessee, and William B. Lewis, Jackson's friend who had been present at the treaties made with the Chickasaw in 1818 and whose greed had resulted in the salt lick scandal.

The group was connected to Jackson both personally and professionally. As young lawyers, Overton and Jackson had roomed together at the home of Rachel Stockley Donelson, the widow of Colonel John Donelson. Jackson would eventually fall in love and marry the widow's daughter,

Rachel Donelson Robards. It was also Overton who joined Jackson and James Winchester in speculating on thousands of acres of West Tennessee land, including the bluffs that would become Memphis. The three made—and sometimes lost—a great deal of money together. It was Overton who chastised Winchester's son, Marcus, for supporting Crockett after the two became friends in Memphis.

Historian Charles Grier Sellers credits this group of Tennesseans with setting up the pieces that would ultimately make Andrew Jackson the seventh president of the United States:

> The accepted interpretation assumes that the men behind Jackson's candidacy...were moved by sincere admiration and affection for their friend. They are also credited with a shrewd perception that the ground swell of democratic discontent building up beneath the surface of American politics might be mobilized to make the popular general president. A close scrutiny of the events of 1821-1823 in Tennessee reveals, however, that the objectives of Judge Overton and most of his associates were by no means so large and disinterested. There is evidence to show that Jackson was nominated for the presidency only in order that specific local political advantages could be achieved...[5]

By 1822, they had already begun planning for a Jackson run for president in the 1824 election. They had one major issue that needed to be addressed; John Williams, representing Tennessee in the Senate, had already indicated that he would be endorsing William H. Crawford for president. The Junto needed to find a suitable candidate to beat Williams in the Senate race of 1823, so they could remove him from office and replace him with someone who would endorse Jackson. After failing to find a viable candidate they thought could actually beat Williams, they had Jackson himself nominated to run against Williams. Crockett, then serving in the Tennessee legislature, came out publicly in favor of Williams.

Ultimately, Jackson won the election to the Senate without Crockett's vote and served from March 4, 1823 until October 14, 1825, when he resigned after the Tennessee legislature nominated him to run for president. As historian Sellers points out, "American history is full of ironies, but surely few are more striking than the situation of these conservative Tennesseans as they unwittingly launched the movement that carried popular democracy to victory in national politics."[6]

That next presidential election was still a year away when Crockett had his meeting with John Erwin in Nashville. As planned, the Crockett family continued on to East Tennessee where they spent time visiting with friends and family before heading on to North Carolina. While on the road, Crockett became ill—likely with more aftereffects of his bout with malaria years earlier. He spent most of the next few weeks in bed recovering and bloodletting, a popular treatment at that time.

He recovered long enough to witness a duel in his wife's hometown between friends-turned-enemies Samuel Price Carson, with whom Crockett would be traveling on to Washington, and Dr. Robert Brank Vance. Carson and Vance had run against each other for the same North Carolina congressional seat. During the campaign, incumbent Vance accused Carson's father of "taking British protection" during the Revolutionary War. After Carson's father later wrote a letter challenging Vance to a duel to defend his honor, Vance replied in a letter, "I can have no altercation with a man of your age; if I have aggrieved you, you certainly have some of your chivalrous sons that will protect you from insult."[7] It was clear he meant Samuel Carson, who had won that congressional seat. Carson surprised his old friend by accepting the challenge, and because dueling was outlawed in North Carolina, a duel was arranged a few feet across the state line in South Carolina. The night before, a mutual friend tried talking Vance out of the fight, but the friend later reported that Vance had replied, "There is no fight in Carson. I wish he would kill me; my life has no future prospect. All before me is deep dark gloom. My way to Congress has been closed forever and to fall back upon my profession or former resources of enjoyment makes me shudder to think of. Understand me McDowell, I have no wish to kill or injure Carson but I do wish for him to kill me, as perhaps it would save me from self slaughter."[8]

Crockett was there at dawn that morning when the word "fire" rang out, and Carson sent a ball through Vance's hip. Vance's purported death wish came true when he died thirty-two hours later. Whether Vance really made that statement or if it was attributed to him to make Carson look less like a murderer and more like he was assisting in a suicide will never be known.

Shortly after the duel, Elizabeth Crockett and her son, John Wesley, headed back home to Northwest Tennessee, and although still suffering from his illness, David Crockett traveled on to Washington with Carson. The two had little experience in the capital, so it was fortunate they traveled with a more seasoned politician, Lewis Williams, a member of Congress representing North Carolina. He was the brother of John Williams, who Crockett had supported in his 1823 Senate battle against Andrew Jackson. As a true testament to the way political parties were evolving, in Lewis Williams's nearly thirty-year career in Congress from 1815-1842, he served under five different parties: as a Republican, as a Crawford Republican, as a Democratic-Republican supporting John Quincy Adams, as an "Anti-Jacksonian," and finally, as a Whig.

The freshman member of Congress from Tennessee arrived in Washington in December 1827 and settled in at Mrs. Ball's boarding house, located on the south side of Pennsylvania Avenue between Sixth and Seventh Streets, near where the National Gallery of Art sits today. Crockett loved adventure, so he likely began exploring right away. Washington City, as it was called, actually included two large sections. The county of Washington lay east of the Potomac River and included the cities of Washington and Georgetown that were governed by Maryland laws. West of the Potomac River, visitors would find Alexandria County and the city of Alexandria that was governed by Virginia laws.

After a visit the same year Crockett arrived, one writer summed up his impression with, "The streets, where streets there are, have been made so unusually wide, that the connexion is quite loose; and the whole affair, to use the quaint simile of a friend at Washington, looks as if some giant had scattered a box of his child's toys at random on the ground."[9] Two years before Crockett's arrival, Prince Carl Bernhard wrote about what he found when visiting Crockett's new home away from home:

> We rode into the Pennsylvania avenue, and eventually came to the houses, which are built so far apart that this part of the city has the appearance of a newly-established watering place. The adjacent country is very fine, and there are several fine views upon the broad Potomac. We passed by the President's house; it is a plain building, of white marble, situated in a small garden.[10]

When Crockett arrived, it was still a city recovering after nearly being destroyed during the War of 1812. Much of the city had been burned to the ground, including the Washington Navy Yeard, president's mansion, and Treasury building. Although it was heavily damaged, a torrential rainstorm saved the Capitol from complete destruction.

Washington also had a temporary feeling to it as the men governing the country, and sometimes their families, came to live there periodically but then left to return home when the sessions were over. At Mrs. Ball's boarding house, Crockett met some of the other boarders with whom he would be rooming including William Clark, representative from Pennsylvania; Nathaniel Claiborne, representative from Virginia; and Thomas Chilton, representative from Kentucky. Chilton's friendship and writing skills would eventually come in handy for Crockett when time came for him to publish his autobiography, and it's possibly his friendship with Chilton that would lead to a religious awakening in a few years.

Although John Erwin had written that Crockett was "more to his proper place, when hunting a bear in a canebreak, than he will be in the capital," David Crockett had arrived and began making himself at home. Although he had a lot to learn, he had begun the next step in his journey that would propel him to worldwide fame.

## Chapter Seven Notes

1. Timothy Flint, *Geography and History of the United States, Volume I*, (Cincinnati: E. H. Flint, 1828), 10-11.
2. George William Featherstonehaugh, *Excursion Through the Slave States, From Washington on the Potomac* (London: John Murray, 1844), 51.
3. Crockett, *Narrative*, XVII.
4. Mary W. M. Hargreaves and James F. Hopkins, eds., *The Papers of Henry Clay: Vol. 6, Secretary of State, 1827*, (Lexington: University Press of Kentucky, 1981), 892.
5. Charles Grier Sellers, "Jackson Men with Feet of Clay," *The American Historical Review* 62, no. 3 (1957): 537.
6. Ibid., 551.
7. John Parris, "Vance, Carson Fought Famous WNC Duel," *Asheville Citizen-Times*, April 14, 1955.
8. John Preston Arthur, *Western North Carolina: A History, 1730-1913*, (Raleigh: Edwards & Brought Printing Company, 1914), 364-365.
9. Basil Hall, *Travels In North America, In the Years 1827 and 1828*, (Edinburgh: R. Cadell, 1830), 1-2.
10. Carl Bernhard, Duke of Saxe-Weimar Eisenach, *Travels through North America During the Years 1825 and 1826*, (Philedelphia: Carey, Lea & Carey, 1828), 170.

*Smithsonian American Art Museum*

For decades after his death, Crockett remained a symbol of western expansion and frontier settlement. At the start of the Civil War, Congress commissioned Emanuel Gottlieb Leutze, known primarily for his 1851 *Washington Crossing the Delaware*, to paint a mural that still spans the entire wall between the second and third stories of the House's Western Grand Stairwell in the United States Capitol. The painting, a small portion of which is seen here, was intended to represent western expansion while hopefully unifying a country that was splitting at the seams over slavery. Leutze loaded his mural with tropes from popular culture, religion, and classic landscapes to illustrate the concept that frontiersmen and women were following a calling from God as they settled the American West. Although Leutze did not include Crockett by name when writing about *Westward the Course of Empire Takes Its Way*, one of the most prominent figures in the painting is wearing buckskin, moccasins, and a large coonskin cap. The figure is seen comforting his family while gesturing west. Leutze described the figure as a frontier farmer from Tennessee.

**Fame is the thirst of youth.**
**—Lord Byron**

## Chapter Eight

# Land

The most pressing issue for David Crockett and many of the West Tennesseeans he served was solving the problem of who would get to own all that valuable land that many of them had already been living on for decades. For some, land ownership was the difference between fortune and failure; for others, it determined life and death.

Thousands of Americans found the idea of owning their own farms on former Native American hunting land irresistible. Many of them knew that they would be able to farm the land until someone showed up with the title to run them off. Their hope was that by the time the land was actually for sale, they would have made enough money to buy it. As squatters cleared the land and built cabins, they also made the land more valuable. Their mere presence contributed to the general economic health of the state by encouraging more settlement. While the state and the person who eventually purchased the title to the land benefited, the squatter was often left with nothing.

Crockett also knew farmers who had legitimately purchased or been given the land they farmed, but because the system of gaining title to land in Tennessee was confusing, constantly changing, and—in many cases—corrupt, the farmers sometimes discovered the official title was actually held by someone else. In those cases, farmers were given no other choice but to move elsewhere with their family with no financial compensation for the land they had cleared, fields they had plowed, and the cabin they had built.

To figure out how Tennessee's land managment had gotten so tangled and gone so wrong, it's helpful to turn the clock all the way back to the first European settlers in America and take a look at their relationship with the land.

In 1663 and 1665, King Charles II granted charters for American land to eight Lords Proprietors. These men had helped defeat the dictator Oliver Cromwell and restore Charles II to the throne. They aided in the return of the monarchy to England after a long period when there had been no king or queen. Their reward, the colony of Carolina—as it was named—included the present-day states of North Carolina and Tennessee along with South Carolina, Georgia, Alabama, Mississippi, and parts of Florida and Louisiana.

The Proprietors were all members of English nobility and had aristocratic titles like Duke, Earl, Baron, and Lord. They knew that if they were going to be successful at generating funds to help support their opulent lifestyles on this new land they had been given, they needed to generate rents, taxes, and crops for export. They needed adventurous workers to populate this new land, so they created an opportunity for families and individuals willing to cross the ocean and settle in the wilderness. The settlers could worship however they wanted, have their needs represented in an assembly that would govern the new colony, and receive fertile land on which to build farms. Those who accepted the Proprietors's offer received 150 acres of farmland per family member. Slaveholders could add one hundred acres for each slave they brought. It would take a lot of workers to achieve the return on investment the Proprietors needed out of Carolina, so indentured servants were allowed to go to the new colony, work off their time with those who sponsored their trip, then receive one hundred acres for themselves. In just forty years, more than six thousand brave men, women, and children risked their lives and immigrated to this new world.

In time, it became clear to these first settlers that while the Lords Proprietors were going to be meddling in their financial and governmental affairs and making unreasonable demands from a distance, they wouldn't be offering any protection from those who wanted to force the settlers off their new farms like the Spanish, Native Americans, and even pirates. Eventually, it seemed the settlers were more trouble than they were worth. By 1729, the monarchy had bought back most of the land from the nearly fifty individuals who had purchased or inherited it from the original Proprietors, and Carolina became a royal colony.

After those early days of settlement, Carolina had evolved into several distinct regions with vastly different cultures. The southern part of Carolina, around present-day Charleston, South Carolina, had a port with easy access to their neighbors across the sea in the British West Indies. This introduced large numbers of slaves and the concept of plantations into the region. Using those slaves, the economy was built on large-scale crops like rice, cotton, and indigo. Proximity to the harbors provided easy access to export those crops to England and other countries. This "low-country" system created great wealth for those who owned the land on which the crops were grown and those in industries supporting agriculture at the time—like barrel-making.

Meanwhile, the northern section of the colony around the Albemarle Sound, near present-day Elizabeth City, North Carolina, was populated by less wealthy settlers who made their living from farming mostly tobacco and surviving on the food and livestock they could grow or barter. Through the decades, this area became a magnet for emigrants from Germany, Scotland, Ireland, and other countries who brought their customs and farming practices with them, creating a very different culture than existed in the southern part of Carolina.

By 1729, tensions and disagreements between the two sections had escalated to the point that Carolina was split into two separate colonies, North Carolina and South Carolina. At the time, North Carolina included all of present-day Tennessee. As more settlers—including slave owners—poured into the area and the export of crops like cotton became even more profitable, the one thing everyone had in common was the need for more and more land.

In 1777, the North Carolina colony had taken control of its land from the British and opened a land office for each of her counties including Washington County, formerly known as the Watauga Association. Located in present-day Tennessee, it had originally been organized as the Washington District in the early 1770s, then was annexed by North Carolina and officially renamed Washington County with the opening of the land office.

North Carolina drew the boundary of that county all the way to the Mississippi River and included the land belonging to the Native Americans. They then passed an act allowing men to purchase up to 640 acres at two pounds, ten shillings for every one hundred acres, plus an additional one hundred acres for every member of their family at five pounds per one hundred acres. Unfortunately for them, those who claimed and purchased tracts of land actually belonging to the Native American tribes quickly found their ownership short-lived; their transactions were invalidated the following year.

North Carolina also needed land to make good on their incentive of giving two hundred acres and one slave to soldiers in exchange for three years of Revolutionary War military service. If they were wounded, the soldiers received even more, and if they were killed, their heirs were given the land. The amount was determined by rank and ranged from 640 acres for a private to twelve thousand acres for a high-ranking officer. As generous as the offer was, many soldiers and their families were already in debt or didn't want to migrate west and settle in an unknown territory, so they sold the land to speculators like William Blount of Tennessee.

Blount was one of the signers of the U.S. Constitution and a friend of George Washington. In 1792, Blount began construction on an impressive new house that overlooked the Tennessee River in present-day Knoxville that would become the first frame house west of the Allegheny Mountains. It also served as the first capitol of the new territory, and much of the first Tennessee Constitution was drafted there in 1796.

Blount had been born to a life of privilege in 1726 in Bertie County, North Carolina, where he and his brothers learned about business from their father and grandfather at an early age. The family built their dynasty from agriculture, turpentine, operating a racetrack, and buying and selling land. In addition to working in the family business, young William Blount pursued a career in politics. By 1783, his service had included a seat in the North Carolina House of Commons, selection as one of the state's four delegates to the Continental Congress, and an appointment to the North Carolina House of Commons steering committee. During sessions of the House in 1783 and 1784, Blount introduced the aptly named "Land Grab Act" that opened North Carolina's land in present-day Tennessee for sale.

While small farmers interested in purchasing land were allowed to do so at that time, Blount's legislation gave speculators great advantage over the farmers. For example, there was a time limit on when the land had to be purchased, and the title could only be given after the farmer visited the land and had its boundaries marked out. That was difficult to do unless you had the knowledge and connections unique to land speculators.

North Carolina found the far West frontier section of the state increasingly expensive and difficult to manage because of settlers' demands for protection from Native American attacks and construction of better roads and waterways leading to and along the Mississippi River. On December 1, 1789, the North Carolina state legislature voted to cede the land to the newly-formed U.S. government, and the region of the country that would become Tennessee separated from North Carolina for good.

Initially called the Southwest Territory, President George Washington appointed his friend, the ambitious William Blount, as governor. Blount's interest in serving as governor was, at least in part, based on his desire to increase the value of his land in the West. He wrote, "The salary is handsome, and my Western Lands had become so great an object to me that it had become absolutely necessary that I should go to the Western Country, to secure them and perhaps my presence might have enhanced their value…I am sure my present appointment will."[1]

Financial success from speculating in land, however, was far from a sure thing. While serving as governor, Blount, along with his brothers and their partners, found themselves stretched financially thin. They had bought a great deal of that Tennessee land to the west on credit, and the price had not risen as quickly as they had anticipated. Blount thought he had a solution. Although much of his plan remains a mystery, he came up with a desperate scheme to conspire with the British to gain control of land in present-day Florida and Louisiana from Spain by encouraging Native Americans and settlers to attack the Spanish. He knew that a British-controlled, rather than a Spanish-controlled, Mississippi river port in New Orleans would make his western land more valuable to settlers. He and his partners would be able to make a lot more money.

Blount was also serving as one of Tennessee's first two senators when he wrote what was essentially a recruitment letter with a few details of his complicated plan to James Carey, a merchant at the Tellico Blockhouse, an outpost where the Tellico and Little Tennessee Rivers come together. Carey, who at times also worked for the U.S. government as a Cherokee interpreter, had been captured by the Cherokee as a small boy and raised in the home of Chickamauga Cherokee Chief Kanaketa or "Little Turkey." Blount knew that Carey's knowledge and skills as an interpreter would be valuable for convincing the Cherokee to go along with his scheme. The letter included a bit of melodrama as it instructed Carey to "read this letter over three times, then burn it."[2] For whatever reason, Carey chose not to burn the letter, and it was passed around among government officials until it made its way into the hands of President John Adams, who frowned upon government officials conspiring in secret with leaders of other countries. Blount, however, knew his constituents back home in Tennessee would not be so quick to judge. He wrote in a Tennessee newspaper, "In a few days you will see published by order of congress a letter said to have been written by me to James Carey. It makes quite a fuss here. I hope, however, the people upon the Western Waters will see nothing but good in it, for so I intended it, especially for Tennessee."[3]

On July 7, 1797, with a vote of twenty-five to one—Senator Tazewell of Virginia voted against—Blount became the first government official in American history to be impeached. Although he was found guilty of "high crimes and misdemeanors," before he experienced any real ramifications in

Washington, Blount had already left the nation's capital and headed back home. Federal charges against him were ultimately dismissed in January 1799 for lack of jurisdiction, since he was no longer a senator. Although guilty in Washington, he was given a hero's welcome back home in Tennessee, where he was quickly elected speaker of the Tennessee state senate. He died in his home in Knoxville in 1800 at the age of fifty, just a year after the charges were dismissed.

Determining who owned what in Blount's Southwest Territory had become nearly impossible by this time. Initially, the territory included two districts: The Washington District in the northeast and the Mero District in the area around present-day Nashville. The remainder belonged to Native Americans, primarily the Cherokee in the east and the Chickasaw in the west. But some settlers, including squatters, paid little attention to the boundaries and set up homesteads wherever they wanted. Adding to the confusion, ambitious speculators were so anxious to make a fortune on the land that was legally available that they sometimes sold property to which they didn't have the rights or sold the same property to multiple buyers who had not yet even laid eyes on their purchase.

The job fell to the secretary of state at the time, Thomas Jefferson, to straighten it out after Congress passed a 1791 resolution requesting that an estimate be made of the "quantity and situation of the Lands not claimed by the Indians, not granted to, not claimed by any of the citizens of the United States, in the territory ceded by the State of North Carolina."[4] Jefferson's report determined that if you took out the areas of the Southwest Territory belonging to the Cherokee and Chickasaw tribes, all remaining land would be needed to satisfy what North Carolina had promised to its soldiers. As a result, once the report was submitted, it was set aside and nothing was done until additional Tennessee land could be taken from the Native Americans, one way or another.

After Tennessee became a state in 1796, the state legislature immediately informed both North Carolina and the federal government that neither had any rights to the state's "western" vacant land that was then in present-day Middle Tennessee. During the next few years, the United States, North

Carolina, and Tennessee battled over who actually had the right to the land in question. A deal was finally struck in 1806 between the three that gave the state of Tennessee the rights to the land west of the Tennessee River and in a strip along the southern boundary.

Specific land was designated for use by the federal government, and the sales from "640 acres out of every six miles of that land" were to be allocated toward the creation of schools. Tennessee was required to provide land for the establishment of a college in both the eastern and western section of the state. Legal challenges to the agreement began almost immediately. The fight between Tennessee and North Carolina over land went all the way to the Supreme Court in 1818, where it was decided that by ceding to Tennessee the right to issue land grants in its own state, North Carolina could no longer do the same within the state of Tennessee.[5] The judgment had little impact; North Carolina continued to issue new land grants, and squatters continued to migrate west, settling on land to which they did not have title.

That 1818 treaty with the Chickasaw for their hunting ground, negotiated by Andrew Jackson and Isaac Shelby, officially made land available all the way to the Mississippi River. On May 1, 1820, a new Tennessee land office was opened in Memphis, and surveyors could be found throughout the region. Sometimes, as they marked, measured, and created a record of what they found, they took note of squatters who had risked their lives, cleared the land, and made other significant improvments to it. If those squatters were lucky, they had money and could purchase the land they had settled from the government or rightful owner if that party was willing to sell at a fair price. If they were not as fortuante, the squatters only options were to fight or move. It would be for those men and women that Crockett would provide the most hope.

**Chapter Eight Notes**

1. Thomas B Jones, "The Public Lands of Tennessee." *Tennessee Historical Quarterly* 27, no. 1 (1968): 20.
2. *Debates and Proceedings in the Congress of the United States, 5th Congress, 2nd Session*, 2349-2350.
3. Zella Armstrong, "Three Tennesseans Impeached," *Chattanooga Daily Times*, April 26, 1936, 42.
4. Clarence Carter, *The Territorial Papers of the United States*, Volume IV, (Washington: The Government Printing Office, 1936), 48.
5. Burton's Lessee v. Williams, 16 U.S., 3 Wheat., 1818, 529.

CROCKETT BLOWING UP A MAN OF WAR, BY A FLASH OF LIGHTNING FROM HIS EYE.

Tall tales about David Crockett's strength and mythological powers were spoken of and written about with increased frequency as he became more famous. After his death, the fictional Crockett became one of the earliest American superheroes. In this woodcut illustration from a *Davy Crockett Almanac*, he's destroying a ship by shooting lightening from his eye.

**"Don't let it worry you," said Ron. "It's me. I'm extremely famous."**

**—J. K. Rowling, *Harry Potter and the Deathly Hallows***

**Chapter Nine**

# Polk

Passage of legislation that protected squatters' rights in West Tennessee was Crockett's priority. But he wasn't the first Tennessean in the nation's capital to have land at the top of his to-do list. That designation goes to Tennessean and future president, James Knox Polk, who began his first term in Congress in 1825.

Polk was the first of ten children born to Samuel and Jane Knox Polk in Pineville, North Carolina on November 2, 1795. He moved with his parents to Tennessee in 1806 where the family eventually settled in present-day Columbia. Polk's father did very well in banking, land speculation, and farming and became quite affluent. A sickly boy, Polk struggled from around age eleven with an ailment thought to be bladder stones and frequently suffered excruciating pain. A difficult surgery at age seventeen—made even more horrific because it was done before anesthesia—cured his medical condition but likely left him unable to father children.

After a private early education, Polk attended the University of North Carolina at Chapel Hill and graduated in 1818. He then studied law in Nashville with Felix Grundy, a lawyer, politician, and member of the Tennessee House of Representatives, who would become a passionate Jacksonian Democrat like Polk. Grundy had left Kentucky and settled in Nashville after a battle with Henry Clay, who was becoming increasingly popular in the state.

After Polk's apprenticeship with Grundy, he moved back to his home in Columbia where he began a successful law practice. In 1824, he married Sarah Childress, another Tennessean from a wealthy and well-connected family. For a couple that later championed education, it's fitting that their introduction came from a mutual tutor in Murfreesboro, Tennessee. Childress was twelve and Polk was nineteen, so they didn't actually meet again and begin dating for several years. According to stories later shared by Polk, Andrew Jackson called Sarah Childress "wealthy, pretty, ambitious, and intelligent" and urged Polk to marry her. Many wives of politicians at that time primarily tended to social affairs. Not Sarah Polk; she assisted her husband with his letters and speeches and played an active role in his campaigns. The Polks were married twenty-five years before his death, but likely because of his operation as a teen, they would be the only presidential couple to never have any children biologically, adopted, or from previous marriages.

Growing up, Polk developed an appreciation for the Republican Party of the day through his father and grandfather. Journalist and Polk biographer John Seigenthaler wrote, "It is quite clear that from early childhood both his father and grandfather engraved on the boy's mind a political creed that never faded. For Ezekiel and Sam Polk, Republican philosophy was their gospel; Jefferson was their Jesus."[1] Party loyalty came first for Polk, and he would be just as loyal to the Democratic Party of Andrew Jackson as his forefathers had been to Jefferson.

At Grundy's recommendation, Polk was elected chief clerk of the Tennessee State Senate in 1819, then later represented Maury County in the State House. Polk was twenty-nine years old in 1824 when he ran for a congressional seat representing Tennessee's Sixth District that included Maury, Giles, Bedford, and Lincoln counties. Among his reasons for wanting a role in the government of the country was his outrage over the "corrupt bargain" that resulted in John Quincy Adams becoming president instead of Andrew Jackson. There were numerous more-seasoned politicians running against Polk in the race including Colonel Andrew Erwin, the father of John Erwin who Crockett visited in Nashville. Polk beat them all and in August 1825 was elected representative of the Sixth District.

No two men representing people from the same state could have been more different than James Polk and David Crockett. While Crockett was loud and charismatic, Polk was quiet and academic. Crockett was known for his sense of humor and told stories to entertain those he was around, while Polk was serious-minded and relied on his business and legal skills to get ahead. Crockett closely identified with the poor of Tennessee and was comfortable toasting flatboat pilots and farmers in Memphis's dingiest taverns, while Polk's friends and contemporaries were among the wealthiest in the entire region. Although Crockett never wore a coonskin cap more than other hunters—and certainly never in Washington—his style of dress was decidedly more frontier casual than Polk's, whose fashion choices allowed him to fit in among the elite of the lawmakers. Crockett would rather be hunting than anything else, while Polk wrote in his diary that "time spent in pleasure was so much time wasted." A reporter for the Nashville *Union* described Polk who was then Speaker of the House:

> I have never seen a man preside over a popular legislative body with more dignity and effect than Mr. Polk. In person he is rather below the middle size, and had a firm and upright carriage which gives great self-possession and command to his manner. His head is finely formed, with a broad and ample forehead and features indicative of a character at once urbane and decided. He is scrupulous in his dress and always appears in the chair as if he were at a dinner party.[2]

In addition to areas in government like improvements, a national bank, and what to do about the Native American "problem," the topic of Tennessee land was high on Polk's list. All the delegates from Tennessee were aware of how important it was to the economy and development of the state.

In becoming part of the fraternity of men representing Tennessee's nine districts in the Twentieth Congress, Crockett was joining a group of proud

Jacksonians—mostly lawyers with degrees from good Tennessee colleges. At least at the time, they strongly supported Andrew Jackson or, at the very least, wanted to take advantage of his success to advance their own careers.

In addition to Polk, who represented the Sixth District, John Blair represented the First, Pryor Lea the Second, James C. Mitchell the third, Jacob C. Isacks the Fourth, Robert Desha the Fifth, John Bell the Seventh, and John H. Marable the Eighth. Each of these men had an interesting back story, and they came to Washington with a wealth of combined experience.

Blair was from Jonesborough, Tennessee, and after graduating from Tennessee's Washington College, had begun practicing law. Lea's election that year had been a close one, beating Thomas Arnold, a passionate anti-Jacksonite, by just 217 votes.

Lea was from Knoxville and had earned the rank of major while fighting in the Creek War under Jackson. He attended what is today Tusculum University and later served on the board of the college that would become the University of Tennessee. Mitchell, who had called Crockett "a citizen of the cane" back when they served together in the state legislature, was a lawyer from Athens, while Isacks, from Winchester, was a noted orator who would hold a seat representing Tennessee for a decade. Desha, who had been born near Gallatin and served as a captain in the War of 1812, was closer to Crockett's working-class background, as he had not attended college and ran a store in his hometown. Bell, born near Nashville, graduated with a degree in law from Cumberland College and was practicing in Franklin when he launched his campaign to represent the Seventh District—previously held by Sam Houston—against Polk's early mentor, Felix Grundy.

More popular with younger voters, Bell easily beat Grundy that year, even though Andrew Jackson had thrown his support behind Grundy. Finally, Marable, the only physician in the group, was from Yellow Creek, where he practiced medicine and served as the county's postmaster. Like Crockett, who was forty-one years old, all the representatives were in their late thirties or early forties, with the exception of Polk and Lee, who were only slightly older than thirty, and Isacks, who was sixty. Also, like Crockett, most of them had gotten their start in Tennessee's state legislature, so he could refer to them as acquaintances if not friends. Lea, Desha, and Bell joined Crockett in Washington as freshman representatives in 1827.

Tennessee would also have strong pro-Jackson Senate representation in 1827 with John H. Eaton from Nashville and Hugh Lawson White from Knoxville. Eaton was twenty-eight years old when he entered the Senate, giving him the title of the youngest U.S. Senator in history. Although the U.S. Constitution sets the minimum age for senators at thirty, it appears that no one asked Eaton how old he was before he was sworn into office. Another Tennessee lawyer and officer in the War of 1812, Eaton had served with Jackson in all of his military battles and would continue to do so in his political battles in the years to come. After an author died before finishing a biography of Jackson, Eaton completed it, and *The Life of Andrew Jackson* was published in 1817.

White, more serious and scholarly than the handsome Eaton, was the son of Knoxville founder James White and had served as secretary to William Blount when he was governor of the Southwest Territory. After receiving his law degree, the list of accomplishments of "Judge White," as he was called throughout his adult life, was long and included serving as judge on the Tennessee Supreme Court, as a U.S. district attorney, and as president of the Bank of Tennessee, a position for which he declined to accept a salary.

Most of these men were loyal to Andrew Jackson, but more importantly, they were loyal to the faction of Tennessee political leadership that had been founded by William Blount. For these men, exploiting land claims, increasing the price and amount of agriculture commodities, and maximizing potential revenue through banking were the ways Tennessee business was going to thrive. While Crockett had little interest in Tennessee business, he was paying especially close attention to the topic of the land claims.

While serving in the Tennessee House of Representatives in 1824, Polk had presented a proposal in which the United States would cede all available land in West Tennessee to the state to sell, partially to bolster the state's fund for education. Polk's argument was that Tennessee already had land offices and had done surveys, so why should the federal government recreate the wheel? The proposal was approved, and Polk, along with a committee, drew up a written request that could be presented to Congress for a vote.

It wasn't until April 24, 1828 that Polk was finally able to get his bill on the floor. He was no doubt curious whether Crockett would fall into place with the other Tennessee members of Congress, as the two had already found themselves on opposite sides of Tennessee land issues in the past. When voting as state legislators on the Hiwassee District, the territory between the Little Tennessee and Hiwassee Rivers, Polk and Crockett had cast opposite votes on each of three amendments.

The first amendment related to setting the price on the land higher than Crockett thought fair for squatters, so Crockett voted against it. Crockett was against and Polk in favor of the second amendment that would eliminate the option of paying for the land with credit, obviously providing an unfair advantage to speculators who were more likely to have access to quick cash. Finally, Crockett voted for and Polk against the third amendment giving widows the land on which they were squatting. In each of these cases, Crockett voted on behalf of the poor, while Polk voted along the party line of maximizing profit for the state of Tennessee from the sale of land.

Now that they were both in Washington representing districts from the same state, Polk could only hope the new West Tennessee representative would fall into line. Most of the representatives from eastern states were opposed to the idea of setting the precedent of giving a state the right to sell its own land. Some of them preferred for the federal government to sell the land in West Tennessee and use the money for improvements to infrastructure. When the value of the land that Polk had disclosed in his report was called into question, Crockett agreed with the other Tennessee delegates and stated that, although there was timber on the land that could be harvested, it took a great amount of labor for the settlers to clear and transport. He no doubt had flashbacks to his attempt at selling barrel staves that left him naked and broke in the middle of the Mississippi River in the middle of the night. He shared with the other members of Congress his first-hand experience with the land in West Tennessee and how much of it was frequently flooded.

As the bill regarding Tennessee land was debated in committees, on the floor, and at Mrs. Ball's boarding house, Crockett was getting a close-up look at how federal government worked. Ultimately, the bill was tabled and would not come up again until the next session. The wheels of change turned slowly—too slowly for Crockett's liking.

He had also come to the conclusion that with Polk's Tennessee Vacant Land Bill, many of the families Crockett represented in West Tennessee were still vulnerable to losing their farms. Polk and the other Tennessee representatives were willing to support a bill that would result in the land being priced so high that much of it would end up in the hands of speculators. The revenue generated would benefit the state and those men in power, some who had their own financial interests in mind. Much to their frustration, Crockett refused to acquiesce. At the beginning of the second session in December 1828, Crockett introduced such drastic amendments to Polk's bill that it essentially made it an entirely new bill. As he said in one of his speeches on the land issue, "the rich require but little legislation. We should, at least occasionally, legislate for the poor."[3]

On January 5, 1829, against the directive of Polk, Crockett officially proposed his amendment to Polk's bill that would allow squatters to each receive 160 acres from the federal government. The state could not sell the land, and no money would be made available for using land to fund education. And what about the land that squatters were not farming in West Tennessee? With Crockett's amendment, that too would remain the property of the federal government rather than the state. He noted that most of the land in question was in his district, and he was obligated to follow the desires of his constituents who were, he noted, "hardy sons of the soil; men who had entered the country when it lay in cane, and opened in the wilderness a home for their wives and children."[4]

It had taken Crockett and his family years of moving from place to place before they finally found a home in which to settle, so when he wrote "to make of your citizen a landholder, you chain down his affections for the soil," he was able to speak personally, from the heart. Crockett stood before the other members of Congress and, with great passion, tried to help them empathize with his people. "They are living there in peace…some of them are widows whose husbands fell while fighting your battles on the frontiers. None of them are rich, but they are an honest, industrious, hardy, persevering, kind-hearted people."[5] In the book *David Crockett in Congress*, James Boylston and Allen Wiener, who researched and wrote in great detail about every aspect of Crockett's congressional career, noted that on this particular issue, Crockett was impressive:

> Crockett's speeches and spontaneous statements during these debates show a man well versed in this issue, in command of the facts, able to push his own agenda, both openly and subtly, and capable of holding his own with his far better educated colleagues. The public record puts the lie to the characterization of Crockett as a virtual illiterate and naive bumpkin.[6]

While Crockett was skilled at pushing his own agenda, a diplomat he was not. If he hoped to eventually find common ground with Polk and the other Jacksonians, any chance was dashed the moment he crossed the line and publicly questioned their integrity. In what must have been surprising for everyone in the chamber that day—even coming from Crockett—he ended a speech by positioning his fellow Tennessee legislators as villains and proclaimed, "if a swindling machine is set up to strip them of what little the surveyors have left them…it shall never be said that I sat by in silence, and refused, however humbly, to advocate for their cause."[7]

He was clearly making good on his declaration to John Erwin back in Nashville that he would go his own way. Those who were against Jackson had taken notice that a popular representative from Jackson's home state was not only publicly breaking from the Jacksonian pack and questioning their motives, but he had also publicly called them swindlers. Crockett wrote back home justifying his statement in a letter published in several newspapers:

> Seeing what I have seen, and feeling what I have felt…I was unwilling to trust your homes to their mercy. I moreover knew that the weight of the State stands in Congress; that is, opposed to my

> proposition, which has been and still is dear to my heart. To make a long story short of the whole affair, I wished you to have your homes directly from the hands of Congress, and then you would, with certainty, call them your own.

Andrew Jackson won the presidential election of 1828 in his campaign against John Quincy Adams. It had gotten dirty, even for that time, and subjects like Jackson's marriage to Rachel were fodder for the newspapers. Pro-Adams newspaper editor Charles Hammond asked in the *Cincinnati Gazette*, "Ought a convicted adulteress and her paramour husband be placed in the highest office of this free and Christian land?"[8] He then published and distributed a pamphlet with the same message. *The United States Telegraph*, published in Washington City, included official documents and interviews with witnesses in their investigation of the candidate and his wife's "adultery."

Running against Adam Alexander once again, Crockett won his second term representing West Tennessee by a large margin. Although Crockett had less mud slung at him than Jackson, Polk and the Jacksonians had openly campaigned against Crockett, making his dramatic win even more remarkable.

Crockett now knew how the game was played. He set up his own committee to tackle the Tennessee land issue, but it differed from Polk's committee in that it included a number of Crockett's new friends from the East. When his bill made it to the floor for debate, Crockett's version of a land bill had more opposition from his fellow Tennesseans than anyone else, and there was even a feeling among some that if a vote were taken, Crockett would have enough votes for the bill to pass. Although he didnt know it at the time, this was his only real chance at getting a land bill passed.

But on January 5, 1829, before the votes could be cast, Pryor Lea moved to postpone the vote on the amendment due to the unexpected death of Rachel Jackson. Many, including Jackson, believed that the embarrassment and stress of having her marriage so publicly discussed was too much for her to handle. She died at the Hermitage of heart failure at age sixty-six.

Considering the way Rachel Jackson was used politically during the campaign, it was not surprising that Lea would use her death as a political maneuver to delay a vote for Crockett's version of a land bill. The tactic, no matter how unseemly, worked. Crockett fought hard during the next few years, but he would never again get that close to seeing the issue addressed favorably for his constituents.

A bill was finally passed in 1841, making Tennessee a federal agent for the disposal of Tennessee land with special accommodations made for squatters. It was ironically brought before Congress by John Wesley Crockett, David Crockett's son and member of Congress, representing the same constituency five years after his father's death.

**Chapter Nine Notes**

1. John Seigenthaler, *James K. Polk: The American Presidents Series: The 11th President, 1845-1849*, (New York: Times Books, 2014), 11.
2. Eugene Irving McCormac, *James K. Polk, a Political Biography*, (Oakland, California: University of California Press, 1922), 9.
3. James R. Boylston and Allen J. Wiener, *David Crockett in Congress, The Rise and Fall of the poor Man's Friend*, (Houston, Texas: Bright Sky Press, 2009), 32.
4. Shackford, *The Man and the Legend,* 94.
5. Ibid., 96.
6. Boylston and Wiener, *David Crockett in Congress*, 39.
7. Shackford, *The Man and the Legend,* 96.
8. W. David Sloan and Lisa Mullikin Parcell, ed., *American Journalism: History, Principles, Practices*, (Jefferson, North Carolina: McFarland & Company, Inc., 2002), 182.

*Wisconsin Center for Film and Theater Research*

Silent screen actor Alan Sears, who was discovered by director D.W. Griffith, played supporting characters in several major films of the day including Griffith's 1915 *Martyrs of the Alamo*. Sears, who played the role of David Crockett, is pictured here in his wardrobe.

**Fame can change a lot of things,**
**but it can't change a light bulb.**
**—Gilda Radner**

**Chapter Ten**

# Whigs

When David Crockett was still new to the ways of Washington, he learned the hard way just how biased newspaper coverage could be at that time. It was a chilly night in Washington City on November 27, 1827 as he entered the White House for a dinner hosted by the sixth president of the United States, John Quincy Adams. The nation was growing up, and Adams was the first president who was not one of the founding fathers. He was also the first son of a president to become president himself.

Crockett and other supporters of Andrew Jackson were still irritated over the election of 1824 that resulted in what became known as the "corrupt bargain." Jackson had won the popular vote against four other candidates, including Adams and Henry Clay, but did not win enough Electoral College votes to be elected. As directed by the Twelfth Amendment to the Constitution, the House of Representatives had to select the next president.

After Adams won, then quickly named Henry Clay as his secretary of state, it confirmed suspicions that the two men had reached a "corrupt bargain." This perceived injustice would go far in fueling Jackson's victory in the next presidential election.

Adams was also criticized because of his and his family's elegant lifestyles that suddenly seemed out of touch with less-privileged Americans. Adams had grown up wealthy and even served as a diplomat in the administrations of George Washington, John Adams, and James Madison. He taught at Harvard, served in the Massachusetts Senate and the U.S. Senate, and was secretary of state under James Monroe. It was partially a response to John Quincy Adams and Washington elites like him that had gotten Crockett elected to Congress and would eventually put Jackson in the White House.

The guest list that evening included other new members of Congress like Gulian D. Verplanck of New York and James Clark of Kentucky. Verplanck was, like Crockett, a supporter of Jackson. Clark, on the other hand, was a Whig and had been chosen to fill the seat vacated by Clay after he had "bargained" himself into the position of secretary of state. In the years to come, Clark would play a significant role in organizing the Whig Party in Kentucky.

As Crockett passed through the doors of the White House, it was surely not lost on him just how far he had come from his father's primitive tavern in East Tennessee. Some attending the dinner who had not yet made his acquaintance but had read about him in the newspapers were likely thinking the same thing and were eager to meet this new member of Congress from the frontier.

While not quite a fish out of water, he was certainly in a different pond. Of course, Crockett was perfectly capable of handling himself in a professional setting where "city" manners were required. He had attended similar dinners in the past without incident. However comfortable he was joining the other legislators for dinner at the White House, it played more to the brand he was building with the voters back home—and his new national audience—to later position the formal setting as a challenge. In the first book to be published about him, *The Life and Adventures of Colonel David Crockett of Tennessee*, the author wrote that Crockett had told him, "I was wild from the backwoods and I didn't know nothing 'bout eating dinner with the big folks of our country, and how should I, having been a hunter all my life? I had ate most of my dinners upon a log in the woods or not at all."[1]

According to those who were present that night, Crockett behaved no differently than any of the other guests. His humor did warrant inclusion in Adams's infamous diary, however. From 1779, when Adams was a twelve-year-old student, until his death at the age of eighty while serving as a member of Congress, he recorded the fascinating events going on around him. About this particular evening, he included a simple note that "Crockett was very diverting at our dinner." It was an indication that the representative from Tennessee had simply kept the president and other guests entertained.

It would not be until a year later that several newspapers including the *Jackson Gazette* and the *National Banner and Nashville Whig* published a planted article about that evening with the intention of positioning Crockett as an ignorant, ill-mannered guest unworthy of dinner at the White House—or of being reelected. The article was written in the first person so that it would appear to be an account written by Crockett himself about his dinner with the president. The phony letter even had the reader believe that Crockett thought a guest being referred to as an attaché was actually named "Tash":

> I went to dinner, and I walked around a long table, looking for something that I liked. At last I took my seat just beside a fat goose, and I helped myself to as much of it as I wanted. But I hadn't took three bites when I looked way up the table at a man they called Tash…but when I looked back again, my plate was gone, goose and all. So I jist cast my eyes down to t'other end of the table, and sure enough I seed a white man walking off with my plate. I says, "hello mister, bring back my plate." He fetched it back in a hurry, as you may think and when he set it down before me' how do you think it was? Licked as clean as my hand. If it wasn't I wish I may be shot.[2]

This fictional Crockett added that for the rest of the dinner, "whenever I looked up and down the table, I held to my plate with my left hand." And when the finger bowls were provided to the guests, he called the server over to him because, thinking they were a beverage, he wanted to taste them first. He wrote, "They were mighty sweet and good—so I took six of 'em. If I didn't I wish I may be shot."[3]

It made for a humorous story, but all who were there that evening knew this never happened. It is unproven who actually placed the article, but it was likely Pryor Lea or one of the other Tennessee Jacksonian Democrats who were eager to see Crockett lose the next election and be replaced with someone whose votes they could control. In the coming weeks, an anonymous letter would run in the *Knoxville Register* blaming Crockett for the defeat of the land bill, among other things. Lea eventually revealed himself to be the author of that letter and continued with more public attacks in Tennessee newspapers.

Regardless of its authorship, Crockett was embarrassed by the article about his dinner at the White House and knew there was some risk that it had done the damage to his reputation that the author had intended. He asked Clark and Verplanck to write letters to the media, sharing their observations from the evening to counter what had been published. Both denounced the article as a fabrication. Clark wrote, "I sat opposite to you at the table, and held occasional conversation with you, and observed noting in your behavior but what was marked with the strictest propriety."[4] Verplank described Crockett's behavior as "perfectly becoming and proper"[5] and confirmed that Crockett had not said or done anything resembling the newspaper account.

Biased content was the norm for newspapers of that period. Reporters frequently concocted fake stories or added details to news coverage in order to position a particular party or politician more or less appealing, depending on the political leanings of the publication. The political parties even paid for the printing of some newspapers, so it was to the editors' benefit to make certain their benefactors stayed in office. For example, in that 1826 letter in the *Jackson Gazette* in which Crockett announced his campaign and included the statement, "I am greatly opposed to our present Representative's vote on the Tariff," the newspaper felt the need to enhance it with a little editorial comment of their own:

> We give, below, Col. David Crockett's circular, announcing himself as a candidate for Congress. It was our intention, when we received

> it, to publish it without comment; but upon reflection, we feel constrained to say, that the direct attack made on the present incumbent, in consequence of his vote on the Tarrif bill, is highly objectionable. It has always been our custom, to admit circulars from candidates, without hesitation; because the candidate is responsible for what he states.[6]

Readers of the *Jackson Gazette* found a much different tone featured in a follow-up to the false account that had been printed about Crockett's dinner at the White House. They praised his "mild, dignified, and forbearing" response to what the editor referred to as a "rude and slanderous insult." The article went on to explain, "His noble bearing on the occasion has convinced us that he is not only more of the man, but more of the gentleman than the miserable caricaturist who has attempted to render him ridiculous in the eyes of a virtuous and intelligent community."[7]

Although Crockett attempted to prove that his behavior at the White House dinner had been nothing like what was reported, his protests simply brought more attention to it. As one newspaper noted, "The fact that Davy produced evidence in refutation of the charges made against him by the 'good Mr. K., of Ohio,' does not detract from the interest of the story."[8]

Crockett had been a somewhat well-known personality in West Tennessee during his early political career as he created the public image that got him elected. But once he made it to the national stage, the stakes became even higher. That public image of an independent, uneducated "man of the people" who was loyal first and foremost to his constituents was about to be tested.

During the late 1820s and early 1830s when Crockett was representing West Tennessee, Andrew Jackson and his supporters were causing a dramatic change in the political party system. Almost as a signal of that change, as the country celebrated fifty years of independence, two former presidents died within hours of each other on July 4, 1826. Thomas Jefferson was eighty-three years old as he took his final breath, then John Adams, at ninety-one, followed just two hours later. Under founding fathers like Adams and Alexander Hamilton, the Federalist Party dominated national government in the country's early decades but had come to an end after the unrelenting opposition to the War of 1812 expressed by some in that party. Then came James Monroe's "Era of Good Feelings," in which the Democratic-Republicans governed mostly unopposed from 1815-1825. The 1824 presidential election, when House Speaker Henry Clay made the "corrupt bargain" that put John Quincy Adams in the White House instead of Andrew Jackson, contributed to the end of that era and resulted in a new, two-party political system—the Jacksonian Democrats versus those who would eventually call themselves Whigs.

The Jacksonian Democrats, in general, championed a country in which governing was mostly left up to the individual states, not handed down by "elites" in Washington who they saw as out of touch with common men. The Jacksonian Democrats favored a strong executive branch and president rather than having a Congress that was too powerful. They claimed to be the protector of the small farmer and supported personal freedom for individuals. For obvious reasons, they benefited greatly from the movement in the early 1800s to expand the right to vote from property-owning men to all White men over the age of twenty-one.

Most of he Whigs, on the other hand, favored Henry Clay's American System. It consisted of tariffs to protect and promote industry, a national bank owned by private stockholders to generate commerce, and federal subsidies to build roads, canals, and other forms of transportation that would support agriculture. Those who aligned themselves with the Whig Party tended to be involved with business and industry rather than agriculture and were more likely to live in a city or town. Many who were religious also favored Whig policies, as they hoped the federal government would further their evangelical agendas. Interestingly, a person's financial status had less influence on whether one was a Jacksonian Democrat or Whig than one might think, and both parties had around an equal number of wealthy, middle-class, and poor supporters.

In summarizing the differences between the two parties, historian Daniel Walker Howe wrote, "the Whigs proposed a society that would be economically diverse but culturally uniform; the Democrats preferred the economic uniformity of a society of small farmers and artisans but were more tolerant of cultural and moral diversity."[9]

There was a growing animosity between those claiming affiliation with one political party or the other, and combined with an increasing number of newspapers that needed to be sold, the line between politics and entertainment was blurring. As historian Howe also noted, "Party politics was our first national sport, and the public played and watched the great games with enthusiasm. Torchlight parades, electioneering songs, and slogans, debates, and speeches were popular entertainment."[10]

And no one was more entertaining than David Crockett. While he never got the chance to officially list his affiliation as Whig—he would be leaving Washington for good after losing the election of 1835—he was clearly encouraged by some of his friends in Washington who were aligning themselves against Andrew Jackson. And once he called his fellow Tennesseans swindlers, Crockett was in a political position where he needed as many friends as he could get.

It was certainly clear to Crockett by 1828 that the Jacksonians, especially those from Tennessee, were going to be actively working against him and his efforts to get a bill passed to benefit the squatters in his district. The last thing the Jacksonians needed was this rogue civil servant from Jackson's own state getting any sort of victory in Congress that could result in his sticking around longer than they desired. They intended to make sure Crockett was out of Mrs. Ball's boarding house and sent back to the Tennessee frontier as soon as possible.

Polk wrote, "they are making a tool of Crockett in order to deal a blow against Tennessee."[11] Lea wasn't the only one submitting anonymous letters to newspapers. Among Polk's personal papers, one historian found undated articles in Polk's handwriting headed "Colonel Crockett & his course in Congress" that slammed Crockett in various ways and was signed "Several Voters." To a friend, Polk wrote, "The whole delegation feels humiliated that Crockett should have Cooperated with some of our bitterest and most vindictive political enemies…we can't trust him an inch."[12]

Polk and the others could hardly have been surprised. Crockett had shown all the way back in 1823 that he was not afraid to "go his own way" when he ran against and beat Dr. William Butler, the husband of Jackson's niece, and then again when he voted for John Williams for the Senate, opposing the directives of the "Nashville Junto."

An ancient proverb states, "the enemy of my enemy is my friend." Crockett must have taken that to heart as he began aligning with the Whigs. While it would seem like they were the antithesis of what Crockett stood for, there were some similarities between Crockett and Henry Clay, one of the most visible leaders of the growing Whig party.

It's been written that "Clay's personal magnetism made him one of America's best-loved politicians; his elaborate scheming made him one of the most cordially hated."[13] Around the time Crockett was having dinner with the president in 1827, Clay was fifty years old and had already experienced a robust political career leading up to that "corrupt bargain" with Adams in 1824 that resulted in his appointment as secretary of state. Clay had launched his career as a lawyer in Lexington, Kentucky and, like Crockett, had improved his station in life by "marrying up" when he made Lucretia Hart his wife. Her father, Thomas Hart, was a prominent Lexington businessman who helped Clay make important connections that quickly grew his influence. He was only twenty-six years old when he began his political career in 1803, being elected to the Kentucky House of Representatives as a Democratic-Republican.

Kentuckians then sent Clay to the U. S. House of Representatives in 1810. As Speaker of the House in 1812, he was one of the leading "War Hawks," advocates for going to war against Britain in spite of the fact that the country had very few soldiers trained to fight. Britain had not only forced young American seamen to serve in the British Navy, but they were also arming many of the Native America tribes with weapons and instigating some of the violence against settlers.

On January 8, 1811, Clay gave an impassioned speech on behalf of a bill that would allow President Madison to increase the number of soldiers in the U.S. Army by fifty thousand. The bill passed, and the United States went to war with Britain. While Clay helped start the War, he also helped end it when Madison sent him and five others to Belgium to negotiate and then sign the Treaty of Ghent on December 24, 1814. Because troops did not receive word that the war was over, the biggest and bloodiest battle of that war came a few days later in New Orleans. Andrew Jackson walked away from that battle a national hero so well loved that he would end up in the White House.

Just like Crockett and Polk, Clay also had a personal connection to the issue of squatters. He had been an early settler in Kentucky, the state line of which was only around forty miles from Crockett's home in Northwest Tennessee. Clay had also speculated in land sales to other settlers very early in the state's history. He was personally acquainted with both the social and economic benefits of land ownership. Just like in Tennessee, Kentucky had a large number of farmers working land to which they did not have the title, and Clay attempted to put legislation in place that would address that problem. In 1823, he even defended some of Kentucky's laws that protected squatters in the highest court in the land. A settler named Richard Biddle was squatting on land actually owned by the heirs of another settler, John Green. There were two Kentucky laws in place that Green's heirs had used in order to have Biddle and his family forcibly removed from the land in question. The case made it all the way to the U.S. Supreme Court where Clay acted as a "friend of the court" on behalf of Kentucky.

Clay testified, "Of all the evils which can afflict an unhappy country, scarcely any is so aggravating as that of having its soil, the source of whence all our riches flow, and our wants are supplied, the subject of endless litigation."[14] Although the court ultimately sided against Kentucky, land ownership in the growing country was an issue that remained closely associated with Clay.

He was, like most others, anxious to see the western lands populated but was in favor of distributing federal land revenue among the states. He was notably against preemption, the idea of providing squatters with the opportunity to buy the land they had settled before it was offered for sale to the public—the very thing Crockett was trying to accomplish for West Tennessee. After 1834, Clay's speeches on the topic are filled with strong language that leave no doubt about his dislike of squatters, calling them "lawless rabble" and "people of the worst character." As far apart as Crockett was from Polk on the issue of land for squatters in West Tennessee, it would seem, philosophically, Clay was even further away.

This introduces a few complex and much-debated questions about Crockett's break from Jackson and rise to fame. In 1927, historian Vernon Louis Parrington observed in his Pulitzer Prize-winning *Main Currents in American Thought* that Crockett was a "minor character" until he broke from the Jacksonians and joined the Whigs. He wrote that Crockett was "paraded at meetings with Daniel Webster, given great dinners, applauded for his rustic wit and homespun honesty, presented with a fine rifle; and he seems never to have realized how grossly he was being exploited."[15]

James Shackford also came to the same conclusion in his much-researched biography of Crockett published posthumously in 1956. In an article for the *Journal of the Early Republic,* author Thomas E. Scruggs summed up Shackford's theory as "the desperate Crockett, following his defeat in 1831, met with aspiring Whig authors and the former clerk of the House of Representatives, Matthew St. Clair Clark…and was drawn into a political-literary conspiracy to recreate himself as a celebrity frontiersman counterpoint to Andrew Jackson and the Democrats. His humble origins would be accented as would his persona as Indian fighter and bear hunter."[16]

Scruggs contends that more recent biographers and historians have been influenced by these two secondary sources. He wrote, "This blind acceptance of secondary sources has led to widespread propagation of an inaccurate theory, and perhaps clouded, rather than illuminated, our understanding of the past."[17]

Ultimately, there is no real evidence to support the hypothesis that Crockett broke with the Jacksonian Democrats and aligned with the Whigs in a "deal" to gain votes for a land bill in exchange for a public break with Jackson. Similarly, there is nothing that proves one way or the other that he was tricked into supporting Whig causes after he got a taste of fame and potential fortune. The true sequence of events and the motivation of Crockett or even the Whig leadership at the time is impossible to know with certainty.

What can be proven is that there was notable improvement in the quality of the speeches, articles, and other content Crockett published after this point in his career, and he found himself increasingly in a brighter spotlight on the national stage. Regardless of exactly how it happened, Crockett the frontiersman, who had become Crockett the politician, was about to evolve again. He next became Crockett the entertainment brand, with a little help from his friends.

**Chapter Ten Notes**

1. James Strange French, *The Life and Adventures of Colonel David Crockett of West Tennessee*, (New York: J. & J. Harper, 1833), 155.
2. Ibid., 157.
3. Ibid.
4. Ibid., 159.
5. Ibid., 160.
6. *Jackson Gazette*, September 16, 1826, 3.
7. *Jackson Gazette*, February 14, 1829, 2.
8. *The Moline Republican*. October 4, 1889. 1.
9. Daniel Walker Howe, *The Political Culture of the American Whigs*, (Chicago: University of Chicago Press, 1979), 20.
10. Howe, *Political Culture of the Whigs*, 15.
11. Thomas E.Scruggs, "Davy Crockett and the Thieves of Jericho: An Analysis of the Shackford-Parrington Conspiracy Theory," *Journal of the Early Republic* 19, no. 3 (1999): 486.
12. Ibid., 487.
13. Eric Foner and John A. Garraty, ed., *The Reader's Companion to American History*, (Boston: Houghton Mifflin Company, 1991), 190.
14. John R. Van Atta, "A Lawless Rabble: Henry Clay and the Cultural Politics of Squatters' Rights, 1832-1841," *Journal of the Early Republic* 28, no. 3 (2008): 345.
15. Vernon Lewis Parrington, *Main Currents of American Thought, Volume Two: The Romantic Revolution in America* (New York: Harcourt, Brace and Company, 1927), 169.
16. Scruggs, Thomas E. "Thieves of Jericho," 482.
17. Ibid., 497.

*Bart Shatto*

Broadway and television actor and singer Bart Shatto pictured during a performance of *The Confessions of Davy Crockett*. The play is set in a tavern in Memphis in 1836 the evening before Crockett departed Tennessee for Texas. It was written by Steve Warren, with original songs by composer Tom Masinter and lyricist June Rachelson-Ospa.

**There's nothing worse than being famous and broke.**
**—Kim Basinger**

## Chapter Eleven

# Lion

It was Christmas 1833, and the audience was settling into their seats at the Washington Theater in Washington City. They were preparing to watch celebrated actor James Hackett perform scenes from his hit play, *Lion of the West*, written by James Kirke Paulding. After opening to great reviews in April 1831 at the Park Theater in New York, a second version had been on tour in cities around America, and a third had even played in London. By now, most in the audience were aware that the main character, performed by Hackett, had been inspired by the famous member of Congress from Tennessee, David Crockett. The rumor around the nation's capital was that Hackett was performing the play specifically at Crockett's request that evening.

As the manager of the theater escorted a VIP to a seat at the front, a growing murmur could be heard throughout the theater. First, one section of the audience and then another began to realize that was no ordinary VIP; that was the man himself, David Crockett. Backstage, Hackett was dressed from head to toe in his exaggerated frontiersman wardrobe made from fur and buckskin. It even included a hat made from the skin of a wildcat. With the head still intact and its tail hanging down the back of Hackett's neck, it looked as though it could leap from his head at any moment. Little had Hackett known when creating the wardrobe for this character just how prominently the cap would figure in the legend of "Davy Crockett" in decades to come.

Hackett must have stood there backstage, smiling as he listened to the audience loudly chanting a few of Crockett's well-known catchphrases including "Go Ahead!" and "I wish I may be shot." His years of performing had given the actor the gift of great timing, so he waited a moment before finally giving the cue to the stagehand to open the curtain.

The audience applauded and then quieted down. Hackett made the spur-of-the-moment decision to walk to the edge of the stage toward Crockett, where he dramatically bowed to the man he was about to portray. Never one to shy away from public adoration, Crockett stood and returned the bow. The audience went wild.

How did a parody of David Crockett end up in a hit play? Crockett biographer Shackford believed the frontiersman was intended to be the subject before Paulding ever put pen to paper. Furthermore, he even proposed the play was originally created as yet another Whig endeavor to build greater public awareness of their most famous anti-Jacksonian. Others believe the characterization of a frontiersman was the natural progression of the work already being done by Paulding and Hackett, and the popularity was simply a result of the nation's appetite for unique American characters representing western expansion on stage.

While the Whig's involvement, if any, will never be proven, what is known for certain is that in 1831, James Kirke Paulding wrote a comedy for actor James Hackett featuring a character named Nimrod Wildfire. Although Paulding wrote Crockett a letter emphatically denying it, there were reports in newspapers long before the play even made it to the stage that the main character of the comedy was based on Crockett. Crockett wrote Paulding back that while he appreciated Paulding's "civility" in letting him know, he knew Paulding was "incapable of wounding the feelings of a Strainger and unlettered man who had never injured him."[1]

We now know that Paulding had, in fact, been looking for Crockett material as he wrote the comedy. A letter surfaced from Paulding to painter John Wesley Jarvis asking for "a few sketches, short stories and incidents, of Kentucky or Tennessee manners, and especially some of their peculiar phrases & comparisons. If you can add or invent a few ludicrous Scenes of Col. Crockett at Washington, You will be sure of my everlasting gratitude."[2]

Of course, when the play was a huge hit, Hackett, Paulding, and Crockett ceased any protests over the identity of the inspiration for the main character. The public's attachment of Nimrod Wildfire to David Crockett was good for both ticket sales and votes.

The play was not only a huge hit then, but it is also noted today as the first American comedy with a frontiersman from the West as the central character. Hackett took pride in the authenticity of his dialects, so many in audiences where he performed were hearing "a westerner" for the very first time. He stood on stage and delivered lines like, "My name is Nimrod Wildfire — half horse, half alligator and a touch of the airthquake — that's got the prettiest sister, fastest horse, and ugliest dog in the District, and can outrun, outkick, outjump, knockdown, drag out, and whip any man in all Kaintuck." Many in the audience assumed they were hearing from David Crocket, and those comments—and others like them—would be associated with him from then on.

The plot of the comedy also sent a not-so-subtle message back to judgmental Europeans about the developing popular culture of America. Just as those in the generation before them had fought for political independence from England, some in the second generations of Americans began seeking creative, artistic, and intellectual independence. After the Revolutionary War, it took some time for American theater to acquire an authentic voice unique to the new country. But by the mid-1820s, a form of entertainment known as "Yankee Theater" began to find enthusiastic audiences in cities like New York, Boston, and New Orleans. As it does today, the term Yankee meant different meanings to different people, but in this reference at that time, a Yankee referred to a stereotypical "American." Some of the characters and plot development of the most successful of the plays were born out of American's growing resentment at the literature published in England and France by tourists after visits to the United States. They wrote of the difficulties of getting from one place to another, eating unusual food, and experiencing a "primitive and unsophisticated" culture. For example, one writer summed up what many thought about American's reading habits at the time:

> They have…no indigenous literature of much consequence, except the angry pages of party spirit,—the snowstorm of newspaper, which, like a perennial cloud of locusts, drifts across their union, blighting everything in its course. They borrow from England only our lighter works, drawing scarcely at all upon the greater stories of literature with which this country is filled, but for which they have neither taste or leisure.[3]

In one two-volume travelogue that was a huge hit during this time, *Domestic Manners of the Americans,* English writer Frances Trollope found little love for the patriotic pride she discovered Americans had for their new way of life:

> If the citizens of the United States were indeed the devoted patriots they call themselves, they would surely not thus encrust themselves in the hard, dry, stubborn persuasion, that they are the first and best of the human race, that nothing is to be learnt, but what they are able to teach, and that nothing is worth having, which they do not possess.[4]

She had moved from England to Cincinnati, Ohio with her husband to open a department store in late 1827. After the failure of that enterprise and the loss of all their money and possessions, Trollope was left with the manuscript of a book of her observations she had written while in the United States. Published in March 1832, it was a phenomenon unlike anything the publishing world had yet seen. The *Harry Potter* of its day, it launched for Trollope a wildly successful career writing more than a hundred novels and travel books. As one New Yorker wrote at the time, "The tariff and Bank Bill were alike forgotten, and the tug of war was hard, whether 'Domestic Manners,' or the cholera, which burst upon them simultaneously, should be the more engrossing topic of conversation."[5] Trollope was likely not impressed by Crockett, as she did not approve of the fact that in America, a man could go from the wilds of the frontier to the halls of Congress, considering it "evil." She wrote, "Any man's son may become the equal of any other man's son, and the consciousness of this is certainly a spur to exertion; on the other hand, it is also a spur to that coarse familiarity...this is a positive evil, and, I think, more than balances its advantages."[6]

French aristocrat Alexis de Tocqueville did include a passage about Crockett in his travel journal, and he was as unimpressed with Crockett as Trollope was with the Americans. He wrote, "Two years ago the inhabitants of the district of which Memphis is the capital sent to the House of Representatives in Congress an individual named David Crockett, who has no education, can read with difficulty, has no property, no fixed residence, but passes his life hunting, selling his game to live, and dwelling continuously in the woods."[7]

American authors and playwrights began responding to the criticism of the new American culture the best way they knew how: with their work. By 1827, American author James Fenimore Cooper had written three romantic novels about frontier adventure and Native American life including *The Spy*, *The Last of the Mohicans*, and *The Pioneers*. The latter is now considered the best portrayal of frontier life in American literature and noted as the first truly original American novel. In many ways, Cooper contributed to Crockett's rise to fame by creating romanticized versions of the wild, western frontier character that Crockett would come to represent for the public. For many Americans, it was early illustrations in Cooper's novels that first introduced the concept of the coonskin cap that came to be so closely associated with Crockett.

When reading Cooper's description of his main character, Natty Bumppo, it is easy to envision the image the public had of David Crockett:

> He was tall, and so meagre as to make him seem above even the six feet that he actually stood in his stockings. On his head, which was thinly covered with lank, sandy hair, he wore a cap made of fox-skin...A kind of coat, made of dressed deer-skin, with the hair on, was belted close to his lank body by a girdle of colored worsted. On his feet were deer-skin moccasins, ornamented with porcupines' quills, after the manner of the Indians, and his limbs were guarded with long leggings of the same material as the moccasins, which, gartering over the knees of his tarnished buckskin breeches, had obtained for him among the settlers the nickname of Leather-Stocking...A leathern pouch hung before him, from which, as he concluded his last speech, he took a small measure, and, filling it accurately with powder, he commenced reloading the rifle, which as its butt rested on the snow before him reached nearly to the top of his fox-skin cap.[8]

Another writer who used his talents specifically for developing American characters for the stage was James Kirke Paulding. Born August 22, 1778 in Pleasant Valley, New York, he left home at eighteen years old and moved to New York City. A self-trained writer, he produced poetry, novels, and plays that were known to be anti-British. After arriving in New York, he became a close friend to Washington Irving, the author of *Rip Van Winkle*, *The Legend of Sleepy Hollow*, and other early American classics. Paulding and Irving, along with Irving's brother, William, created *Salmagundi*, an early satirical magazine that lampooned New York City culture and addressed topics like politics, women's rights, corruption, and other social issues. Filled with humorous stories, poems, and illustrations, it was *Mad* magazine and *Saturday Night Live* rolled into one. *Salmagundi* even gets the credit for introducing the world to the word "Gotham" as a nickname for New York.

The three men were also part of the Knickerbocker Group, a loosely-formed association with other pioneering American writers like Cooper, William Cullen Bryant, and Lydia Maria Child. One of the goals of many of these writers was to create an authentic American culture through literature, art, and journalism. As one early scholar wrote, "the Knickerbockers practically originated artistic literature of pleasure,"[9] or in other words, reading for fun.

While Paulding was developing an authentic American voice in his writing, James Henry Hackett was doing the same with his comedic performances on stage. He was born March 15, 1800 in New York City to a father from Holland and a mother from Long Island, New York. He dropped out of Columbia University because of illness and began studying law and working as a wholesaler. The escape from a boring life of business came when he met and married Catherine Lee Sugg, a successful stage actress. Thanks to important connections from his mother's family, and the proven ability of Hackett's wife to draw an audience, the couple quickly began headlining in major New York theaters. Hackett became a master of mimicry and was able to completely embody the characters he portrayed on stage. While he played many different types, the one that was most popular with audiences was "the Yankee." Hackett had a very specific character in mind when presenting a Yankee to an audience. He wrote,

> Yankees are: Enterprising and hardy—cunning in bargains—back out without regard to honour—superstitious and bigoted—simple in dress and manners—mean to degree in expenditures—free of decep.—familiar and inquisitive, very fond of telling long stories without any point, which just as they appear to approach is diverted by some new digression—when they finish, will laugh themselves, and never care whether the listener does or not—the only sure way of knowing when they are done is their throwing away a chip or stick, which they invariably keep whittling while telling a story, and putting a knife in their waistcoat pocket after sitting an hour on a wood-pile.[10]

The one thing Hackett needed most to continue his rise to fame was good material. He could and did write some of his own dialogue and was, like other successful stage performers at that time, adept at improvising. Comics typically altered their performances based on the laughter they were receiving from the audience. They added, removed, or changed dialog all while listening, watching, and analyzing how the audience responded to their performance.

In 1830, Hackett placed advertisements for a contest to provide a three-act play featuring an "American," for which the winning playwright would receive $300. The winner was James Kirke Paulding who submitted his play, *The Lion of the West*. While the original play was rewritten at least twice, the primary character remained Colonel Nimrod Wildfire, an adventurous Kentuckian with common sense and a sharp wit who represented many Americans as they saw themselves.

While no copy of Paulding's original version of the play remains, much of the plot and main characters are known because of the newspaper coverage it received. In the play, Cecilia Bramble, a wealthy heiress and daughter of a senator, is being courted by numerous bachelors including a phony French count who is pretending to be wealthy. Her frontiersman cousin, Wildfire, is a member of Congress from Kentucky. Around this time, Kentucky had begun to represent all of the West for Americans living in the East, and numerous stories of Kentucky and Tennessee filled the newspapers. The first name of the protagonist in the play came from Genesis 10:8–9 where Nimrod, one of the descendants of Ham, was described as "a mighty hunter before the Lord."

In spite of his lack of education and slapstick behavior, Nimrod Wildfire is much smarter than the foreigner, sees through the Frenchman's charade, and works to reveal the arrogant imposter's true intentions. According to a review in the *Morning Courier and New-York Enquirer*, the premiere was a success:

> The city is at present full of western merchants—'strangers" from Kentucky, Tennessee, Ohio and the contiguous states. They crowded to the theater…and received with great applause the successful hits of the author and actor…the author has made this character an extremely racy representation of western blood, a perfect non-pareil—half steam-boat half alligator, &c. It possesses many original traits, which never before have appeared on the

stage.[11]

Although the play seems to have been a success, Hackett was not satisfied. Working with comedic actor and playwright John Augustus Stone, he created an entirely new production with a new cast of characters to support the protagonist, Nimrod Wildfire. Stone had become something of a celebrity himself after the success of a play he had written in 1829, *Metamora; or, The Last of the Wampanoags*. Set in seventeenth-century New England around the arrival of the Puritans, the plot of Stone's play centered around the conflict between the English settlers and the Wampanoags. Metamora, a "noble Native American hero," ultimately turns violent only when he sees no other way for his tribe to survive.

Hackett took the new production written by Stone on the road, and it received an even better response than the original. When it appeared at New York's Park Theater in mid-November 1831, the play broke box office records, bringing in an average of $900 in ticket sales each night, an unheard-of amount at the time. As the play toured theaters around the country, newspapers published reviews and articles about the play's success, exposing an even wider audience to Nimrod Wildfire—and David Crockett.

Readers opening their newspapers on December 10, 1831 first met Wildfire without knowing his connection to David Crockett or even the fact that the character was from a play. An article using the dialogue appeared in one newspaper and then was copied by many others. Included was Wildfire's proclamation that would eventually be associated with Crockett, "I am half horse, half alligator and a touch of the airthquake—that's got the prettiest sister, fastest horse, and ugliest dog in the District, and can outrun, outkick, outjump, knockdown, dragout, and whip any man in all Kaintuck."[12]

With the most successful theatrical production in American history on his hands, Hackett then created an entirely new version working with English actor and playwright William Bayle Bernard. A prolific writer, Bernard had his first professional production in London at age twenty. The new comedy featuring Wildfire that Bernard created with Hackett, *A Kentuckian's Trip to New York in 1815*, opened at Covent Garden Theatre in London in April

1833 and was as successful in London as the first two versions had been in America. A critic in the *London Times* wrote of the Wildfire character,

> He may be compared to an open-hearted, childish, giant, whom any one might deceive but none could daunt. His whimsical extravagance of speech arises from a mere exuberance of animal spirits; and his ignorance of the conventional restraints he overbalances by a heart that would scorn to do a mean or dishonest action.[13]

While copies of the first two plays do not exist, a copy of the third thankfully does. When the play was first performed in London, Hackett had to submit a copy to the Lord Chamberlain's Office for approval. Fortunately, this version was later stored at the British Museum, where it was discovered by James N. Tidwell in 1954.

In this third version, Crockett was not the only celebrity lampooned. A new character was introduced that was based on the author of *Domestic Manners of the Americans*, Frances Trollope. Amelia Wallope, as she was called in the play, is an Englishwoman who intends to improve the manners and refinement of Americans. Many of the laughs in this version come from the clash of the cultures and misunderstandings between Wildfire and Wallope.

Thanks to the newspaper coverage of the first two versions and the discovery of the script of the third, we know the Wildfire character based on Crockett was presented as unrefined, boastful, and prone to wild exaggeration, while somehow remaining an appealing hero for the audience.

One excerpt from the third version of the play illustrates the "tall tales" that those in the theater heard delivered from Hackett as Wildfire described an encounter with a riverboat pilot:

> Mister, says he, I'm the best man—if I ain't, I wish I may be tetotaciously exflunctified! I can whip my weight in wildcats and ride straight through a crab apple orchard on a flash of lightening—clear meat axe disposition! And what's more, I once back'd a bull off a

> bridge. Poh, says I, what do I keer for that? I can tote a steamboat up the Mississippi and over the Alleghany mountains. My father can whip the best man in old Kaintuck, and I can whip my father. When I'm good natured I weigh about a hundred and seventy, but when I'm mad, I weigh a ton.[14]

As author and arts educator Vera Jiji summarized in a handbook of source materials for the study of *The Lion of the West*, "The country's territorial expansionism found a counterpart in the boasts of Nimrod Wildfire."[15] At the end of the play, Wildfire departs New York for "old Kaintuck" where "the ground's so rich…that if you but plant a crowbar overnight perhaps it will sprout tenpenny nails afore mornin'."[16]

While Wildfire departed stage after stage around the world, Crockett found his spotlight was growing steadily brighter. He had found fame after years of personal and professional struggle; now it was time to seek his fortune.

**Chapter Eleven Notes**

1. Boylston and Wiener, *David Crockett in Congress*, 195.
2. Ralph M. Aderman, *The Letters of James Kirke Paulding* (Madison: University of Wisconsin Press, 1962), 113.
3. George Walter Prothero, "Review of Domestic Manners of the Americans by Mrs. Trollope," *The Quarterly Review* (March 1832): 47-48.
4. Ibid., 47.
5. Edward Thomas Coke, *A Subaltern's Furlough: Descriptive of Scenes in Various Parts of the United States, Upper and Lower Canada, New-Brunswick, and Nova Scotia, During the Summer and Autumn of 1832*, Volume 1 (New York: J. J. Harper, 1833), 148.
6. Frances Trollope, *Domestic Manners of the Americans* (New York: Alfred A. Knopf, 1949), 121.
7. Alexis de Tocqueville, Journal Entry, Memphis, Tennessee, December 20, 1831, 267.
8. James F. Cooper, *The Pioneers*, (New York: Stringer and Townsend, 1852), 25-26.
9. Stockton Axson, "Washington Irving and the Knickerbocker Group," *Rice Institute Pamphlet - Rice University Studies*, 20, no. 2 (1933): 179.
10. Maura L. Jortner, "Playing 'America' on Nineteenth Century stages; or, Jonathan in England and Jonathan at Home" (PhD diss., University of Pittsburg, 2005), 115.
11. Nelson F. Adkins, "James K. Paulding's Lion of The West," *American Literature* 3, no. 3 (1931): 252.
12. Richard Boyd Hauck, *Davy Crockett, A Handbook* (Lincoln and London: University of Nebraska Press, 1982), 68.
13. Adkins, "Lion of the West," 220.
14. James Kirke Paulding, ed. James N. Tidwell, *The Lion of the West*, (Stanford University, 1954), 64.
15. Vera Jiji, *A Sourcebook of Interdisciplinary Materials in American Drama J.K. Paulding, "The Lion of the West"* (Brooklyn, New York: City Univ. of New York, 1983), 6.
16. Melvin Rosser Mason, "'The Lion of the West': Satire on Davy Crockett and Frances Trollope," *The South Central Bulletin* 29, no. 4 (1969): 144.

*Discovery Park of America*

The Davy Crockett Hotel was built in Union City in Northwest Tennessee in the early 1930s to cater primarily to travelers using the railroad lines. The hotel was advertised as having 100 "air-cooled" rooms featuring Beautyrest mattresses. One of the main features of the hotel was its location "just thirty-minutes' drive to Reelfoot Lake." The hotel hosted hunters and fishermen who visited the area from around the nation. For a period, the hotel was managed by noted outdoorsman Ralph Morton who also founded the Davy Crockett Hunting Club. Later, it was managed by the family of future Tennessee governor Ned Ray McWherter. The hotel took advantage of its name and capitalized on the free publicity provided by the Davy Crockett craze ignited by Walt Disney beginning in 1954. The hotel closed in 1977 and was reopened later as apartments for senior citizens.

**Money and fame made me believe I was entitled. I was wrong and foolish.**

**—Tiger Woods**

Chapter Twelve

# Comeback

When Crockett was having what must have been a surreal experience of seeing a version of himself parodied on stage in 1833, he was at the beginning of a comeback of sorts. The previous two years had not been good ones for the member of Congress from Tennessee, and his professional, personal, and financial situations were all, simply put, a mess. In the election of 1831, voters in District Nine of West Tennessee had selected someone else to represent them in Congress. Meanwhile, his financial situation was so bad, all the land and much of the property he owned had been sold to help pay off his enormous debts. And his family, who he had spent little time with in recent years, had grown acustomed to his absence.

His future in politics was also looking bleak. As part of the launch for his campaign for reelection in 1831, Crockett finally made it known that he was no longer a supporter of then-president Andrew Jackson; he had joined the Henry Clay camp. As one newspaper put it, "Crockett is no longer a half-horse, half-alligator Kentuck; but has become a whole hog Clay man."[1] Crockett's sixteen-page circular, reprinted in numerous newspapers, explained why in simple terms—Jackson had changed, not him:

> I thought with him, as he thought before he was President: he has altered his opinion—I have not changed mine. I have not left the principles which led me to support General Jackson; he has left them and me; and I will surely not surrender my independence to follow his new opinions, taught by interested and selfish advisors, which may again by remolded under the influence of passion and cunning.[2]

Once he split from Jackson, there was no going back—not that he ever wanted to. In an 1834 speech made in Philadelphia a few years after his public break with Jackson, his talking points remained similar:

> I was one of the first men that fired a gun under Andrew Jackson. I helped to throw around him that blaze of glory, that is blasting and blighting every thing it comes in contact with. I know I have equal rights with him, and so does every man that is not a slave; and when he is violating the constitution and the laws, I will oppose him, let the consequences to be be what they may.[3]

It was certainly a gamble. Would the voters return Crockett to Washington for a third two-year term now that he was taking such a public stand against the president, a fellow Tennessean? The failure of the Tennessee Vacant Land Bill to gain traction was certainly an albatross around his neck for voters. He attempted to explain that away by blaming Polk and the other Tennessee representatives' vendetta against him.

While the land bill had been his primary focus while in congress, he had also not shied away from taking a stand on a variety of other issues that were divisive at the time. He had come out strong against federal funding of the U.S. Military Academy at West Point, writing in the *Jackson Gazette* that "no one could ever gain admittance who had not rich or influential friends to aid him."[4] He likely reflected back to his own service as an untrained volunteer in the Creek War and the time General John Coffee made Crockett feel unimportant by dismissing the report he had been so excited to give. Coffee himself had done well after Andrew Jackson was elected president and, along with secretary of war John Eaton, was chosen to head up the negotiations with remaining Native American tribes in the southeastern U.S. to move them far west once and for all. Of course, Crockett wasn't going to lose too many West Tennessee voters over the West Point issue since few of them had "rich or influential friends," and most of their sons were not headed to West Point.

Jackson's Indian Removal Act, signed into law on May 28, 1830, was yet another issue that found Crockett publically in strong opposition with the president. It authorized Jackson to set aside land west of the Mississippi River in present-day Oklahoma in exchange for receiving all remaining Native American land within existing state borders. As though Crockett could see the horrors that were coming, he publicly called the act "inhumane" and wrote that Jackson's policies concerning Native Americans "brought shame and reproach on the American name."

Another matter of the day that got more attention from Crockett's constituents had to do with internal improvements and building a strong transportation infrastructure in Tennessee. One big question was whether the national government or the states would be responsible for the selection and management of the projects. Some legislators, especially those in southern states, feared a more powerful federal government would ultimately lead to the abolition of slavery.

Although he was absolutely against using his constituents' money for projects from which they would not benefit, he did side with the Whigs against the Jacksonians if he thought there was something in it for West Tennesseans. On the much-debated issue of a federally funded and managed project that would see a road built from Buffalo, New York to Washington and then on to New Orleans, Louisiana, Crockett even submitted an amendment that would have the road stop in Memphis, Tennessee. In a bit of dark foreshadowing, he pointed out that if the road should terminate in Memphis, it would be on a "direct route to the province of Texas." He added that he hoped that Texas would belong to the United States one day. Crockett's amendment was rejected, as was the bill.

Crockett's votes, circulars, articles printed in newspapers, and speeches on various issues prove that he was a politician willing to take a stand, regardless of the consequence, if he thought it helped those he served. He certainly was not in favor of spending their money unnecessarily. One of his most referenced public speeches, though, was likely not even given by Crockett. The speech in question was said to have been made during a debate regarding whether or not Congress should approve giving financial support to the struggling widow of a veteran who contracted a disease during military service that resulted in his eventual death. It was while objecting to this act that Crockett has been given credit for a speech declaring public relief as being unconstitutional. For decades, it has been commonly referred to as the "Not Yours to Give" speech. After much research, authors James Boylston and Allen Wiener determined that the speech, as reported for decades, is most certainly a fabrication.

The *Register of Debates in Congress* did record that during the first session of the Twentieth Congress on April 2, 1828, Crockett and Thomas Chilton had both been absent the previous day for the discussion and vote of a bill to provide financial support for the widow of a General Brown. Crockett "delivered their sentiments in opposition to the principle of the bill" and requested a public vote. It was also noted that Crockett personally offered to pay the sum that had been proposed, ironic considering his own precarious financial situation. John C. Clark, a member of Congress from New York who was obviously in favor of the bill, rose and sarcastically thanked Crockett and Chilton and stated that he was grateful for the opportunity to publicly vote in favor. The bill passed with ninety-seven for and seventy-four against, and then it went on to pass in the Senate.

The first appearance of this impassioned speech that Crockett allegedly gave in reference to this congressional vote came from Edward S. Ellis who, later in the century, wrote dime novels about the "Wild, Wild, West" for young readers. The speech can first be found in an 1867 issue of *Harper's New Monthly Magazine* written by Ellis, using the pseudonym James J. Bethune.

He then included it in his 1884 Crockett biography, *The Life of Colonel David Crockett.* Since Ellis was not even born until four years after Crockett's death, and no other evidence has been found for the existence of the speech, the most logical conclusion is that Ellis actually fabricated one of the speeches most frequently attributed to Crockett today.

Running against Crockett in 1831 to represent the people of the Ninth Congressional District was William Fitzgerald. He was born in Port Tobacco, Maryland in 1799. Some sources indicate that at seven years old, he (and possibly his brother) moved with his father to Dover, Tennessee.

Letters to Fitzgerald as an adult from his mother indicate that there was a long estrangement from her and that he had a grandmother, two sisters, and a brother still in Port Tobacco. One letter notes that she had not seen him since he "quit this, the County of his Childhood and his birth"[5] and that she had assumed he was dead. Fitzgerald studied law, possibly in England, then returned to Dover where he was admitted to the bar in 1821. He married Elizabeth Wells of Clarksville, Tennessee in 1822, and they purchased a farm on the bank of the Big Sandy River in present-day Henry County. They later moved to Dresden, Tennessee.

In previous elections, Crockett—the "uneducated" underdog—had been underestimated by his opponents, who usually had law degrees and successful careers. Fitzgerald was no different and, before running against Crockett, had served as a state legislator and a Tennessee circuit judge. But unlike previous opponents, Fitzgerald had the benefit of knowing what he was up against.

It was a different type of campaign for Crockett as well. In the past, with no pressure of having to justify a stance on specific issues, Crockett had been able to connect with voters as one of them by using his charm, humor, and charisma. A vote for him meant sending a "common man" with little experience to Washington to show the elites in the nation's capital how things are done on the Tennessee frontier. But in many ways, he was now what he had once made fun of and campaigned against. There was a record of his votes for constituents to consider and four years of work that his opponent could use against him. There was also the case of his frequent absences. Unable to sit for hours upon hours listening to his fellow members of Congress pontificate on issues he felt were not relevant to West Tennessee, he was often absent and was accused of missing a large number of votes. Early on, he struggled with the format of some of the congressional legislative sessions, writing to a friend, "Thare is no chance of hurrying business here like in the legislature of a State thare is Such a desposition to Show Eloquence..."[6]

The campaign got ugly, and Crockett was now on the defensive. Fitzgerald's camp pulled stunts like advertising appearances by Crockett in newspapers without his knowledge, then showing up and claiming the incumbent was too afraid to appear. They would then attack his record and present Fitzgerald as the best candidate.

The more defensive he got, the more Crockett was behaving and sounding like all the other angry politicians. In one response to accusations made by Fitzgerald, Crockett wrote, "Did you think little Fitz, that I would suffer myself to be squeezed to death like a mouse, without at least a squeak? It was a bold attempt to think I could impose upon the good people of this District such a thing as truth; well done Fitz, you are not accustomed to it I suppose."[7]

Fitzgerald was also accusing Crockett of being a drunk and of having affairs instead of tending to business while in Washington. When Crockett found out, he publicly threatened to "thrash" his opponent. When the chance came to make good on his threat, it turned out to be a big political misstep. Crockett and Fitzgerald were both at the same campaign event in Paris, Tennessee.

As Fitzgerald began his speech, some in the audience may have wondered what the candidate had placed in front of him, wrapped in a handkerchief. They found out when Crockett stood up and charged the stage to make good on his threats of a thrashing. When Crockett was just a few feet from the stage, Fitzgerald pulled a pistol from the handkerchief in front of him and pointed it at Crockett's chest, warning, "one step further and I shall fire." Stunned, Crockett turned around and retreated to his seat. Some later said it was at that moment the election was decided.

Jackson and the Democrats did all they could to help Fitzgerald and hurt

Crockett. Jackson wrote to his nephew, Samuel Jackson Hays, "I trust, for the honor of the state, your Congressional District will not disgrace themselves longer by sending that profligate man Crockett back to Congress."[8]

The *Jackson Gazette*, along with other newspapers, also came out in favor of Fitzgerald. As the editor of the *Gazette* wrote, "He can't 'whip his weight in wild cats,' nor 'leap the Mississippi,' nor 'mount a rainbow and slide off into eternity and back at pleasure,' but we believe, that Mr. Fitzgerald will make a better legislator."[9]

Enough of the voters of West Tennessee agreed, and Crockett lost the election, although by an extremely narrow margin and primarily due to the loss of votes in Madison County. Crockett contested the election, but Fitzgerald's victory held. In a letter to a friend that Crockett wrote with "at home in Weakley County" written in bold letters across the top, he blamed his loss on Andrew Jackson and on not being willing to be a "puppy dog" running after Jackson's Democratic party:

> The truth is I was one of the first men that ever crossed the Tennessee river into the Creek war with him and I served two tours of duty with him and voted for him for President...I supported him as far as he pursued the principles he professed to possess before he was elected. I never did support men and forsake principles...The Jackson partizans here is exulting that they have me beaten. I thank God I would rather be beaten and be a man than to be elected and be a little pupy dog, to yelp after their party. I love my country and I would not give one chaw of tobaco for a man that will not make a sacrifice of himself before he will have his country imposed on....I have no doubt but the time is not far distant when the American people will see the purity of my making. I have truth on my side... and it will prevail.[10]

At least in letters, he expressed no regret. In one, he wrote, "I have acted fearless and independent and I will never regret my course...I have always believed I was an honest man and if the world will do me Justice they will find it to be the case."[11]

Crockett was now forced to leave the excitement of Washington and return home to Northwest Tennessee. To make matters worse, the attention he had placed on his career rather than his family seems to have taken a toll. He had not been present at the weddings of his son, William, or his daughter, Margaret, in the spring of 1830, and many Crockett biographers believe that he and Elizabeth had amicably separated after years of essentially living separate lives. She lived with her children and with relatives on her side of the family. Elizabeth's father, Robert Patton, and five of her sisters ended up living in Northwest Tennessee so she was surrounded by family.

No one volunteered to work off Crockett's loans, as he had done so many years earlier for his father. He was forced to sell property—primarily to family members—to pay off debts accumulated during his political campaigns and from living in Washington. Interestingly, it was assumed for many years he had scrawled a version of what had become his catchphrase, "Be always sure you are right then Go ahead" on one of the deeds. It was later determined that flourish had been added by an overzealous registrar.

Crockett asked for and received an extension on a loan he had gotten from the Bank of the United States. In his request, he noted that he had come out in favor for an extension of the bank's charter, while his opponent, Fitzgerald—or "the thing that had the name of beating me," as he called him—was aligned with Jackson against the bank. He added, "Times is hard in this country I will do the best I can."[12] He received the requested extension. Later, the loan was personally forgiven by Nicholas Biddle, the president of the bank—an example of the very reason Jackson was so against the bank in the first place.

With much of his property sold, Crockett leased a few acres near some of his children and put up a simple cabin. He had no law practice, plantation, or land speculating to return to like many other legislators who lost their campaigns for public office.

A writer, who later authored the first book about Crockett, wrote of visiting him at his cabin around this time. After traveling on an overgrown path, he came to a small opening through which he found the cabin that was "rude and uninviting situated in a small field of eight or ten acres"[13] He described the inside as being clean and neat, with the trophies of wild animals spread around the house and in the yard.

While there are few records or newspaper articles to show how Crockett spent his two years out of Congress, it's likely that he spent at least some of the time strategizing how he would win the next election. If he had any doubts at all about running again during that time, they were not recorded.

Crockett was ready to campaign. Although Fitzgerald had an unremarkable two sessions in Congress, he had the president and the Jacksonians in his corner. When population growth demanded District Nine be divided, they made sure that Crockett's new district included Madison County, whose more urban voters had caused Crockett to lose the previous election. Crockett would be running to represent the new Twelfth District of Tennessee that included Haywood, Madison, Dyer, Obion, Gibson, Weakley, Henry, and Carroll Counties.

One of those Jacksonians working to make sure Crockett lost again was Adam Huntsman, who was a rising star in the party. He put his writing skills and sense of humor to work against Crockett. Huntsman was born in Charlotte County, Virginia on February 11, 1786 and was educated in Virginia. He moved to Knoxville, Tennessee in his early twenties, where he studied law under John Williams. It had been Crockett's support of Williams in 1823 that so angered Jackson back when Crockett was a state legislator. Huntsman passed the bar in Knoxville and began what would be a successful law career only interrupted by his service fighting in the Creek War.

Huntsman lost a leg serving in that war, which resulted in a constant reminder of his service: a wooden leg. He moved to Madison County, Tennessee in 1821, where he became a well-respected criminal attorney, speculated in land, and was selected as another of the early commissioners. From 1827-1831, he served as a Tennessee state senator representing Madison, Fayette, Hardeman, Haywood, Shelby, and Tipton Counties.

Crockett and Huntsman actually had a number of areas where they agreed. Huntsman fought for legislation in Tennessee that would limit the speculators in favor of squatters and was an advocate of internal improvements. He introduced bills for creating toll bridges over the Forked Deer River and the Hatchie River and for a canal from the Hatchie River to the Mississippi River. He also introduced legislation for the creation of numerous roads throughout West Tennessee, making towns like Trenton, Troy, Brownsville, and Union City more accessible for settlement.

Huntsman was a passionate advocate for the Jacksonian Democratic party, however, and was appalled at Crockett's betrayal of the president and the party. During the election of 1833, he used his writing skills and the alias Black Hawk to publish a biblical parody of Crockett that accused him of making a bargain with the Whigs in order to get his land bill passed. It was a clever way to attack Crockett's record, and there was certainly no confusion among readers as to who the main characters were or the meaning of the story.

Huntsman's bible story opens with, "And it came to pass in those days, when Andrew was chief ruler over the children of Columbia, that there arose a mighty man in the river country, whose name was David; he belonged to the tribe of Tennessee, which lay upon the border of the Mississippi and over against Kentucky." The story continues with a reference to the squatters of West Tennessee who "loved David exceedingly, because he promised to give them lands flowing with milk and honey." In Huntsman's *Book of Chronicles*, David is denied his request, which results in his betrayal and secret deal with Daniel Webster, Henry Clay, and the Whigs. In the end of the parable, the people sided with Andrew Jackson and William Fitzgerald.

Surprisingly, even with everything against him, Crockett's celebrity status and support from the Whigs proved to be enough to push him over the edge. Unlike in Huntsman's story, he actually won the election—but just barely. In reflecting on his victory, Crockett wrote, "I had Mr. Fitzgerald, it is true, for my open competitor, but he was helped along by all his little lawyers again, headed by old Black Hawk, as he is sometimes called...Adam Huntsman, with all his talents for writing 'Chronicles,' and such like foolish stuff."[14]

For the "Davy Crockett" brand that would appear more than one hundred years later, winning the election of 1833 was one of the biggest milestones on the path to Crockett's status as a folk hero. Without it, he would have likely stayed in Tennessee. He would have lived out the remainder of his life carving out what living he could on a small farm and hunting around Reelfoot Lake. Today, like William Fitzgerald and Adam Huntsman, he would be a mere footnote in history, remembered by few. But thanks to his growing fame, the voters of West Tennessee had given Crockett a second chance and sent him back to Washington City.

**Chapter Twelve Notes**

1. Boylston and Wiener, *Crockett in Congress*, 80.
2. Ibid., 297-298.
3. David Crockett, *An Account of Col. Crockett's Tour to the North and Down East* (Philadelphia: E. L. Carey and A. Hart, 1835), 31.
4. David Crockett, *Jackson Gazette*, April 10, 1830, 2.
5. George C. Osborn, "Some letters of William T. and Sarah Firtzgerald," *Tennessee Historical Quarterly* 6, no. 2 (1947): 183.
6. Shackford, *Crockett*, 89.
7. David Crockett, *The Southern Statesman*, July 02, 1831, 2.
8. Emma Inman Williams, *Historic Madison: The Story of Jackson and Madison County, Tennessee* (Jackson, Tennessee, 1946), 403.
9. William C. Davis, *Three Roads to the Alamo: The Lives and Fortunes of David Crockett, James Bowie, and William Barret Travis* (New York Harper-Collins, 1998), 181.
10. Crockett to James Davison, August 18, 1831, Estate of Robert A. Davison
11. Boylston and Wiener, *Crockett in Congress*, 217.
12. Shackford, *Crockett*, 146.
13. Sketches 115
14. Crockett, *Narrative*, 220.

*Hanna-Barbera, Imaged by Heritage Auctions*

*Davy Crockett on the Mississippi* was one of many animated television specials that aired on CBS from 1970 to 1984 as part of the anthology series *Famous Classic Tales*. The episode featuring Crockett aired on November 20, 1976. In addition to Crockett, it featured the characters Matt Henry, Honeysuckle the Bear, and Mike Fink. Crockett was voiced by veteran actor Ned Wilson.

**Fame is the perfume of heroic deeds.**
**—Socrates**

## Chapter Thirteen

# Tears

Playwright John Augustus Stone worked with James Hackett on the second version of *The Lion of the West*. He came to the project having contributed to the creation of a nineteenth-century archetype for the American stage that was, in many ways, the opposite of the western frontiersman: the noble savage. This character's way of life was about to be destroyed in the name of progress. Actor Edwin Forrest sponsored a contest in 1828 similar to the one held by Hackett and offered $500 to the playwright who could provide the best tragedy featuring a Native American as the main character. Stone won the prize with his entry, *Metamora; or, The Last of the Wampanoags*.

While David Crockett inspired the creation of Nimrod Wildfire in *The Lion of the West*, Stone selected Metacomet, a chief of the Wampanoag tribe, as the inspiration for his leading man. And just as *The Lion of the West* was a vehicle for Crockett and, by association, the Whigs, *Metamora* furthered the agenda of the Jacksonian Democrats regarding Native American removal and resettlement.

The script was based on King Philip's War, a conflict from 1675-1678 between New England colonists and the Wampanoag tribe led by Metacomet, otherwise known as King Philip. Because the colonists faced their enemies without support from any European government or military, the war is said to mark the birth of an independent America. *Metamora* was the most successful and frequently performed American play of the nineteenth century. Its success also resulted in Forrest becoming the highest-paid and most-celebrated actor in America for the next two decades. And just as Hackett as Nimrod Wildfire was the first encounter with a "Westerner" for many audiences around the world, Forrest as Metamora was their first "Indian." While the play brought to life the romantic ideal of the beauty and wisdom of Native Americans, it also included a strong primary message—the "savages" had to be sent somewhere else for their own good. As author B. Donald Grose noted, "it was seen as a pro-removal vehicle, one that illustrated the necessity of moving Indians to keep them from extermination." He added,

> *Metamora* not only exhibits all the stereotypic traits of the noble savage, he also incorporates the attributes of the noble savage's antithesis, the red devil. With its foundation in Renaissance primitivism, the stereotype of the noble savage exemplifies the Indian as a creature of physical beauty and natural grace, filled with an intuitive knowledge of nature and secrets, elegant in speech, stoic and totally loyal to friends, relatives and loved ones. When this stereotype was brought into conflict with white civilization, three possibly methods of adjustment were available: willing victimization, acculturation, and extermination.[1]

Whether or not that was the original intent of Stone and Forrest in presenting the play is debated, but they did put on stage a dramatic representation of how many Whites in the country felt during that time. Books, newspapers, periodicals, and plays during this period featured the image of the proud Native American warrior unable to assimilate into a White man's world. For them, the only solution was to move the Native

Americans far away. For many, it was a way to justify their desire to quickly remove Native Americans so they could take their land.

Removal was not a new solution on how to deal with non-Whites. In 1817, the American Colonization Society was formed to emancipate slaves and send them, along with free Blacks, to Africa. It included such esteemed members as Abraham Lincoln and James Monroe. In 1822, the organization established a colony on Africa's west coast that later became the independent nation of Liberia. Eventually, more than twelve thousand free and formerly enslaved Blacks were sent to make new lives there.

Around this same time, another unique method of colonizing Blacks in America was championed by British writer Frances Wright. She believed she could create a system that would result in the eventual abolishment of slavery and the resettlement of former slaves in other countries.

She returned to England in 1821 after a two-year visit to America and wrote and published a popular book about her transformative experience in the new country. *Views of Society and Manners in America* was the opposite of books like Trollope's that positioned American society as boorish and the people ill-mannered. In Wright's view, America was a "republican utopia" where liberty created a culture unlike anything else in the world. She wrote, "It is singular to look around upon a country where dreams of sages, smiled at as utopian, seem distinctly realized, a people voluntarily submitting to laws of their own imposing…respecting the voice of a government which their breath created and which their breath could in a moment destroy."[2] Her travels also inspired her to do something about the only negative thing she saw in America—slavery. Although she was against slavery as an institution, she believed that years of captivity had rendered Blacks inferior to Whites and thought they were not yet able to function independently.

The popularity of her book resulted in a friendship with the Marquis de Lafayette, and she traveled to America as his assistant during his celebrated return and tour of the country in 1825. While exploring the South, she began developing a plan to create a utopian farming community that would educate enslaved people and pay them for their work, allowing them to purchase their own freedom. They could then join other Blacks in communities in other countries.

A talented politician, she capitalized on her friendship with Lafayette and got her plan in front of powerful men including Thomas Jefferson, Andrew Jackson, James Monroe, Henry Clay, James Madison, Mayor Marcus Winchester of Memphis, and Chief Justice John Marshall. While some offered advice and kind words of vague support, what she was really after—financial investment—was harder to come by.

Of course, the Jackson, Winchester, and John Overton trio was always eager to sell Tennessee land. With her own money, Wright purchased a little over a thousand acres of wilderness along the Wolf River just east of Memphis and named her farm "Nashoba," inspired by the Chickasaw word for wolf.

Wright developed a friendship with Mayor Marcus Winchester and his wife, Mary, who had experienced such racism from many of the White settlers in Memphis. Early Memphis historian James Davis wrote of Wright, "she was of large masculine figure, strong voice, and most remarkable oratorical powers." He also noted that she had "unbounded confidence" in Marcus Winchester.[3]

Without investors, she could only afford to buy seven slaves to begin her experiment rather than the one hundred she originally had in her grand plan. It was just as well, since Nashoba fell apart quickly. There were numerous reasons why it didn't work including her lack of farming experience, the brutal heat and humidity of West Tennessee summers, and her liberal ideas on relationships and sexuality that departed greatly from the norms of the day. In the end, her own illness and pregnancy resulted in a return to her home in England to recover. She later came back to America, where she freed and resettled her slaves in Haiti after the Haitian president agreed to place them "as cultivators on land belonging to kind and trustworthy persons."[4]

For Blacks in America in the early 1800s, the issue of slavery and the forced labor they provided ultimately kept them tethered to the country. Native Americans, however, were expendable, and the reward for their removal was what Americans needed most—land. While many in the country at the time played a part in their near annihilation through the early decades of American history, perhaps no single individual is more closely identified with Native American genocide than Andrew Jackson. Some historians point to his actions and come to the conclusion that he had an intense hatred for Native Americans. Others argue that his actions were based on a desire to preserve their society, while taking their land away and making it available for expansion. Regardless of his motivation, there is little doubt that solving the "Indian problem" was at the top of his agenda after Chief Justice John Marshall administered the presidential oath of office on March 4, 1829. Among Native Americans, Jackson had earned the nickname "Sharp Knife." Now that he was president, they were about to find out just how cutting that blade could be.

In his first annual message to Congress on December 8, 1829, Jackson made his intentions clear. He spoke of how the government had long tried to incorporate the Native Americans into civilization in the hope of "gradually reclaiming them from a wandering life." But he noted that because the government ignored its own policy, the Native Americans had "retained their savage habits."[5] In reality, he knew that was far from the truth.

The Cherokee tribe, for example, had assimilated into the "White man's world" with many of them farming thousands of acres and some even becoming slaveholders. The Cherokee had done exactly what White Americans said they had to do if they wanted to continue to live on their land. They wore the same clothes as their White neighbors, built the same type of houses, and filled them with the same furniture. Some Cherokee communities in Georgia and Tennessee had schools and churches, and many members of the tribe valued education to such a degree, those with money sent their children up north to private schools.

The Chief of the Cherokee from 1828-1866 was John Ross, the son of a Cherokee mother and Scottish father, who was raised speaking both languages and attending schools specifically for mixed-race Cherokee. He served as a second lieutenant of a Cherokee regiment under Jackson in the War of 1812. After the war, he started several businesses including a tobacco plantation and ferry service in present-day Chattanooga at what came to be called Ross's Landing on the Tennessee River. He was able to read and write both English and Cherokee fluently and was successful, articulate, and charismatic. Ross quickly rose to prominence among both his tribe and the politicians in Washington.

Thanks in part to Ross, on February 21, 1828, the first Cherokee newspaper rolled off the presses in the Cherokee Nation's capital city, New Echota, Georgia. The *Cherokee Phoenix* was published each week with adjacent columns of Cherokee text set next to English. Editor Elias Boudinot, a mixed-race Cherokee, had been sent to school in Connecticut. It was there he met Harriet Gold, the daughter of a wealthy and prominent family. After their marriage created controversy, Boudinot took his White wife to live in New Echota, where they raised six children as Cherokee.

Many Cherokee had clearly not "retained their savage habits" as Jackson claimed. In fact, some had become more literate and more cultured than the White settlers living around them. The Cherokee Nation even mimicked the government of America in forming their own constitution and bill of rights, something the state of Georgia had no intention of following. On the symbolic date of July 4, 1827, Ross (like George Washington forty years earlier) led a constitutional convention and then became his nation's first leader—an act that journalist Steve Inskeep applauds in his book, *Jacksonland*:

> There was poetry in this parallel, since the Cherokee constitution was the ultimate achievement to grow out of Washington's civilization program. Ross and the Cherokees were committing an act of political jujitsu—taking the force of an opponent's blow and turning it against him. The Founding Fathers had offered civilization as a means to humanely pacify and displace the Indians; Cherokees accepted the offer and used it to strengthen themselves in place.[6]

In spite of an eventual Supreme Court decision in favor of the Cherokee, the state continued to torment them and, as Jackson instructed a Georgia member of Congress, "build a fire under them. When it gets hot enough, they'll move."[7] They were not allowed to vote, pass laws, make legally binding contracts, or even travel. They were harassed, bullied, and—in many cases—even killed, with their murderers never brought to justice. Although the law of the land was on the side of the Cherokee, Jackson made it clear in his first address that he was on the side of Georgia and anyone else who wanted to force the Native Americans out once and for all:

> I informed the Indians inhabiting parts of Georgia and Alabama that their attempt to establish an independent government would not be countenanced by the executive of the United States, and advised them to emigrate beyond the Mississippi or submit to the laws of those states…our ancestors found them the uncontrolled possessors of these vast regions. By persuasion and force they have been made to retire from river to river and from mountain to mountain, until some of the tribes have become extinct and others have left but remnants to preserve for a while their once terrible names. Surrounded by the whites with their arts of civilization, which by destroying the resources of the savage doom him to weakness and decay, the fate of the Mohegan, the Narragansett, and the Delaware is fast overtaking the Choctaw, the Cherokee, and the Creek. That this fate surely awaits them if they remain within the limits of the states does not admit of a doubt.

On February 24, 1830, Jackson turned his rhetoric into reality and introduced the Indian Removal Act. The bill gave him, rather than congress, the right to negotiate for "an exchange of lands with the Indians residing in any of the states or territories, and for their removal west of the Mississippi River." The act appropriated $500,000 that the president could use to relocate tribes still in Mississippi, Alabama, Tennessee, and Georgia to land set aside far out west, that few Americans had ever even seen. Jackson, with the grateful support of the majority, was about to build a fire hot enough to make them move.

Ultimately, it was an offense to two minority groups, as it would result in White slave owners using the land for agriculture, which required even more enslaved people to work the land that had belonged to the Native Americans. As author and historian Daniel Walker Howe wrote, "In the first place it was about the extension of white supremacy across the North American continent. By his policy of Indian Removal, Jackson confirmed his support in the cotton states…and fixed the character of his political party."[8]

Not everyone was in favor of the Indian Removal Act. Some lawmakers, church leaders, and social groups could see through the rhetoric and fought for the Native Americans. Included in that number was David Crockett. Although he had been troublesome for the Democrats since arriving in Washington, his break with Jackson had not yet occurred publicly. If there had been even a slight chance that the relationship between the party and the representative from Northwest Tennessee could have been repaired, it evaporated during the debate and vote over the Indian Removal Act.

The bill was passed in the House of Representatives by a vote of 102-97 and in the Senate by a vote of 28-19. Crockett was the only member of the Tennessee delegation to vote against the bill. John Ross thanked Crockett for his vote and wrote to him, "the day of retributive justice must and will come, when, integrity and moral worth will predominate and make the shameless monster hide its head. Whether this day will come in time to save the suffering Cherokees from violence and fraud, it is for the wisdom, magnanimity & justice of the United States to determine."[9]

While John Ross was grateful, many believe the price Crockett paid for his vote came when he lost the next election. In a speech given later, Crockett said, "I stand alone from my state; but I glory in what they consider my sin and shame."[10] Like other aspects of his life and career, his public response to the Indian Removal Act is muddled in a combination of bluff, bravado, and public relations.

While the speech did not appear in the *Register of Debates in Congress*, it was printed in the *United States' Telegraph* and other newspapers. In this case, there is indication that Crockett delivered a speech against the bill in the House of Representatives on May 19, 1830 that was later reprinted in newspapers and a book of speeches about the bill. But because it did not appear in the *Register of Debates in Congress*, some historians think the speech was never actually given and, instead, submitted later to justify his vote against the bill. Biographer Shackford even implied that the speech was written by Whigs and noted sarcastically, "Evidently someone wrote a speech for Crockett he never got around to delivering."[11]

Whether given verbally in the House of Representatives, written later by Crockett, or even written later by a Whig in his name, Crockett's opinion regarding the bill and his reasons for voting against it were clear. He noted that he did not know if any other member of Congress within five hundred miles of his home would vote like he was going to, but he had to vote with his conscience, no matter what. He did not approve of the bill for various reasons including his dislike of putting money in the hands of the president with no oversight. He also noted that four of the counties he represented bordered Chickasaw country and that he personally knew many individuals in the tribe. He acknowledged that while nothing could ever induce him to drive them from their homes, he would support it if they wanted to go willingly. A transcriber who recorded one of Crockett's speeches for the *Telegraph* wrote,

> He had been told that he did not understand English grammar. That was very true. He had never been six months at school in his life; he had raised himself by the labor of his hands. But he did not, on that account, yield upon his privilege as the representative of freemen on this floor. Humble as he was, he meant to exercise his privilege. He had been charged with not representing his constituents. If the fact was so, the error (said Mr. C.) is here, (touching his head) not here (laying his hand upon his heart). He never had possessed wealth or education, but he had ever been animated by an independent spirit; and he trusted to prove it on the present occasion.

In his autobiography, Crockett wrote of the vote against Andrew Jackson's bill:

> His famous, or rather should I say in-famous, Indian bill was brought forward, and I opposed it from the purest motives in the world. Several of my colleagues got around me, and told me how well they loved me, and that I was ruining myself. They said this was a favorite measure of the president, and I ought to go for it. I told them I believed it was a wicked, unjust measure, and that I should go against it, let the cost to myself be what it might. [12]

While the bill did not give Jackson the right to remove Native Americans against their will, that is exactly what happened. In 1835, a few self-appointed representatives of the Cherokee Nation, without the approval of Chief John Ross, negotiated the Treaty of New Echota with Jackson. Included in the minority faction who saw removal as the only answer was Major Ridge, John Ridge (Major's son), and Stand Waite. Joining them was Major Ridge's nephew, Elias Boudinot, who resigned his position as editor of the *Cherokee Phoenix* in protest because Ross would not even consider a move west to Oklahoma. Stand Waite was Boudinot's younger brother. Although they were viewed as traitors by the majority of Cherokee who did not want to leave their homes, they and their small group of supporters considered themselves patriots. They believed—correctly, as it turned out—that Jackson and others had no intention of furthering any scenario that allowed the Cherokee or any other tribe to retain any portion of their land.

They traded all Cherokee land east of the Mississippi for $5 million, relocation assistance, and compensation for lost property.

John Ross wrote to the Senate, "The instrument in question is not the act of our nation. We are not parties to its covenants; it has not received the sanction of our people." A petition protesting the treaty signed by sixteen thousand Cherokees was submitted to Congress and then summarily ignored.

In 1838, then-president Martin Van Buren, Jackson's vice president and hand-picked successor, sent General Winfield Scott with seven thousand soldiers to force around two thousand Georgia Cherokee into stockades at gunpoint, while Whites ransacked their homes and businesses and walked away with their belongings. The Cherokee were not allowed the appropriate clothing or tools and were shoved into poorly built stockades for days before their departure. In numerous smaller groups, they were forced to walk more than twelve-thousand miles on what is now called the "Trail of Tears."

A soldier sent as an interpreter later wrote of the morning a group of Cherokee departed:

> I witnessed the execution of the most brutal order of the History of American Warfare. I saw the helpless Cherokee arrested and dragged from their homes, and driven at the bayonet point into the stockades...One can never forget the sadness and solemnity of that morning. Chief John Ross led in prayer and when the bugle sounded and the wagons started rolling many of the children rose to their feet and waved their little hands good-by...The trail of the exiles was a trail of death...I have known as many as twenty-two of them to die in one night of pneumonia due to ill treatment, cold, and exposure.[13]

Each morning, the dead were buried along the side of the trail.

More than one hundred thousand Native Americans were forced from their land to "Indian Territory" from 1830-1850, some in chains. Although the exact number is unknown, thousands died along the way. Alexis de Tocqueville witnessed a group of Choctaw on the trail while in Memphis. He wrote,

> At the end of the year 1831, whilst I was on the left bank of the Mississippi at a place named by Europeans, Memphis, there arrived a numerous band of Choctaws (or Chactas, as they are called by the French in Louisiana)...It was then the middle of winter, and the cold was unusually severe; the snow had frozen hard upon the ground, and the river was drifting huge masses of ice. The Indians had their families with them; and they brought in their train the wounded and sick, with children newly born, and old men upon the

> verge of death. They possessed neither tents nor wagons, but only their arms and some provisions…No cry, no sob was heard amongst the assembled crowd; all were silent.[14]

Three months after the final group of Cherokee survivors arrived to their new home in present-day Oklahoma, Elias Boudinot, Major Ridge, and John Ridge were murdered in retaliation for their role in the Treaty of New Echota.

There are many tragic aspects to the story of the removal of the Native Americans from their homeland. But perhaps one of the cruelest was that on the Trail of Tears, those who died were usually the youngest and oldest of the tribe. As a result, the Native Americans who survived arrived to what would become their home having lost much of their past and their future.

## Chapter Thirteen Notes

1. Donald B. Grose, "Edwin Forrest, 'Metamora', and the Indian Removal Act of 1830," *Theatre Journal* 37, no. 2 (1985): 191.
2. Frances Wright, *Views of Society and Manners in America* (London: Longman, Hurst, Rees, Orme, and Brown, 1821), 188.
3. James Davis, *History of Memphis* (Memphis, Tennessee: Hite, Crumpton & Kelly, 1873), 71.
4. Robert Dale Owen, "An Earnest Sowing of Wild Oats," *Atlantic Monthly* (July 1874): 75.
5. President Jackson's Message to Congress "On Indian Removal," December 6, 1830; Records of the United States Senate, 1789-1990; Record Group 46; Records of the United States Senate, 1789-1990; National Archives.
6. Steve Inskeep, *Jacksonland* (New York: Penguin Press, 2015), 121.
7. Boylston and Wiener, *David Crockett in Congress*, 68.
8. Daniel Walker Howe, *What God Hath Wrought: The Transformation of America, 1815–1848* (New York: Oxford University Press, 2007), 357.
9. Gary Moulton, ed., *The Papers of Chief John Ross: Volume I 1807–1839, Volume II 1840–1866* (Norman, Oklahoma: University of Oklahoma Press, 1985), 1.
10. Crockett, *Travels*, 42.
11. Shakeford, *Crockett*, 116.
12. Crockett, *Narrative*, 206.
13. R. Satz, "The Cherokee Trail of Tears: A Sesquicentennial Perspective," *The Georgia Historical Quarterly*, 73(3) (1989): 459.
14. John Stone and Stephen Mennell, ed., *Alexis de Tocqueville on Democracy, Revolution and Society* (Chicago: The University of Chicago Press, 1980), 330.

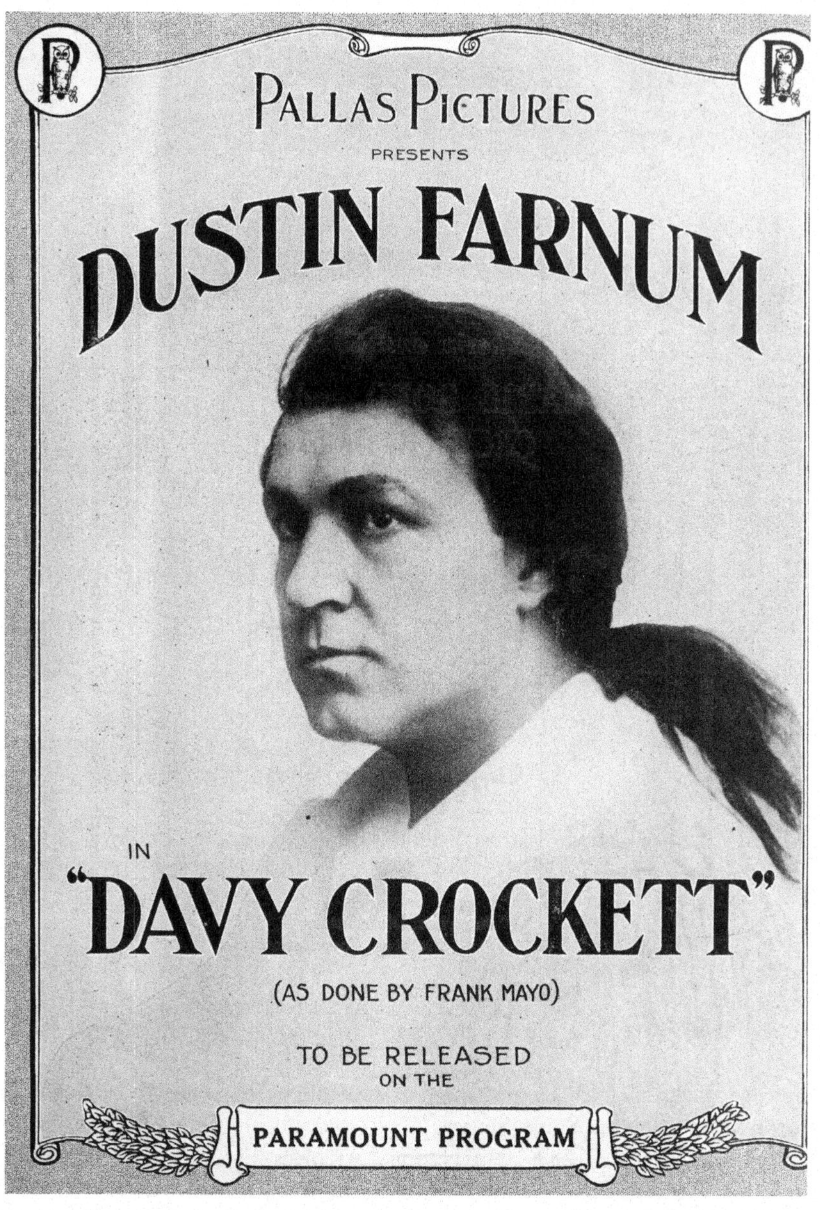


Actor and film director William Desmond Taylor directed silent screen star Dustin Farnum in *Davy Crockett*. Released in 1916, it was based on the play featuring Frank Mayo and was produced by the Pallas Pictures studios in Los Angeles with some scenes filmed in the San Bernardino Mountains. In its review of the film, a reporter for the *Knoxville Sentinel* noted, "Real bears and hungry wolves make the outdoors right there before you, and Mr. Farnum has the advantage in such roles of being a real lover of nature and knowing how to paddle and shoot and do all the out-of-doors 'stunts' almost like a real native American Indian—and ride? You can always expect some fine horsemanship in a 'Dusty Farnum' picture." No copies of the film exist.

**The three terrible karmas are beauty, wealth, and fame — they're the things that stop you from finding true happiness.**

**—Brad Pitt**

Chapter Fourteen

# Fame

By the spring of 1834, David Crockett had achieved a level of fame and popularity in America that was unprecedented, especially for someone who had done so little to earn it. As Crockett biographer Joseph Arpad pointed out,

> Unlike George Washington and Andrew Jackson, he was not a military hero, not a savior of his country...Unlike Alexander Hamilton or Thomas Jefferson, he was not a statesman, not a great political philosopher. Unlike John C. Calhoun, Henry Clay, or Daniel Webster, he was not a great political leader, not a great orator, not even an effective political leader...And unlike Daniel Boone, he was not a great American pioneer.[1]

Arpad determined that Crockett's fame had little to do with what he did; it had to do with who he was. He added, "His sole distinction appears to have been something inherent, an originality of character so innately American that it caused his elevation in public esteem."[2]

And the more he was exposed to the public, the more famous he became. Crockett himself had a hard time explaining what was happening. He wrote, "I know, that obscure as I am, my name is making a considerable deal of fuss in the world. I can't tell why it is...everybody seems anxious to get a peep at me...there must be something in me, or about me, that attracts attention, which is even mysterious to myself."[3]

In the early decades of the nineteenth century, there were plenty of heroes. But somewhere along the way, Crockett transitioned from hero to his status as America's first superhero. Reporters and editors looking to sell newspapers and magazines wrote and reprinted tall tales about the outrageous "congressman from the wilderness of Tennessee," whether they were true or not. One article that made its way around the country reported that then-president Andrew Jackson had to hire Crockett to climb the Allegheny Mountains to wring the tail off a comet and save the world. One would like to have been a fly on the wall to observe Jackson reading that bit of fake news.

The public ate it up and wanted more, and Crockett was more than happy to give it to them. Everywhere he went, fans wanted to see the frontiersman from the West in person or hear him speak. In one instance, he was with friends at Mrs. Ball's Boarding House when a Washington tour guide showed up with visitors from out of town. According to the guide, they had come from far away, specifically to meet Crockett. He not only met those fans, but he also spent some time sharing a few Tennessee stories with them, as only he could. After they left, he said to his friends, likely with an air of false modesty, "Well, they came to see a bear, and they've seen one. Hope they liked the performance—it did not cost them anything anyhow."[4]

Crockett was no fool, and it was apparent that he needed to figure out a way to financially capitalize on his national popularity, since he vacillated between being in debt and heavily in debt. But it wasn't just money he was after. His fame also provided a platform for Crockett to blast his political enemy, Andrew Jackson. And he was far from being the only politician in that era to nurse a hatred for Jackson—or leave the party—as it was an especially divisive period in American politics. Crockett was a trailblazer, though, when it came to using down-to-earth humor that appealed to the "common man" to get his political points across.

While in Boston's Charlestown Navy Yard on a tour to promote his new autobiography, Crockett was shown a number of ships including the iconic USS *Constitution.* The famous ship was nicknamed "Old Ironsides" after victories against numerous British battleships during the War of 1812. After years of service, the ship was scheduled to be scrapped. In response to an outcry inspired by an early sense of patriotism, Andrew Jackson directed that it be saved and dry-docked. As a display of gratitude, the commandant of the navy yard had a ten-foot-tall figurehead of Jackson carved and placed on the front of the great ship.

When shown the carved representation of Jackson while in the company of reporters, Crockett couldn't help wryly commenting that "they had fixed him just where he had fixed himself, that was—before the Constitution."[5]

Crockett was among the last to see that particular Jackson figurehead on the USS *Constitution.* The voices of descension against Jackson, especially in the east, were growing louder. Around the time Crockett made his comment, a handbill was circulating around Boston that read, "For God's sake save the ship from this foul disgrace."[6] A few months later, a storm blew into Boston, making the ship harder for security to see. Samuel Worthington Dewey, a local captain who also happened to be an angry Whig, was able to climb up the USS *Constitution* with a saw during the dark, stormy night. As the sun rose the next morning, those arriving to the navy yard were surprised by the sight of a headless Andrew Jackson on the front of the ship.

The continued success of *The Lion of the West*, combined with the popularity of Nimrod Wildfire's unique delivery of southwestern humor—often attributed to Crockett himself—inspired others to capitalize on this public figure that had quickly taken on a life of its own. In modern vernacular, the Crockett brand had wide appeal in a broad demographic. In other words, he was hot. He was still at the "Get me David Crockett" level of fame, but the "Get me someone like David Crockett" level was just around the corner.

In early 1833, an anonymous and unauthorized biography titled *The Life and Adventures of Col. David Crockett of West Tennessee* was published in Cincinnati, Ohio by Harper & Brothers. It was an immediate success. Copies flew off the shelves, and the presses couldn't keep up with the demand. After a few edits, a second version of the Crockett biography was quickly published in New York and London with a new title, *Sketches and Eccentricities of Colonel David Crockett of West Tennessee.*

Books of this nature usually sold for less than sixty cents, but *Sketches and Eccentricities* was selling for five dollars in some places, and bookstores even began renting copies. By 1847, the book would go through at least eleven editions in the United States and two in England.[7]

The publishing firm J. & J. Harper was established in 1817 by James and John Harper. Their first published work, John Locke's *An Essay Concerning Human Understanding*, led to their reputation for quickly producing quality books. By 1825, brothers Wesley and Fletcher had joined the firm, and around the time the Crockett biography was published, the name was changed to Harper & Brothers. Their early adoption of stereotype printing, or using a metal plate, allowed them to become the largest printer in New York at the time.

Although written by someone else while Crockett was at home in Northwest Tennessee, nursing his political wounds between his twenty-first and twenty-third sessions of Congress, the book was clearly a work in which he himself had input of one kind or another. The author makes multiple references to spending time with Crockett while researching the book, even stating that the two hunted together. However, the possibility exists that the author actually got his information secondhand from Crockett's friends and associates.

Regardless, *Sketches and Eccentricities* is filled with images of the bear-hunting frontiersman, who only has the interest of his poor West Tennessee constituents at heart. In the introduction, the author explains that he is writing about Crockett because although "his humors have been spoken of in every portion of our country...less is known than of any other individual who obtained so much notoriety."[8] Included in the book are some factual details from Crockett's life, along with a few exaggerations and tall tales. Unlike the stories about Crockett that would appear in later years, these were delivered tongue in cheek, clearly intending to entertain while making a political point.

In one incident in *Sketches and Eccentricities*, the author writes that Crockett was asked about campaigning against Fitzgerald, who was known for his good-natured smile. When asked if Crockett was going to let Fitzgerald "grin them out of their votes," he replied that "Fitz" couldn't outsmile him because a raccoon couldn't even stand up to Crockett's grin. He shared a story to prove it:

> That night was very moony and clear, and old Ratler was with me; but Ratler won't bark at a 'coon—he's a queer dog in that way. So I thought I'd bring the lark down in a usual way, *by a grin*. I set myself—and, after grinning at the coon a reasonable time, found he didn't come down…I went over to the house, got my axe, returned to the tree, saw the 'coon still; there and began to cut away. Down it come, and I run forward; but d—n the 'coon was there to be seen. I found that what I had taken for one, was a large knot upon a branch of the tree—and, upon looking at it closely, I saw that *I had grinned all the bark off and left the knot perfectly smooth.*[9]

Like newspaper editors, book publishers had a liberal view of plagiarism at the time, so the book also included the words of Nimrod Wildfire from *The Lion of the West* as though they were spoken by Crockett.

Much of the book positions Crockett so favorably for the reader, some thought he wrote it himself. It does, however, include some chapters he no doubt found disturbing. The author reprinted both Huntsman's *Book of Chronicles* circular and the fake news story of Crockett's dinner at the White House. But there were other political stories and propaganda that he surely appreciated. The final chapter addressed Crockett's break from Jackson with, "the chief circumstance which characterized Colonel Crockett's second term in congress is the change which is supposed to have undergone in his sentiments towards the present executive."[10] The author then shared the Crockett talking points and explained that Crockett was in favor of improvements and, unlike Jackson, believed they were consistent with the directives of the Constitution of the United States. The author wrote that Crockett felt that his constituents lived in poverty, and the West was so sparsely populated that the only way land would be cleared, roads opened, or bridges built was if those projects were planned, implemented, and paid for by the federal government rather than by the state.

It's clear that Crockett or someone else shared enough information with the author that he got much of the early biographical content and political spin correct. When it was published, however, Crockett was either disappointed in the finished piece or pretended to be and called the book a "highly infectious disease of Crockett fiction."[11] He wrote that he thought it "had done him much injustice" and was filled with "catchpenny errors."[12]

Who was this unauthorized author who wrote the first book about Crockett? Biographers and historians have debated the identity of the author of *Sketches and Eccentricities* since it was first published. The actual list of suspects has long been narrowed down to one of two candidates: James Strange French or Matthew St. Clair Clarke. Although there is proof that French received royalties and applied for the book's copyright, biographer James Shackford made a case for Clarke's authorship that became the prevailing theory for decades.

Clarke, a good friend of Crockett's and a well-connected Whig, was secretary of the House of Representatives. In his 1956 Crockett biography, Shackford claimed the autobiography was part of the grand Whig conspiracy to position Crockett as a worthy nemesis to Jackson among a voting public hungry for "common men." According to Shackford's theory, *Sketches and Eccentricities* and *The Lion of the West* were early efforts at shaping the public's image of someone they thought might be able to beat a Jacksonian Democrat in the election of 1836. Decades of biographers and historians embraced the Shackford theory, and Clarke came to be the accepted author of *Sketches and Eccentricities*.

More than fifty years after Shackford's book was published, James R. Boylston and Allen J. Wiener released *David Crockett in Congress: The Rise and Fall of the Poor Man's Friend*. Their book includes a meticulous exploration and analysis of original Crockett source material including speeches, letters, newspaper articles, and political circulars. They point to contracts with publishers in both Ohio and New York signed by French and a copyright for the book endorsed by the author to the publisher. They also uncovered an 1833 *Boston Gazette* newspaper story reporting that French not only worked with Crockett on the book, but he also shared earnings with him. Whether or not Crockett participated or shared in the earnings, after a thorough examination, Boylston and Wiener believed French was the author of *Sketches and Eccentricities*.

A look at French's unique life and the other work he created during this phase of his career certainly indicates that a book about Crockett fits in nicely. Born at their plantation in Dinwiddie County, Virginia in 1807, James French was the first-born child of William and his wife, Maria Brooke DuVal. Like Crockett, French's father, William French, was a tavern keeper. Unlike Crockett's father, though, French's father was upwardly mobile and found great success in the early hospitality business. He eventually became the proprietor of French's Hotel in Richmond, Virginia. In a stroke of good luck or promotional savvy, the hotel's first guest when they opened in April 1837 was Louis Bonaparte, the future emperor of France.

Young French enjoyed a privileged life attending the College of William and Mary in Williamsburg and later transferring to the University of Virginia at Charlottesville, where he was a classmate of writer Edgar Allan Poe. French began studying law with his uncle, North Carolina senator Robert Strange, in Fayetteville, North Carolina and then moved back to Petersburg, Virginia, where he began his own law practice.

Another trait that French shared with Crockett—and possibly why the two connected in the first place—was that French had a very curious mind and had trouble staying in one place. He packed up and traveled west to get to know the frontiersmen and the Native Americans he had been hearing stories about since childhood. He spent time in Arkansas, Kentucky, Tennessee, and Mississippi getting to know the people of the West. He later wrote, "Traveling much throughout most of our western states, I often met with persons who were present in many of the engagements which took place along our north-western line of Posts, during the war with Great Britain."[13]

French returned home to Virginia by 1831, in time to play a small role in a pivotal moment in the evolution of slavery in America. To justify the horror of enslaving humans, many Americans had convinced themselves that slaves actually enjoyed their lives and were satisfied with their status as enslaved people. In August of that year, slave Nat Turner led a rebellion in Southampton County, Virginia that struck fear in the hearts of slave owners around the country by proving just how badly many slaves hated their White owners and how far they were willing to go to gain their freedom.

As a young child, Turner had learned to read and received religious training from one of his master's sons. By fall of 1831, he had undergone a fanatical transformation and felt he was called by God to lead his people out of bondage. Turner, along with a small group of his closest followers, brutally murdered more than fifty-five White men, women, and children, hacking some of them to pieces with machetes. Most of the slaves involved were quickly captured, and more than a hundred free and enslaved Black people were killed by militia as suspected collaborators.

Forty-eight others were eventually tried in court; of these, twenty-eight were convicted and eighteen hanged. According to family legend, French represented some of the accused during the trial and even won the acquittal of some Blacks who were not involved. Turner was not so fortunate and was hanged in Jerusalem, Virginia on November 11, 1831. According to a 1920 article in the *Journal of Negro History*, he was "skinned to supply such souvenirs as purses, his flesh made into grease, and his bones divided as trophies to be handed down as heirlooms."[14]

Although it is unknown what French did after the trials, he possibly continued to travel in the West and began writing about his experiences. In 1832, at just twenty-five years old, he possibly encountered Crockett and spent enough time with him to get the biographical information he needed.

Several characters and plotlines in books written by French in future years would include Crockett-like characters and would reference the region in which Crockett lived, further suggesting that he was the author of *Sketches and Eccentricities*. French wrote a six-page short story in *The Knickerbocker* magazine titled "Buck Horn Tavern." In the story, a man from the east is traveling in Northwest Tennessee and stops in a tavern on the highway between Bolivar and Paris, less than fifty miles from Crockett's cabin. The list of writers at the time who were even aware there were towns named Bolivar and Paris in Tennessee was short.

French authored a two-volume historical novel published by Harper & Brothers in 1836 titled *Elkswatawa; or, The Prophet of the West. A Tale of the Frontier*. While the protagonists of the story are Shawnee brothers Elkswatawa and Tecumseh, another character in the book is a frontier hunter from Kentucky nicknamed Earthquake. In the novel, Earthquake, who is written as a character with a great sense of humor, marries a girl named Polly.

Unlike his biography of Crockett, *Elkswatawa* was not considered a success for French and was panned by most critics of the day. His former classmate, Edgar Allan Poe, wrote a critical review of the novel in the *Southern Literary Messenger*, concluding, "What has Mr. French here done for his reputation?—we would reply possibly, upon the spur of the moment —'very little.' Upon second thoughts we should say—'just nothing at all'."[15] He did add that French's style was "intrinsically good—but has a certain rawness which only time and self-discipline will enable him to mellow down."[16] Poe also considered French to be the writer of *Sketches and Eccentricities* in "A Chapter on Autography." Of French, he wrote, "Mr. French is the author of a 'Life of David Crockett,' and also of a novel called 'Elkswatawa,' a denunciatory review of which in the 'Southern [Literary] Messenger,' some years ago, deterred him from further literary attempts."[17]

Poe was correct, and after the negative response to *Elkswatawa* by critics, French stopped writing and returned to practicing law in Virginia. He later tried his hand at his father's profession of hospitality, purchasing the Hygeia Hotel in Old Point Comfort, Virginia on the Chesapeake Bay. In his later years, French became a hypnotist, invented alternatives to the steam train engines of the day, and worked in the U.S. patent office.

It will likely never be proven beyond a doubt that French wrote

Crockett's biography. Whether Crockett worked with the author on the "unauthorized" look at his life will never be known for certain. What is undeniable is that Crockett decided he needed to produce a look at his life, written—as the title would eventually indicate—"by himself." It was time he started making money off the brand he had created.

**Chapter Fourteen Notes**

1. John Joseph Arpad, "David Crockett, An Original, PhD diss., (Duke University, 1968), 2-3
2. Arpad, "An Original," 3
3. Crockett, *Narrative*, 7.
4. Curtis Carroll Davis, "A Legend at Full-Length," *Proceeding of the American Antiquarian Society* 69 (October 1959): 173.
5. Crockett, *Travels*, 64.
6. Sam Roberts, "President's Features Reunited After 176 Years," *The New York Times*, April 4, 2010.
7. Arpad, "An Original," 39.
8. French, *Sketches and Eccentricities*, 19.
9. Ibid., 126.
10. Ibid., 200.
11. Curtis Carroll Davis, *A Legend at Full-length: Mr. Chapman Paints Colonel Crockett and Tells About It* (Worcester: American Antiquarian Society, April 1960), 558.
12. Crockett, *Narrative*, 3.
13. Curtis Carroll Davis, "Virginia's Unknown Novelist: The Career of J. S. French, a Southern Colonel of Parts." *The Virginia Magazine of History and Biography* 60, no. 4 (1952), 556.
14. John W. Cromwell, "The Aftermath of Nat Turner's Insurrection," *The Journal of Negro History* 5 (1920): 218.
15. Davis, "Career of J. S. French," 566.
16. Ibid.
17. Ibid., 568

*Raybert Productions, imaged by Sunshine Factory*

In "Hillbilly Honeymoon," an episode of *The Monkees* that originally aired October 23, 1967, Peter Tork played the role of Uncle Racoon. The character, loosely inspired by David Crockett, comically spoke his first lines with a German accent. Once corrected, he changed his accent to "hillbilly."

**All fame is infamy, and all infamy is fame.**
**—Yoko Ono**

## Chapter Fifteen

# Tour

On January 10, 1834, David Crockett wrote to his son, John Wesley Crockett, who was twenty-seven years old at the time:

> I am ingaged in writing a history of my life and I have completed one hundred and ten pages and I have Mr. s to correct it as I write it…I may take a trip through the eastern States during the recess in Congress and Sell the Book a great many have perswaded me to take a towar through the Eastern States that my presents will make thousands of people buy the book that would not by it and I intend never to go home until I am able to pay my debts…[1]

John Wesley Crockett was practicing law in Paris, Tennessee—another town named in honor of Marquis de Lafayette's visit—and was following in his father's footsteps by serving in various roles in county and state government. David Crockett had been an absentee father for much of John Wesley's life, and the elder Crockett's committing to getting out of debt before returning home indicates that was possibly an area of contention between the two.

The elder Crockett's political career had taken a toll on both his family and his finances. After all the sacrifices, it would seem that winning the election against William Fitzgerald in 1833 should have provided some measure of satisfaction. But Crockett found that he was beginning to tire of the demands of serving as a representative. Compared to his newfound status as a celebrity, the hours of having to listen to one long argument after another had become tedious. The cost of running campaigns and of living in Washington also resulted in that growing debt that nagged at him, so it is not surprising he felt it was time for him to cash in on his popularity as others had done.

Crockett engaged the influential Philadelphia publishing firm managed by partners Edward L. Carey and Abraham Hart to publish his life story. He was in good company as the list of authors that Carey and Hart published included William Makepeace Thackeray, Henry Wadsworth Longfellow, and James Fenimore Cooper. Crockett had a very specific vision for his autobiography, likely inspired by *The Autobiography of Benjamin Franklin*, one of the few books he was known to have owned. He directed that his biography be set in large type to make it "open and plain," and he wanted the book to be at least two hundred pages. He also asked the publishers to refrain from correcting any spelling and grammatical errors and wanted it "printed as written."

From his personal and professional letters and other written documents, it's clear that Crockett's lack of formal education left him unable to author a book of any kind, so it was fortunate that he had a friend he could trust in his roommate, Thomas Chilton. At first glance, Chilton and Crockett would seem to be an unlikely duo, but after years of rooming together at Mrs. Ball's Boarding House, they had become close friends. Chilton, twelve years younger than Crockett, was a Baptist minister and lawyer. Born near Lancaster, Kentucky, he was a representative for his home state in Congress.

Like Crockett, he had been a passionate supporter of Andrew Jackson, and in addition to sharing a passion for their mutual region, they both shared similar frustrations with the president and the party he represented. Possibly strengthening their friendship, they both abandoned the Jacksonian party around the same time. Some even credit Chilton with Crockett's spiritual awakening that appears to have occurred around 1829. In a letter to his brother-in-law, George Patton, on January 27 of that year, Crockett wrote,

> I have altered my cours in life a great deal since I reached this place [Washington City] I have not taisted one drop of Arden Sperits since I arrived here nor never expects to while I live nothing stronger than Cider I trust that god will give me fortitude in my understanding I have never made a prentention to Relegion in my life before I have run a long race tho I trust that I was called in good time...[2]

Early March of 1834, *A Narrative of the Life of David Crockett of the State of Tennessee, Written by Himself* was released and quickly became a best seller. Crockett initially received 62.5 percent of the profit from sales of the book. He split that with Chilton and either sold or gave Chilton half of the copyright of the book. The first chapter opens with an explanation of the motivation for writing his autobiography that was part snapshot of life on the southwestern frontier and part Whig propaganda:

> As the public seem to feel some interest in the history of an individual so humble as I am, and as that history can be so well known to no person living as to myself, I have, after so long a time, and under many pressing solicitations from friends and acquaintances, at last determined to put my own hand to it, and lay before the world a narrative on which they may at least rely on being true.[3]

And the narrative was mostly true. Other than a few factual errors that could be attributed to a faulty memory or a desire to paint a slightly more positive image, the book does provide a factual representation of much of Crockett's life story up to that point. For a public hungry for original American heroes, the true tale of a poor, young boy working hard and rising from nothing to a place where he could even be considered as a candidate for president resonated like no story had before. *A Narrative of the Life of*

*David Crockett* also did a remarkable job of capturing the humor and wit of Crockett's people, the settlers of Tennessee. It inspired an entire generation of humorists, and some historians claim the world would not see its equal until the publication of Mark Twain's *Adventures of Huckleberry Finn* fifty years later.

Of course, what the public actually read was Chilton's version of what Crockett had written or shared verbally with his friend. Much to Crockett's frustration and despite his earlier directive, the publisher had also added a few misspellings they felt would add more authenticity and edited out some of the text about violence against Native Americans that Crockett had witnessed during the Creek War.

As the book was being finished, Crockett was having to force himself to do the work his constituents had voted him into office to do. He procured mail service for the small town of Troy, Tennessee in Obion County and continued to unsuccessfully push for a land bill that would benefit squatters in West Tennessee. He was also vocal about his anger toward Jackson regarding the Second Bank of the United States, one of the biggest political issue around that time.

A national bank had been founded by George Washington and Alexander Hamilton in 1791 as a central repository for federal funds. Five years after that bank's charter expired, the Second Bank of the United States was founded. The bank developed a reputation among many, especially those in the south, of being biased toward the urban and industrial northern states. It was run by a board of directors from industry and manufacturing that was less inclined to support agriculture.

During the summer of 1832, Henry Clay led Congress in a bill renewing the bank's charter that was set to expire in 1836. Jackson was against what he saw as economic and political elitism and immediately vetoed the bill. Battle lines were drawn on what came to be called the Bank War.

In a controversial move that also became a lightning rod for the issue of the power of the federal government versus the states, Jackson ordered his secretary of the treasury to divert federal funds from the Second Bank of the United States to state banks. Jackson's secretary of the treasury at the time refused, as did the second who was appointed later. The third appointed secretary followed through on the president's orders, effective October 1, 1833.

The president of the Bank, Crockett's friend Nicholas Biddle, began a series of moves he thought would prove to the nation the necessity of a national bank. Ultimately, his move backfired, and the Jacksonian Democrats were able to point to Biddle's actions as proof of the danger of giving the federal government too much power. The president lived up to his nickname, Old Hickory, and remained firm. When the bank's charter expired in 1836, it was never renewed. Jackson had won another war.

Crockett was beyond frustrated by the lack of progress on any legislation relating to Tennessee land and sick of the constant battles between the Whigs and the Jacksonian Democrats. He was also suffering from frequent illness and tired of being broke. He was ready to leave Washington and sell some books. When Crockett was later criticized for leaving his duties to go on a book tour while Congress was still in session, he would use the excuse that his doctor told him he needed to get away for his health. He also wrote, "the House of Representatives was engaged on the appropriation bills, and I knew they would consume some two or three weeks, and as I determined and declared that I would not vote on an appropriation bill…it was of little consequence for me to remain there while those bills were under discussion."[4]

On April 25, 1834, Crockett departed for a three-week book tour organized by his Whig friends that would take him to various cities throughout Maryland, New York, New Jersey, Massachusetts, Rhode Island, and Pennsylvania. Crockett would experience firsthand just how nice the world of "celebrity" could be with state-of-the-art transportation, first-class accommodations, and gifts presented at nearly every stop.

While his sense of humor remained intact and he loved making audiences laugh, he had no intention of playing the role of jester. Early during his book tour, he was at a dinner on a steamboat headed to Philadelphia. Reverend Obadiah Brown, a Baptist minister and clerk of the U.S. Post Office, smugly called on Crockett to make a toast. The dining car quieted as the other guests waited for a laugh. Crockett stood, raised his glass, and said, "Here's wishing the bones of tyrant kings may answer in hell, in place of gridirons, to roast the souls of Tories on. Never heed; it was meant for where it belonged."

Surprised, Reverend Brown and the other diners returned to conversations at their own tables, and Crockett was left to enjoy his evening in peace.

Later that evening, he saw the captain hoisting up three flags and received another hint of the heights to which his fame had risen. The captain explained he had promised "the people of Philadelphia" that if the famous Crockett was onboard the ship, he would display the flags as a sign. When they arrived, Crockett was surprised to find a huge crowd shouting his name and waiting to get a look at the frontiersman from Tennessee. He was even further stunned and caught off guard when he found himself surrounded by the shouting crowd at the pier. Fortunately, he was rescued by one of the Whigs assigned to pick him up at the dock:

> Some gentleman took hold of me, and pressing through the crowd, put me up into an elegant barouche, drawn by four fine horses; they then told me how to bow to the people. I did so, and with much difficulty we moved off. The streets were crowded a great distance, and the windows were full of people, looking out, I supposed, to see the Wildman.[5]

At first, he found that speaking to the large crowds was intimidating. He wrote, "It struck me with astonishment to hear a strange people huzzaing for me, and made me feel sort of queer."[6] Although he was used to speaking to his West Tennessee constituents and his peers in Congress—some of whom he referred to as "little office yelpers who opposed me,"[7]—this was something entirely different. The crowds seemed to get larger and louder at each appearance. Early on in the tour, he was scheduled to speak from the porch of the newly built Merchants' Exchange Building in the heart of Philadelphia. It was the first office building in the city and it was there much of the business of the city took place.

As he rounded the corner and got a look at the size of the crowd gathered to see him, he developed a sudden case of nerves and considered backing out. As the carriage made its way through the crowd, people were clamoring to get as close as possible so they could get a look inside at the "Wildman." Finally, he made eye contact through the carriage window with a young boy who pumped his fist with excitement and shouted part of Crockett's catchphrase, "Go ahead, Davy Crockett!"[8] That was enough to steady his nerves and give him the courage he needed.

This speech was like others he would give on the tour in which he humbly expressed gratitude, shared a funny story or two, then reserved much of his passion for his anti-Jackson, pro-Constitution message. Of course, Philadelphia provided the perfect backdrop to include a mention of those who had fought for the country's freedom a little over fifty years earlier. He shouted, "Our forefather's toils and struggles are all forgotten, and we have returned to the good old days of '76—to the government of one man."[9]

Many politicians were speaking out against Andrew Jackson, but for the Whigs, Crockett was one in a million. He had somehow tapped into the imagination of the public, who were looking for heroes among "regular people," and being from the same state as Jackson, he could speak with even more authenticity. There were surely Whig leaders backstage that day, watching to see how Crockett's speech went and evaluating how the people and the press responded to him and his message. Even a few months earlier, the idea of David Crockett running for president would have been laughable. But with the public response he was somehow generating, Crockett was suddenly a candidate worth exploring for those who were more interested in winning than governing. As Crockett spoke out against "King Jackson" and the people cheered, Whig leadership must have looked at each other and wondered if David Crockett, an uneducated frontiersman from the wilderness of West Tennessee, could actually become the next president of the United States of America. From the balcony of the Merchants' Exchange Building, he shouted,

> I was one of the first men that fired a gun under Andrew Jackson. I

> helped to throw around him that blaze of glory, that is blasting and blighting every thing it comes in contact with. I know I have equal right with him, and so has every man that is not a slave; and when he is violating the constitution and the laws, I will oppose him, let the consequences to me be what they may…it is said, and truly that all power is in the people; and if so, the time is shortly coming when they must and will show their power, by sustaining the laws and the constitution. The stars and stripes must never give way to the shreds and patches of party.[10]

Earlier in the year, when asked about a possible run for president by a group of Mississippi Whigs, Crockett had declined but added, "If I am elected, I shall just seize the old monster, party, by the horns, and sling him right slap into the deepest place in the great Atlantic sea."[11] It was a hyperbolic response, at best, but one that was clearly on brand for a politician that was morphing into a fictional superhero. In his autobiography, Crockett slipped in a few lines that alluded to the possibility of a Crockett presidency including, "It is true, I had a little rather not; but yet, if the government can't get on without taking another president from Tennessee, to finish the work of 'retrenchment and reform,' why, then, I reckon I must go in for it."[12]

The book tour served Crockett's objective of creating publicity to sell books so he could pay off some of his debt. The Whigs also accomplished their mission of having a popular personality denounce the president.

One unanticipated benefit of the tour for history lovers came from the book that was written and published after the tour, *An Account of Col. Crockett's Tour to the North and Down East*. It provides a unique look at a country undergoing rapid technological and cultural change experienced through the eyes of a visitor who was more used to traveling through the wilderness on horseback and sleeping in a cabin with a dirt floor.

It began with David Crockett's first ride on a train. In the years just prior to Crockett's 1834 book tour, the eastern states had been undergoing what has been called a "transportation revolution." New roads and turnpikes, stagecoach lines, and canals for steamboats greatly contributed to increased mobility for both business and pleasure travel. But no mode of transportation introduced in Crockett's lifetime would make an impact more powerful than the train. About his first ride, Crockett wrote,

> About a dozen big stages hung on to one machine, and to start up a hill. After a good deal of fuss we all got seated, and moved slowly off; the engine wheezing as if she had the tizzick. By-and-by she began to take short breaths, and away we went with a blue streak after us. The whole distance is seventeen mile, and it was run in fifty-five minutes.[13]

Like others experiencing train travel for the first time, the speed understandably fascinated Crockett, who could see the benefit of getting from one place to another so quickly. During another portion of his travels taken by train, he wrote, "…they say we run twenty-five miles to the hour. I can only judge of the speed by putting my head out to spit, which I did, and overtook it so quick, that it hit me smack in the face."[14]

Stagecoaches traveled less than ten miles per hour, while small engines of the 1830s, like the ones Crockett experienced, could travel more than twice that fast. This was only the beginning. In the next twenty years and after continued innovation and improvement, train travel would become the primary mode of transportation, making other forms, like stagecoaches and many steamships, obsolete.

This progress impacted travel in other ways as well. Most of the first generations of Americans had been too busy carving a country out of the wilderness to spend time on something as frivolous as pleasure travel. Subsequent generations with the resources and willingness to visit other cities for fun began changing that. With more visitors to large metropolitan hubs like New York and Philadelphia, came the birth of the hospitality industry that included hotels, attractions, and live entertainment.

As a guest of the Whigs, Crockett was able to experience the first luxury hotels the country had to offer. In Baltimore, he stayed at David Barnum's City Hotel, built in 1825. Known as Charles Dickens's favorite hotel, the list of those spending at least one night under its roof would eventually include John Wilkes Booth, John Quincy Adams, and Confederate spy Belle Boyd. Crockett had extravegant accommodations at the brand new American Hotel in New York, and while in Philadelphia, he lay his head to rest on the fancy pillows in one of the opulent suites at the United States Hotel. In that city, it was no accident that his Whig hosts selected the hotel directly across the street from the building that housed the Bank of the United States.

Crockett also visited some of the first tourist attractions in the cities. He explored Peale's Museum of New York City at 252 Broadway in a building then known as the Parthenon. It was founded by Rubens Peale, whose father was Charles Wilson Peale, early American painter and founder of the Philadelphia Museum. Like most early museums of the day, the Peales' museums followed the concept of a "cabinet of curiosities" of exhibits and displays. The term originally described a room rather than a piece of furniture as it does today. Collectors who owned a cabinet of curiosities would include items belonging to natural history, archaeology, religious or historical relics, works of art, and antiquities.

Rubens Peale's museum included snuff boxes, whale teeth, stuffed animals—positioned in their natural habitat—along with live tigers, snakes, and bears. The collections of butterflies and insects made Crockett scratch his head. He had spent many sleepless nights hunting around the Obion River and Reelfoot Lake trying to avoid swarms of mosquitoes and other pests. He noted that he couldn't help wonder "what pleasure or curiosity folks could take in sticking up whole rows of little bugs, and such varmints." A boy born without arms used his feet to cut Crockett's name out of paper using a pair of scissors. "This I called a miracle,"[15] he wrote.

Peale did not have the flamboyancy or show business flair of his biggest competitor, who moved in down the street and opened the American Museum. That competitor, showman Phineas T. Barnum, eventually purchased the entire Peale collection but kept the museum open. Competition, he explained, was good for business.

While in Boston, Crockett visited Bunker Hill where a monument was being built. Begun in 1823, construction had to be halted twice because of lack of funds, and it would not be completed until 1843. While he cheered this monument that was being built to pay tribute to those who fought for America's freedom, he found another Boston tribute to a forefather to be disturbing. He noted that the sculptor of the statue of George Washington in Boston's courthouse had chosen to dress Washington in a Roman gown. Crockett wrote, "They have a Roman gown on him, and he was an American: this a'n't right. They did things better at Richmond, in Virginia, where they have him in the old blue and buff. He belonged to this country—heart, soul, and body: and I don't want any other to have any part of him—not even his clothes."[16]

With an increase of visitors to cities around this time came a growth in the business of live entertainment, which Crockett, known to play the fiddle, certainly enjoyed. At New York's Park Theatre, the finest in the city at the time, he caught the act of Fanny Kemble. He noted that the "fixings" looked nicer at the Park than at the theater in Philadelphia but added that any of them would be good enough if they had as "pretty play-actors" as Miss Kemble. He described her as being like "a handsome piece of changeable silk; first one colour, then another, but always the clean thing."[17] Crockett was catching Kemble, a beautiful Shakespearean actor and writer from England, toward the end of her two-year engagement in America. Audiences fell in love with Kemble but no one more so than Pierce Butler, wealthy grandson of the founding father with the same name. Butler and Kemble were married the month after Crockett saw her perform in New York.

Unfortunately, the two did not live happily ever after. They divorced in 1849, in part because slave-owning Butler did not appreciate his wife's growing passion for abolitionism. After their two daughters were grown, Kemble published *Journal of a Residence on a Georgian Plantation in 1838–1839*, her firsthand account of the horrors she witnessed on her ex-husband's plantation.

Attitudes of White male supremacy were very much present in all areas of culture in both the northern and southern states at the time. Because of issues relating to slavery, they were growing even more pronounced. At the Walnut Street Theatre in Philadelphia, Crockett caught the act of Thomas

Dartmouth Rice. The twenty-seven-year-old Rice, who was White, had recently become famous himself with a song and dance called *Jump Jim Crow*, named after a Black character he created called "Daddy Pops Jim Crow."

Rice darkened his face with burnt cork, wore tattered clothing, and spoke in an exaggerated version of slave vernacular. His tall, lanky frame lent itself to a shuffling dance he performed as he sang. Rice, and others who copied him, created an entirely new entertainment genre—the blackface minstrel show—and Rice became known as the "Father of Minstrelsy." As Crockett's popularity grew, references to him began showing up in the lyrics of minstrel performances. That evening, Rice worked Crockett's "Be sure you are right, then go ahead" into one of his song and dance numbers. At the conclusion, Rice bowed to Crockett in the audience. In a repeat performance from his exchange with James Hackett before the performance of *The Lion of the West*, Crockett stood and returned the bow. The audience appreciated it as much as Rice.

While he got to visit some of the earliest tourist attractions in America and enjoy live entertainment at the finest theaters, this was not a pleasure trip. The Whigs wanted to make certain to take advantage of the biggest celebrity of the day—and the reporters who were following him around—to promote eastern business and industry. In Philadelphia, he was given a tour of the impressive modern water system, a mental health facility, a Naval hospital, and the Navy yard. In Boston, they showed Crockett around the new market, while in Lowell he was shown shiny, new examples of modern industry including a clothing manufacturer, a shoe factory, and an Indian rubber factory.

At one stop, he observed workers pouring out of the factories when the dinner bell rang and described the female workers as looking as though they had come from "a quilting frolic":

> I could not help reflecting on the difference of condition between these females, thus employed, and those of other populous countries, where the female character is degraded to abject slavery. Here were thousands, useful to others, and enjoying all the blessings of

> freedom, with the prospect before them of future comfort and respectability; and however we who only hear of them, may call their houses workshops and prisons, I assure my neighbors there is every enjoyment of life realized by these persons, and there can be but few who are not happy.[18]

The tour also provided new audiences at every stop for Crockett's unique version of anti-Jackson propaganda. In Philadelphia, he pointed out that many brave patriots had perished in the Revolutionary War so that Americans could have "a constitution and government of laws." He added that for the past fifty years since, the citizens had been "the most happy people under the sun"—until Jackson came along, that is. "Alas! In 1834, we again see one man seize the sword in one hand, and the purse in the other, and saying, 'I am the government—my will shall be the law of the land.'"[19]

In his speech to a crowd in New York, he said, "Is it come to this, our happy country destroyed to gratify the ambition one man?"[20] In another, he raged against Jackson and declared, "I may be beaten, and struck from the rolls of public servants: be it so; I will rejoice in my fate; for I would rather retire into private life with clean hands and a good conscience, than live and breathe in an atmosphere of sycophants and time-servers."[21]

Those he met were excited to meet a celebrity, and he was presented with expensive gifts. After a tour of a mill in Lowell, Massachusetts, the owner gave Crockett a wool suit that was especially symbolic of the relationship growing between northern industry and southern agriculture. While the suit was manufactured in Lowell, the wool for the fabric had been purchased from Mark R. Cockrill, the nephew of James Robertson (one of the founders of Nashville, Tennessee). Cockrill was one of the leading experts on agriculture innovation in the country at the time. The wool from the sheep he bred in Middle Tennessee was celebrated for its exceptional quality, earning him the nickname "Wool King of the World."

Cockrill's five-thousand-acre farm, Stock Place, was located just outside Nashville. In addition to breeding the Merino sheep that provided the wool for Crockett's suit, Cockrill also imported Durham cattle from England and introduced the breed to American farmers. Crockrill was also a pioneer in horse breeding.

The 1874 book *Introduction to the Resources of Tennessee*, published by the Bureau of Tennessee Agriculture, noted that after studying the wool of every country, Cockrill determined the weather and soil of Tennessee would make it the best wool-growing region "under the sun."[22] He must have been right. According to Crockett, it was the best quality cloth he had ever seen.

The suit was far from the only expensive gift he was presented during his tour. From the "young men of Philadelphia," he received a gun, a tomahawk, and a knife. He was also given a watch seal engraved with "Go Ahead," and he received six boxes of gun powder personally from chemist and entrepreneur Eleuthère Irénée du Pont.

While the fuzzy idea of a "President David Crockett" began to take shape during his three-week book tour in April and May 1834, it never came completely into focus. It disappeared forever during his next campaign and the eventual loss of his seat in Congress in the election of August 1835.

Making that an even more bitter pill to swallow, he lost against Adam Huntsman, the author of the pamphlet *Book of Chronicles* that had made such a joke of Crockett's image.

One of the biggest strikes against Crockett during the campaign was his absence from Washington during his book tour. Ironically, it was during the tour that cost him the election, that the real David Crockett reached the pinnacle of his fame. Any dreams of the White House or huge crowds shouting his name ended. He packed his belongings and returned to his Northwest Tennessee cabin.

## Chapter Fifteen Notes

1. Boylston and Wiener, *Congress*, 232.
2. Boylston and Wiener, *Congress*, 49.
3. Crockett, *Narrative*, 13.
4. Crockett, *Travels*, 12.
5. Ibid., 18.
6. Ibid., 17.
7. Ibid., 23.
8. Ibid.
9. Ibid., 30.
10. Ibid., 31.
11. Boylston and Wiener, *Congress*, 111.
12. Crockett, *Narrative,* 71.
13. Crockett, *Travels*, 15
14. Ibid., 37.
15. Ibid., 44.
16. Ibid., 77.
17. Ibid., 38.
18. Ibid., 92.
19. Ibid., 26.
20. Ibid., 43.
21. Ibid., 107.
22. J. B. Killebrew, *Introduction to the Resources of Tennessee*, (Nashville, Tennessee: Tavel, Eastman & Howell, 1874), 137.

*Library of Congress*

This illustration by Will Crawford appeared in a June 1912 issue of *Puck* magazine. David Crockett, pictured in the front closest to the boy scout, joins other settlers of the "Wild West" including William Frederick "Buffalo Bill" Cody, John Wilson "Texas Jack" Vermillion, Kit Carson, Moses Embree "California Joe" Milner, and Daniel Boone.

**My fame had become annoying for my enemies, and a little trying, I confess, for my friends.**

**—Sarah Bernhardt**

**Chapter Sixteen**

# Image

What did David Crockett look like? In various places, he was described by those who laid eyes on him as "tall in stature and large in frame" and "about six feet high—and stoutly built." Crockett's neighbor, John L. Jacobs, remembered that he was "about six feet high, weighed about two hundred pounds, had no surplus flesh, broad shouldered, stood erect, was a man of great physical strength." One of Crockett's sons wrote in 1889, "My father was a fraction over six feet tall and weighed over 200 pounds, in good health, and was not fleshy."[1] One observer wrote that he was "a respectable looking personage, dressed decently and wearing his locks much after the fashion of our plain German farmers."[2] Journalists also attempted to capture the image of Crockett in words for their readers.

After an appearance in Boston, a reporter for the *Boston Tribune*—who had clearly been charmed—described Crockett as "an uncommonly fine looking man." He added, "His face has an exceedingly amiable expression and his features are prominent and striking. He wears his hair which is black, (with a light shade of brown) parted down the center of his forehead, combed back from his temples, and ending in a slight curl at the neck—not unlike the simple manner of many of the clergy."[3] When writing about Crockett's appearance in York, Pennsylvania, another reporter was equally impressed:

> In person he is rather above the medium height, about fifty years of age—his features are expressive, and we may even say handsome, particularly when he smiles; he is muscular, and wears all the indications of excellent health—a bright and laughing eye, a ruddy cheek, and a row of teeth that would shame the whiteness of ivory—he says he can out grin a panther, but he never grinned the bark off a tree. He is not witty, yet, there is a dryness in his anecdotes, and a kind of blunt good humor which makes them amusing & even instructive.[4]

If Crockett had lived even a few more years past his forty-ninth birthday, there would certainly be photos of him for reference. The first photographic process, the daguerreotype, was invented by Louis Jacques Mandé Daguerre. It spread rapidly around the world after its presentation to the public in Paris in 1839, three years after Crockett's death. Andrew Jackson would be the first president whose image was captured for posterity by a camera. Matthew Brady, known now as the father of photojournalism, photographed the seventy-eight-year-old former president at the Hermitage in 1845. Jackson disliked the photo and said Brady made him look "like a monkey." Brady was also responsible for the first surviving photo of a sitting president, Tennessean James K. Polk. In the fifteenth presidential election held in 1844, Polk, running as a Democrat, beat Henry Clay, running as a Whig. Polk was photographed on February 14, 1849 and wrote in his diary, "I yielded to the request of an artist named Brady, of New York, by sitting for my daguerreotype likeness today. I sat in the large dining room." Henry Clay also had his turn in front of Brady's camera in New York in 1849. Brady later described Clay as having "a light complexion and quick, running, laughing eyes and a grin that went from ear to ear."[5]

While there are no photographs of Crockett, there were at least six artists who captured his likeness in watercolor or oil in his lifetime. Crockett's star was rising, so some of his portraits were reproduced commercially in etchings, wood engravings, and lithography.

The earliest portrait is thought to have been painted around 1830. While historically it was attributed to Rembrandt Peale, it was more likely painted by a lesser-known artist named Cornelius T. Hinckley. In the mid-1850s, Crockett's son, Robert, had ambrotype copies of that portrait produced and distributed to family members.

Crockett sat for watercolors by James Hamilton Shegogue and Anthony Lewis DeRose and oil paintings by Samuel Stillman Osgood, Chester Harding, and John Gadsby Chapman. During Crockett's lifetime, the paintings produced by DeRose and Osgood were engraved, reproduced as lithographs, and sold to the public. It is unknown whether Crockett participated in any of the proceeds from the sales of his likeness, but it is likely. If so, the agreement to reproduce and distribute lithographs was one of the earliest celebrity licensing deals. The two lithographs were certainly endorsed. Written in Crockett's handwriting underneath the engraving by Albert Newsam of the Osgood portrait is, "I am happy to acknowledge this to be the only correct likeness that has been taken of me. David Crockett."

Crocket must have liked the Osgood painting. An engraving of it by Thomas B. Welch was included at the front of the book based on Crockett's book tour. What many of those who purchased a lithograph of the Osgood portrait or saw it in the tour book didn't realize was that they were only getting a partial reprint of the original. It hung for many years in the home of Crockett's son, Robert. His descendants remembered the large painting was of their famous ancestor sitting at a desk, holding a goose quill pen in his hand. Robert Crockett donated the original to the state of Texas.

The DeRose watercolor was of Crockett's profile and was engraved by Asher B. Durand. Those who purchased a copy of this engraving for fifty cents received a portrait of Crockett's likeness along with his catchphrase and signature at the bottom: "I leave this rule for others when I am dead. Be always sure, you are right, then go, a head. David Crockett."

His last two portraits, one bust and one life-size, were painted by John Gadsby Chapman. Pictured in hunting gear from head to toe and posed with hunting dogs, the life-size portrait is the one most closely associated with Crockett, the bear-hunting frontiersman. The process the two men went through during the creation of the painting provides insight into how Crockett was very deliberate in the public image he was presenting to the public once he became famous.

The twenty-six-year-old Chapman was already enjoying a celebrated art career by late spring of 1834 when he began painting the portrait of Washington's most celebrated politician after he returned from his book tour. Chapman was born in Alexandria, Virginia in 1808 to an affluent and influential family with a long history in Virginia and Washington. Although Alexandria is across the Potomac River from Washington, it was considered part of the nation's capital city until 1846, and the family was well established in both communities.

Chapman's maternal grandfather was John Gadsby, the namesake of Gadsby's Tavern in Alexandria and the founder of Washington's National Hotel at the corner of Pennsylvania Avenue and Sixth Street. It was across from Crockett's home away from home, Mrs. Ball's Boarding House. In later years, the Newseum, the museum of the news and the First Amendment, would be built where the National Hotel had previously stood.

Chapman's talent was spotted early in life, and his supportive parents even built a studio adjacent to their home. His cousin Maria Heath married artist George Cooke. Chapman and Cooke studied together under the mentorship of portrait artist Charles Bird King in King's Washington studio located at Twelfth and F Street. By 1825, Cooke had acquired enough commissions from painting portraits, that he and his wife moved to Europe for him to continue his education. After a period studying at the Pennsylvania Academy of the Fine Arts, Chapman followed his cousin and spent time copying the masters in Rome.

One of Chapman's early paintings even captured the eye of author Frances Trollope who gave the artist a mention in *Domestic Manners of the Americans*. Although Chapman was still out of the country during her visit, one of his paintings had already been shipped home:

> It was at Alexandria that I saw what I consider as the best picture by an American artist that I met with. The subject was Hagar and Ishmael. It had recently arrived from Rome where the painter, a young man of the name of Chapman, had been studying for three years. His mother told me that he was twenty-two years of age and passionately devoted to the art; should he, on returning to his country, receive sufficient encouragement to keep his ardour and his industry alive, I think I shall hear of him again.[6]

Chapman returned to America in 1831, and he must have received more than sufficient encouragement to "keep his ardour and his industry alive." His reputation as an illustrator and artist of history-related landscapes and portraits grew quickly. Being from a notable family with important connections served him well, and he was able to travel around Virginia and Washington painting portraits of the distinguished citizens of the day. A fan of historic sites, he also painted landscapes of historically relevant places around Washington including Mount Vernon and Arlington. Among his most notable subjects were former president James Madison at Montpelier and members of George Washington's family at Mount Vernon. Interestingly, Chapman and Crockett would soon share a mutual connection in James Kirke Paulding, writer of *The Lion of the West*. In the spring of 1835 in New York City, Chapman showed seven of his landscapes from sites relating to George Washington. All seven were purchased by Paulding, who included them as engraved illustrations in his biography of the first president, *A Life of Washington*.

It is unknown how exactly Crockett connected with Chapman. Proximity was in their favor; the young artist had a studio in Washington near the house where Crockett boarded. Chapman opened an exhibition of his work on Pennsylvania Avenue in April 1834 that included copies of Italian masters and Virginia landscapes. Crockett had returned to Washington from his book tour in May of that year, so it's likely that Crockett saw Chapman's work on display. Chapman had certainly heard of Crockett and was aware of his growing fame. Once the two connected and Crockett sat down in front of Chapman's easel, Crockett surely hoped that he had found someone who could finally capture the true essence of a frontiersman from the wilds of Tennessee. Crockett complained to Chapman that all the previous painters had made him look "sort of like a cross between a clean-shirted member of Congress and a Methodist Preacher."[7]

After a quick glance at the first painting of Crockett's head and shoulders, he was only slightly impressed with what he saw. Perhaps he was just thinking out loud or mumbling to himself, but his observation came out almost as a challenge. Many years later, Chapman wrote his memory of that moment when the idea for the final painting of Crockett was born. Crockett had mused, "If you could catch me on a bear-hunt in a 'harricane,' with hunting tools and gear, and team of dogs, you might make a picture better worth looking at."[8]

Chapman responded that he would certainly be happy to try, but it would have to be painted on a large canvas, and as he had never seen either a bear hunt or a harricane, Crockett would have to show him what those things looked like. That was all the encouragement Crockett needed.

Although there is no recorded mention of it, one does wonder if Chester Harding's portrait of Daniel Boone, painted in 1820, provided a bit of inspiration. Harding, and others, painted replicas, and Harding worked with James Otto Lewis to produce an engraving that was mass-produced and included in books, newspapers, and magazines. In the painting, Boone is dressed in buckskin and a hunting jacket with rifle and brimmed hat in hand. Next to him is a hunting dog. Lewis and Harding sold 150 limited-edition prints in the 1820s. The original painting hung unsold in the Frankfort, Kentucky capitol building. The state tired of the painting and planned to replace it with one painted by another artist. Before he picked it up, Harding made one last attempt to sell it to the state with an anonymous letter placed in the *Frankfort Daily Commonwealth*:

> Mr. Editor: Are the members of the legislature aware that the portrait of Daniel Boone—pioneer of Kentucky—which is now in the Governor's office is about to be removed from the state by Mr.

> Harding, the painter of it? This is the only painting of the old hunter ever taken from life, and Kentucky should never permit it to go. $200 will keep it. If the legislature will not vote the money to buy it, will not each member subscribe $1 towards the object? The balance could be easily raised. Mr. Harding has been offered $500 for this portrait by a historical society of Boston--but having once offered it to Kentucky for $200 he still gives her a chance to keep it.[9]

The people of Kentucky were unmoved, and Harding retrieved his painting of Boone. To his horror, when he began to unroll the canvas, the painting was damaged to such a degree, only the face was salvageable.

Working with Chapman to create a similar life-size painting of himself was much more fun than anything Crockett actually should have been doing just down the street in the House Chamber. As Chapman later noted, Crockett embraced the production aspects of the painting with a level of enthusiasm he never anticipated. From the faded and soiled hunting shirt, leggings, and moccasins to the tools he arranged in his belt, Crockett painstakingly agonized over every detail. A few elements needed for the painting were harder to come by in Washington, far from his Northwest Tennessee cabin. After considering several guns, he finally found one belonging to a hunter across the Potomac River in Alexandria that he thought could be made to work.

Although the painter and the frontiersman could not have been from more different worlds, they became friendly while working together. In addition to sitting for the portrait in Chapman's Washington studio, Crockett spent time in the painter's Alexandria home. On one visit there, he talked Chapman into going with him to visit the owner of the gun who lived nearby. Chapman quietly listened as the two hunters exchanged stories and compared notes on the best hunting tools to use. As they departed, the old hunter, clearly charmed, presented Crockett with the gift of a powder horn, a pouch, and a piece of leather that Crockett used to make a cover for his hatchet.

When it came to selecting the hunting dogs that were to be included in the painting, Crockett quickly dismissed Chapman's valuable full-blooded hound. Not wanting to hurt Chapman's feelings, he conceded that the painter's dog could be "stuck in the corner." Chapman and his famous subject hit the Washington streets together where Crockett found several dogs that he explained had the traits needed for a Tennessee bear hunt. While Crockett sang their praises, Chapman thought they were "the ugliest mongrels" he had ever seen, but the artist deferred to the hunter's knowledge on the subject. It's likely that after that experience, Chapman thought of the member of Congress from Tennessee anytime a painting called for a dog.

With so little in common, what must the two men have discussed during the weeks Crockett sat for the painting? The artist had attended the best schools in the country and was used to socializing with the elite in both America and Europe. Chapman wrote that he found Crockett's communication skills impressive:

> Col. Crockett's command of verbal expression was very remarkable, say what he might his meaning could never be misinterpreted. He expressed opinions, and told his stories, with unhesitating clearness of diction, often embellished with graphic touches of original wit and humor, sparkling and even startling, yet never out of place or obtrusively ostentatious.[10]

One morning, Crockett arrived to the studio, and Chapman could tell something was bothering him. He held a crumpled letter, and as Chapman later wrote, "The whole man seemed to have undergone a change." When Chapman inquired about the source of Crockett's stress, he became privy to a bit of the strained relationship between Crockett and his family back in Tennessee. Crockett replied, "a son of mine out west has been and got converted. Thinks he's off to Paradise on a streak of lightening. Pitches into me pretty considerable. That's all."[11]

Although the painting was coming along nicely and the artist and his subject had developed a bond of sorts, it felt to Chapman that Crockett was not completely satisfied; something was not quite right. When Crockett arrived for a sitting one morning, he startled Chapman with a greeting that he described as "raising the entire neighborhood." That morning, Crockett not only brought the type of hat he wanted to be seen holding, he brought an idea. To bring the painting to life, he thought he should be waving the hat in the air as though he were greeting his neighbors. Chapman was certainly accommodating and incorporated the idea into the painting, ultimately deciding it had been a great idea.

Around the same time that Chapman was painting Crockett, member of Congress Henry A. Wise, a close friend of Chapman's, arranged to have Chapman's name submitted as a candidate to paint additional works of art to be hung in the rotunda of the Capitol. The new paintings would be part of a series that were being added to four by John Trumbull that had been hung in 1826, just two years after the rotunda was completed.

Although the design for the Capitol had been awarded to Dr. William Thornton in 1793, a lack of funds, the War of 1812, and the fire set by the British in 1814 slowed completion. It was finished in time to welcome the Marquis de Lafayette during his famous visit to Washington in October 1824. He was a fitting early visitor since the space was intended to be used for ceremonial events, lying in state for important citizens, and displaying works of art that represent the nation's history. The four paintings of historical moments painted by Trumbull were of the signing of the Declaration of Independence, the surrender of General Burgoyne, the surrender of Lord Cornwallis, and George Washington resigning his commission as commander-in-chief of the Continental Army.

Each of Trumbull's paintings depicts a pivotal moment before, during, and after the Revolutionary War. By the early nineteenth century, expansionism was clearly on the American mind, and the next four paintings commissioned by Congress featured early exploration and the arrival of Europeans to the New World. John Vanderlyn painted a scene depicting Christopher Columbus and members of his crew after stepping off the *Santa Maria* in the West Indies. Robert Weir's painting is of the Pilgrims on the deck of the *Speedwell* on July 22, 1620 as they prepared to depart from Holland for North America, seeking religious freedom. William Henry Powell's painting, the last to be added, is of explorer Hernando de Soto in 1541, pictured triumphantly arriving on a white horse to become the first European to see the Mississippi River.

Then there was Chapman's contribution. While his painting of Crockett would certainly provide a place for the artist in the history of popular culture, it was his painting of a famous Native American that would result in his most frequently seen work of art, *Baptism of Pocahontas*—an ironic connection considering Crockett's passionate opposition to Jackson's 1830 Indian Removal Act. Chapman's *Baptism of Pocahontas* portrays the moment that the daughter of Algonkian chief Powhatan was baptized and had her name changed from Pocahontas to Rebecca. Considered the first Native American convert to Christianity, Pocahontas's marriage to Pilgrim John Rolfe contributed to a brief moment of perceived peace by the pilgrims. In another moment from history bathed in irony, an engraving of Chapman's painting of Pocahontas appeared on the first twenty-dollar bills issued in 1863 and 1875; this honor was shared by Andrew Jackson, whose face was added to the same denomination in 1928.

As they neared completion of the portrait, Chapman asked Crockett where he could insert his name into the painting. Looking over the artist's shoulder, Crockett instructed, "Name on the butcher knife—'Go ahead' on the rifle." And with that, the painting was done.

It was first publicly shown in 1835 in New York at an annual exhibition held by the National Academy of Design. A reporter for the *New-York Mirror* gave it a positive review:

> In this bold picture, size of life, Mr. Chapman shows that he is master of the grand as well as the minute style. He has in several pictures here exhibited, displayed a delicacy that is unrivaled. In this large composition of the backwoodsman…the accuracy proves that the artist is not confined to the small and the smooth, but can encounter with the success the broad and bold in subjects.[12]

Not everyone was impressed, however. One reviewer wrote, "We are told that it is an excellent likeness. The face has less ruggedness than one would expect in the bear-hunter, but whether his fault or the artist's we are not advised."[13] Humorist Alexander E. Sweet later wrote that he thought Chapman's Crockett looked more like "the effeminate youth of the present day who suck at the end of a [candy] cane."[14] For whatever reason, the painting did not sell. It was displayed again in 1838 and 1839 at exhibitions held by the Apollo Association of New York, where it was for sale for $1,000. It was not an unreasonable price, especially considering in 1839 that Crockett had been dead nearly three years and had become even more famous than he had been when he was alive.

Apparently, a buyer for a life-size painting of a frontiersman was hard to come by, no matter how famous he was. Forty years would pass before Chapman, then seventy-one years old and in much need of money, touched up the painting and offered it to the state of Texas. In a persuasive letter to Texas governor Richard B. Hubbard dated December 4, 1879, Chapman explained that he had been holding on to it for more than forty years in anticipation of it going to Texas. In a case of poetic salesmanship, he wrote that the painting should go to Texas because it was a "unique, veritable and historic record of a hero prominently associated with her national existence."[15] He further explained that the value of the painting was estimated at $5,000, but he was willing to take whatever amount the state wanted to pay him, as long as it was no less than $3,000. The painting was finally purchased and hung, along with the portrait that had been donated by Robert Crockett, in the three-story state capitol building in Austin. It would have been much safer had it stayed with Chapman.

The capitol building was in shambles at the time, and there was little money in the state budget to make the necessary repairs. On November 9, 1881, Henry McBride, a janitor who was working in the courthouse, smelled fire. Upon entering the attorney general's office on the first floor where he had been cleaning, he was surprised by the sight of a room full of smoke and flames shooting up around where the chimney pipe connected to the wall. The *Texas Siftings* newspaper described what happened next:

> The fire's demon cruel tongues licked the fair proportions of the historic pile, while huge volumes of black smoke poured in from the doomed building, and settled over the fair city...while the toot, toot, toot of the fire engine, and the hoarse profanity of the enthusiastic volunteer firemen, seemed a solemn and appropriate dirge as the old sarcophagus crumbled… the architectural monstrosity...at the head of Congress Avenue is no more. The venerable edifice that bore such a resemblance to a large size corn crib, with a pumpkin for a dome... took fire on Wednesday.[16]

In less than two hours, the courthouse had been reduced to an empty limestone shell. Some were actually grateful for the fire. Plans for a new, more modern courthouse on the same spot had actually been underway for some time, and the fire likely saved the state the cost of having to haul much of the old courthouse away.

What was less appreciated by many at the time was the loss of the items from Texas history that were destroyed that day. More than eight thousand valuable books in the courthouse's library were reduced to ash including six volumes of records of early Mexico. Numerous irreplaceable artifacts were also destroyed. Gone were items including early Native American weaponry and a coat of mail from a Spanish conquistador from the 1700s. It had been removed from a dead Comanche known as "Iron Shirt." Many pieces of art also went up in smoke including portraits of Sam Houston, George Washington, and Stephen F. Austin, known as the "Father of Texas."

But those were not the most valuable of the lost paintings. Both the Samuel Stillman Osgood painting donated by Robert Crockett and the life-size portrait by Chapman that had only recently been purchased were gone forever. Also reduced to ash were two paintings, *Dawn at the Alamo* and *Lee at the Wilderness*, painted by artist Henry Arthur McArdle. An Irish transplant to Texas, his Alamo painting was eight feet tall by thirteen feet wide and included an image of David Crockett swinging "Old Betsy" at his enemies as he defended the Alamo.

As the *Galveston Daily News* reported after the fire, "While the loss of some of these may be lightly borne on account of the little art value they possessed, there is still one painting the absence of which on the walls of the future capitol will ever form a source of regret. It is the historic portrait of David Crockett, a painting that bore the true mark of genius in conception as well as in artistic treatment."[17] Fortunately, Chapman had produced a second, much smaller version of his famous portrait of Crockett that is in the collection of the Harry Ransom Center at the University of Texas at Austin.

As Chapman and Crockett finished the painting in June 1834 and went their separate ways, Crockett headed to Philadelphia where he had been booked to participate in a Fourth of July celebration. He shared the stage with Senator Daniel Webster, also a vocal opponent of Andrew Jackson and his policies. While there, Crockett made numerous anti-Jackson speeches, but he also made time to pick up a new rifle that had been given to him by a group of Philadelphia Whigs during his book tour. He named the gun, believed to be a percussion cap rifle, "Pretty Betsy." Along the muzzle was inscribed "Go ahead." It was not the first time he had been given a gun. In honor of his work on the state legislature, his constituents in Lawrence County had given him a .40-caliber flintlock rifle crafted by James Graham around 1822. Crockett named that gun "Old Betsy" after his sister or his wife.

The time for gifts came to an end. Crockett was already hearing rumblings that the Jacksonian Democrats were using his book tour, failure to get any traction on legislation to help squatters, and general spotty attendance in Congress against him. If he really believed he had any chance of running for president, he knew he had to get back to Tennessee and get his congressional reelection campaign going.

**Chapter Sixteen Notes**

1. Shauna Williams, "David Crockett," *Weekly Gazette Stockman*, August 1, 1889.
2. Shackford, *Crockett*, 169.
3. Frederick S. Voss, "Portraying an American Original: The Likenesses of Davy Crockett." *The Southwestern Historical Quarterly* 91, no. 4 (1988): 457.
4. "Col. David Crockett," *York Gazette York Pennsylvania*, December 17, 1833.
5. Robert Wilson, *Matthew Brady, Portraits of a Nation* (New York: Bloomsbury Publishing, 2013), 29.
6. Trollope, *Manners*, 326-327.
7. Davis, "Legend at Full Length," 165.
8. Ibid.
9. Leah Lipton, "Chester Harding and the Life Portrait of Daniel Boone," *American Art Journal* 16 (1984): 13.
10. Davis, "Legend at Full Length," 170.
11. Davis, "Legend at Full Length," 171.
12. Ibid., 473.
13. Ibid.
14. Sam DeShong Ratcliffe, *Painting Texas History* (Austin, Texas: University of Texas Press, 1992), 24.
15. *The Austin Weekly Statesman*, January 23, 1879.
16. Mike Cox, *Legends & Lore of the Texas Capitol* (Charleston, South Carolina: The History Press, 2017), 46.
17. "Destroyed Art Treasures," *The Galveston Daily News*, November 11, 1881.

*Columbia Pictures*

In *Davy Crockett Indian Scout*, released in 1950, George Montgomery played the famous frontiersman's nephew. He donned buckskin once again for the 1952 film *The Pathfinder* that was loosely based on James Fenimore Cooper's novel first published in 1840.

**There are times when I've thought if I'd known fame was going to be like this, I wouldn't have tried so hard.**

**— Madonna**

**Chapter Seventeen**

# Loss

The second generation of Americans led the way in creating the first authentically American voices in art, theater, and literature. Seba Smith joined David Crockett in doing the same for political humor and satire. Young writers in the new country also had innovative, modern tools to deliver their work to a public hungry to consume it. Around 1830, an American inventor and politician in Boston named Isaac Adams invented a printing press that revolutionized book publishing:

> It was the bed and platen machine that became the predominant press in American printing offices. With skilled handling, it could rival the best work of the hand press, with far greater speed and economy of labor. Between 1830, when Isaac Adams patented his first press, until about 1880 when the bed and platen press finally neared its end, an estimated ninety percent of American book printing was done on Adams' presses.[1]

Meanwhile, new technologies in newspaper printing meant publishers could lower the price, and nearly every American could afford one. Benjamin Day, a New York City printer, began publishing the *New York Sun* for a penny in 1833, and the "penny press" was born. Reading a newspaper became a daily habit in many parts of the country. The number of newspaper publications in America grew from around thirty-five in 1783 to over twelve hundred by 1833.[2] By 1860, there would be more than three thousand.

As the readers of those newspapers evolved from the wealthy elite to the working-class Americans around the country, publishers needed entertaining content that would appeal to those new consumers. It was the perfect moment for "America's first political satirist," Seba Smith, to arrive on the scene.

Smith was born in 1792 in Buckfield, Maine, but his family eventually settled north of Portland. After graduating from Bowdoin College with honors in 1818, he taught school and then began work as a journalist. He founded his own newspaper, the *Portland Courier*, in 1829. Smith soon introduced his readers to a fictional character, Major Jack Downing, as a way to create content and incorporate local politics into his newspaper in a more entertaining way.

Smith wrote that his Downing character was from the small town of Downingville and visited Portland to "sell his load of ax handles, and mother's cheese, and Cousin Nabby's bundle of footings."[3] The fictional Downing wrote letters to his friends and family back home, sharing observations about the political happenings of the day. Smith biographers Dr. Patricia and Dr. Milton Rickels noted, "The taste for his down east company grew strong among Americans who were still wondering exactly how they were different from Englishmen and where they were going as a nation."[4] As Smith himself later reflected, "The first letter made so strong a mark that others had to follow as a matter of course. The whole town read them and laughed; the politicians themselves read them, and their wrathful, fire-eating visages relaxed to a broad grin."[5]

Eventually, Smith began writing about the national political scene by having his fictional character Downing travel to Washington to begin work as an advisor to then-president Andrew Jackson. At first, Smith made it a point to be non-partisan, although he was presenting a parody of the common man's divisive president. The portrait of Jackson that he painted with his words was, as his biographers described, "understated, sometimes affectionate, but never so gross and so unrestrained as the ones many newspapers of the times permitted."[6]

The fictional Downing wrote sympathetically that, "President Jackson opens his heart about the difficulty of governing a country where 'folks will act pretty much as they are a mind to.'"[7] The point being, Jackson would prefer governing a country where folks acted as *he* wanted them to.

It wasn't long before readers began drawing connections between the "Col. David Crockett" character that Crockett himself had created and Smith's fictional politician. Much of Downing's dialect was written phonetically, as though it were taken out of the mouth of the working class of Maine. Crockett's, on the other hand, represented an exaggerated version of settlers living on the wild frontier. They may have sounded different, but both were likable characters who were "fish out of water" and wiser than any of the more educated and experienced politicians they were each around. Both characters had found themselves "unexpectedly" engaged in the political and social issues of the day, in spite of a lack of formal education, Crockett and Downing were able to draw upon their natural common sense to make wry observations about current events. From time to time, readers would even find Crockett's "go ahead" used in Downing's letters.

Crockett the politician and Smith the journalist also both benefited from the growth of the book publishing industry. In 1833, the same year Crockett's autobiography was released, Smith published *The Select Letters of Major Jack Downing, of the Downingville Militia, Away Down East, In the State of Maine. Written by Himself.* Like Crockett's book, it was also a big hit with readers around the country, and the two books were frequently advertised together.

The connection between Crockett and Downing made by readers became a reality in print in September 1833. One of the Downing letters that appeared in newspapers included an exchange of letters between Crockett and Downing.

Crockett loved the connection to the fictional character. Around Thanksgiving of that year, he ran into John Quincy Adams in Washington. After losing the presidential election of 1828 to Andrew Jackson, Adams had been elected to the House of Representatives, where he represented Massachusetts from 1831 until his death in 1848. Adams inquired about where Crockett was living. Crockett replied to the former president that he "had taken for lodgings two rooms on the first floor of a boarding-house, where he expected to pass the winter and to have for a fellow-lodger Major Jack Downing." He added, "the only person in whom I have any confidence for information of what the Government is doing."[8]

While Crockett was on his book tour during the spring of 1834, he noted that he had an "honest-to-goodness meeting with the real Major Jack at dinner." Most biographers agree that he likely dined with Seba Smith that evening. If that was the case, it's certainly possible that the two men brainstormed about how, together, they could capitalize off what they had separately created. The public had responded favorably to recent exchanges of letters between Smith's version of Colonel Crockett and his Major Jack Downing character. Some readers were even understandably confused and thought Downing was a real man and the letters really were to and from the Tennessee politician.

Like Crockett, Smith had also grown increasingly frustrated by Jackson's leadership. On July 4, 1834, he issued the first of a weekly newspaper titled the *Downing Gazette.* In one feature, an anti-Jackson Downing and Crockett exchanged frequent letters, bashing the president and the Jacksonian Democrats. In the March 14, 1835 issue, Downing wrote, "Hoorah, if there isn't a letter from my old new friend Col Crockett, to the one I sent him a week or two ago in Washington. I'm so tickled I don't know what to do…I guess between us we shall keep matters pretty straight clear from here to Tennessee."[9] The reply from Crockett, also written by Smith, referenced Jackson's desire to force France to pay a debt to America incurred during the Napoleonic Wars and the upcoming presidential campaign:

> …the dimocrats tried to give the Gineral three millions of dollars

> to make ready to go to war with France. But the Senate vetoed the proposition, and said we will wait a while before we give the General that much of the people's money…I must say now something about how little Van and the dimocrats look since Judge White has come into the field. I think they are scared badly; and well they may be, for the Judge is one of the best men in the world, and it will not take long to make the people believe it. He is the only man in the General's government that can be looked upon to take charge of the deranged state of affairs, and make peace with our once happy country. I do believe he would put down party strife and restore our country to peace and harmony.[10]

The inclusion of Crockett in the *Downing Gazette* certainly increased his visibility in the public, as did a pair of books that were published in 1835. *An Account of Col. Crockett's Tour to the North and Down East* was published in late March while *Life of Martin Van Buren* was published in June. Although his autobiography had sold well, Crockett's earnings had not led to the great wealth he had anticipated. Simply put, he consistently spent more money than he made. Sometimes, he was borrowing from one source to pay back another.

After the success of his autobiography, he saw great promise for generating a big paycheck in the future from publishing. In a move that today would be described as "meta," Crockett came up with the idea to produce a book about his book tour. In many ways, it was brilliant, especially for someone who needed quick cash. Crockett simply gathered newspaper articles from his tour and the notes for his speeches and then added a few personal details. He then gave that to William Clark, a friend and member of Congress from Pennsylvania, who compiled them into book format. Crockett was well aware that he wasn't actually *writing* a book and suggested to the publishers that the title page could position this one slightly different than his autobiography had:

> You have stated that it is written by my self I would rather if you

> think it could sell as well that you had stated that it was written from notes furnished by my self But as to this I am not particular more than it will perhaps give some people a chance to cast reflections on me as to the correctness of it...[11]

As they seemed to be doing with greater frequency, especially when he was asking for advances of royalties against future book sales, they ignored Crockett. The book would be titled, *An Account of Col. Crockett's Tour to the North and Down East in the Year of Our Lord One Thousand Eight Hundred and Thirty-four... Written by Himself.* The subtitle left little doubt that Whig fingerprints were both on the tour and the book: *His object being to examine the grand manufacturing establishments of the country; and also to find out the condition of its literature and morals, the extent of its commerce, and the practical operation of 'The Experiment.'"* The frontispiece of *An Account of Col. Crockett's Tour* featured the Thomas B. Welch engraving of the portrait of Crockett painted by Samuel Stillman Osgood. True to Crockett's comment regarding his portraits, as readers flipped to the first page, they gazed upon a David Crockett who looked every bit like the cross between "a clean-shirted member of Congress and a Methodist preacher."

There was a delay in completing the book about the tour after William Clark fell ill, but that was just as well since it would not be popular with the public or the critics. Edgar Allan Poe wrote, "We see no reason why Col. Crockett should not be permitted to expose himself if he pleases, and to be as much laughed at as he thinks proper—but works of this kind have had their day, and have fortunately lost their attractions."[12]

The release of the third book attributed to Crockett followed just months after *An Account of Col. Crockett's Tour* hit the shelves. While this one would also have an impressively long title, it would suffer from even worse reviews and lackluster sales. *The Life of Martin Van Buren, Heir-apparent to the "government," and the Appointed Successor of General Andrew Jackson. Containing Every Authentic Particular by which His Extraordinary Character Has Been Formed. With a Concise History of the Events that Have Occasioned His Unparalleled Elevation; Together with a Review of His Policy as a Statesman* was a no-holds-barred, mean-spirited diatribe against Jackson's chosen successor for president, Martin Van Buren.

Crockett frequently called the vice president of Jackson's second term "Little Van" and, like others, pointed out Van Buren's ability to negotiate himself onto the right side of any issue in the back rooms of Washington. For that skill, he earned the nickname "little magician." His political skill and organizational powers were a major reason the Jacksonian Democrats had risen to such power, and his methods of promoting party politics would become the prototype for state political machines in the future. Jackson, loyal to those who supported him, selected Van Buren to succeed him as the next resident of the White House. Van Buren was not a universally popular choice in the party for several reasons. He spoke English as a second language—his parents were Dutch—and he made southerners especially nervous. Many of them were suspicious of any politician from up north who may begin legislating away their right to run their plantation using the labor of enslaved people.

Crockett wrote, "it is true little Van was smuggled into the vice-presidency, in the seat of Jackson's breeches..."[13] Quite the opposite of Jackson, Van Buren appreciated the finer things in life and was made fun of for his fashion choices—a fact that was driven home rather harshly in Crockett's book:

> When he enters the senate chamber in the morning, he struts and swaggers like a crow in a gutter. He is laced up in corsets, such as women in a town wear, and, if possible, tighter than the best of them. It would be difficult to say, from his personal appearance, whether he was man or woman, but for his large red and gray whiskers.[14]

Crockett actually had even less to do with the Van Buren book than he had with the book about the tour. Augustin Smith Clayton, a lawyer and representative from Georgia, gets the blame for that. Like Crockett, Clayton had been pro-Jackson but had denounced the president over many of the same issues. Crockett, Clayton, and others who were evolving into the Whig Party were equally against Van Buren because he would surely champion Jackson policies if elected to serve as president in the election of 1836. Clayton had become one of the primary organizers of the Whig Party in Georgia, and they could use all the organizers they could get, as there were no men with the skills of Van Buren bringing them together.

In the early days of the party, the Whigs were still a loosely-formed group of anti-Jacksonians, National Republicans, leftover Federalists, anti-Masons, and southern slaveholders who were building a party based on a variety of beliefs that often conflicted. They really had only one basic tenant that held them together: "King Andrew" had gone too far in elevating the power of the president at the expense of Congress.

In a questionable move intended to split votes and throw the election into the House of Representatives, the Whigs did not run one candidate against Van Buren in 1836; they ran four. North Carolina senator Willie Person Mangum and Tennessee senator Hugh Lawson White from the South, Massachusetts senator Daniel Webster from the East, and former Ohio senator William Henry Harrison from the West were all on the ballot.

Hugh Lawson White came to the election with an extensive pedigree in Tennessee law and government, as the eldest son of the founder of Knoxville, General James White. With his father's financial success and professional connections, young White was able to study law with Archibald Roane, later a governor of the state, and then secure a position as secretary to Tennessee governor William Blount. At just twenty-eight years old, he was elected to serve on the Superior Court of Law and Equity, the highest judicial body in Tennessee. Andrew Jackson was a member of the court at that time and, before White's election, stated publicly that to see White elected was his greatest wish."[15] Like Crockett, White answered the call when the Tennessee legislature was looking for young soldiers to fight under Jackson's leadership in the Creek War.

According to White's descendants, it had been White who convinced his brother-in-law and commander of the Thirty-ninth Regiment, John Williams, to march with six hundred men to fight with Jackson in the Battle of Horseshoe Bend. White went on to an impressive career in Tennessee and then federal government, serving in a variety of legislative positions including state supreme court judge. He was called "Judge White" for the rest of his life. Although not deferential enough to be considered a member of Jackson's "Kitchen Cabinet," White was a long-time supporter and friend of his fellow Tennessean. White felt the group that included Van Buren, William B. Lewis, and John Overton were "yes-men" simply backing up whatever whims the president put before them. That wasn't his way.

Without question, however, White was an asset to the Jacksonian Democratic party. After Jackson resigned his Senate seat in 1825, he heartily endorsed White to take his place. White was then unanimously elected to fill the vacancy left in the Tennessee legislature.[16] He served as chairman on the Committee on Indian Affairs, and while he was in favor of moving Native Americans west, he wanted it done only if they chose to go voluntarily. With a background in both law and banking, as former president of the Bank of Tennessee, he was an important part of Jackson's Bank War. He came out publicly against a national bank but warned Jackson not to remove the government deposits as "public opinion would not approve such a course."[17]

Obviously, Jackson ignored his friend's advice. White supported Jackson in many ways both publicly and behind the scenes and, according to all accounts, was one of Jackson's most trusted allies and frequent advisors during his first term. The two even looked a little alike. As historian Robert V. Remini noted, "White rather resembled Andrew Jackson in appearance except that his long, lean, bony outline radiated none of Jackson's aggressiveness and tension. White was more contemplative, more cerebral."[18] White's biographer, Nancy N. Scott, wrote, "His abundant gray hair was thrown back from his forehead, and curled at considerable length upon his shoulders; its silvery waves adding to his venerable and remarkable appearance. The usual expression of his face in repose was sad."[19]

During Jackson's second term, White's feelings toward the president began to cool as he found himself more frequently concerned about the direction Jackson's leadership was taking the country. When it became clear that Jackson was going to endorse Van Buren as his successor, he offered White the position of secretary of war. White had wanted that position early in the Jackson administration, but it had been given to John Eaton instead. White declined, and when a group of Tennessee political leaders who had broken with Jackson suggested that White run for president against Van Buren as a Whig, his decades-long friendship with Jackson came to an end. Jackson was infuriated and felt betrayed by White and those Tennessee legislators who dared campaign against his chosen successor.

Not only had the group of Tennesseans been persuasive, but White also suddenly found great motivation at home as well as at the office. He had suffered great personal loss with the death of his wife, Elizabeth Carrick, and eight of their ten children from tuberculosis between 1825 and 1831. He met his second wife, Ann Peyton, because she ran the boarding house he stayed in when in Washington. She was rumored to be ambitious and could likely see a move from the boarding house to the White House in her future.

The new Mrs. White would be disappointed. The 1836 U.S. presidential election was held from Thursday, November 3 to Wednesday, December 7, 1836, and a Hugh Lawson White presidency was not to be. White carried Tennessee and Georgia but finished third in the electoral college. In the end, the Whigs were only able to capture 124 electoral votes to Van Buren's 170. A Jacksonian Democrat would reign four more years in the White House.

White was not the only Tennessean to lose in an election in 1836. Crockett lost his as well, and it is not hard to see why. He had once been a man who harshly judged his opponent, William Butler, for having a fancy rug on the floor of his Jackson, Tennessee home. Crockett himself now stayed in the most expensive hotels, dined in the best restaurants, and sat for portraits by the same artists who painted the elite politicians he once criticized. Almost as bad, he didn't even try to hide who he had become; he wrote books about it.

Although his fame had risen to heights he found personally rewarding, when it came to doing the job West Tennessee voters had elected him to do, he was frequently missing in action. That was something Jackson's political machine was more than happy to point out during Crockett's 1834 congressional campaign against the one-legged Adam "Timber-toe" Huntsman.

Huntsman had made his home and businesses in Knox and Overton counties in Tennessee, then moved west in 1821 and became one of the earliest settlers of Madison County. Unlike Crockett's previous opponents, Huntsman had spent years on the Tennessee frontier and knew the people and the politics just as well. Huntsman represented Overton, Jackson, and Smith Counties in the Tennessee General Assembly from 1815-1821. He returned to the legislature as state senator representing Madison, Fayette, Hardeman, Haywood, Shelby, and Tipton Counties from 1827-1831. He served as a delegate to the Tennessee Constitutional Convention of 1834. By all accounts, Huntsman served his constituents well. In 1951, historian Chase C. Mooney opined that nearly one hundred years after his death, Huntsman had "remained buried in the oblivion of records, with only a brief reference here and there to his activities that stretched over more than four decades of the history of Tennessee."[20]

Mooney also noted the impact Huntsman made regarding transportation in West Tennessee in the years immediately prior to his campaign against Crockett:

> As the inhabitant of a relatively undeveloped region, Huntsman continued his efforts in behalf of internal improvements. He successfully introduced bills for the establishment of toll bridges over the Forked Deer and Hatchie rivers; for the authorization of a lottery for the cutting of a canal from the Hatchie to the Mississippi; for the levying of a tax by Haywood County for the building of bridges and causeways and for the cutting of roads; for the substitution of work on roads for work on the rivers; for the building of bridges and causeways in a direction from Trenton to Troy, from Brownsville to Trenton, and from Denmark to Memphis; for declaring the middle fork of the Forked Deer navigable from its mouth to Spring Creek in Madison County; and for clear obstructions in the Wolf River.[21]

Not only was he an experienced civil servant with a proven record of service, he was also an excellent speaker, creative writer, and could deliver witty anecdotes on the campaign trail just as effectively as Crockett. Even though his opponent was now famous, Huntsman thought he had a chance of winning, with one caveat—that Tennessee land bill. In January 1835, Huntsman wrote Polk, "I begin to believe I can beat Davy…I have been in all the Counties but one in this District and Crockett is evidently losing ground or otherwise he was never as strong as I supposed him to be—Perhaps it is both…"[22] Crockett's adversarial position against Jackson would very likely cost him votes. Huntsman added, "He is eternally sending Anti Jackson documents here and it has had its effect. If he carried his land Bill I will give him strength Otherwise the conflict will not be a difficult one."[23]

A Tennessee land bill that would accommodate the needs of squatters was not to be, at least not in Crockett's lifetime. His blind rage toward Jackson and Van Buren and his resentment of the Jackson political machine had resulted in him becoming a single-minded, ineffective member of Congress with no ability to compromise or even contribute to legislation; in fact, since they refused to let him bring his land bill to the floor for discussion, he would simply oppose everything that did.

Finally, on February 20, 1835, William Claiborne Dunlap, member of Congress from Tennessee's Thirteenth District, moved to suspend the rules for a moment and take up the Tennessee land bill, likely as a favor to Crockett. Protecting Tennessee's squatters had been the first thing Crockett talked about from the floor of the House. Would it now be the last?

Crockett stood that day to make his case, knowing it was also a last-ditch effort at saving his political career. There were immediate objections, and the request to hear any argument was denied. Crockett took his seat without being allowed to utter a word, a metaphor for the state of his political career.

Jackson wrote numerous letters to friends and associates around this time that made his opinion of Crockett crystal clear. Crockett and Jackson had been political enemies for years, but now he was part of that bigger betrayal by White and the other Tennesseans who supported White's run for president against Van Buren. Jackson instructed his followers to "hurl Crockett and Co. from the confidence of the people." In advance of the

Democratic convention in Baltimore, he had written of the "high talents" of those who would be attending and declared that Tennessee would appear "degraded and humiliated." He claimed that "Crocket and Co. cry out that Judge White was brought out by the people" when, in fact, he was brought out by "this miserable little caucus." Jackson left no question about their fate and wrote, "...like all others who, have abandoned the principles that gave them popularity, for the sake of office, [they] must fall politically, never to rise again in the affections of the people..."[24]

When the votes were counted, Crockett would indeed fall politically. Adam Huntsman had beaten the incumbent but not by much. Crockett lost the election to Huntsman 4,400 votes to 4,652. One Jacksonian newspaper gleefully wrote, "Crockett will find the business of 'Coon hunting' which he will now resume, much better suited to his genius than legislation. The Whigs have used him until he is used up."[25]

Not only had his enemies won, but long periods away from home and the cost of his frequent travels and life in Washington had exacerbated Crockett's already precarious financial problems. He was facing numerous legal battles relating to debt and settlement of the estate of his father, who had recently died after moving to Northwest Tennessee. Some of his wife's relatives were now even claiming that he had not administered his father-in-law's estate properly. If there was ever a time for an explorer with an aversion to settling down to head west, this was it. In advance of the election, Crockett wrote a letter to a friend and mentioned what he would do if Van Buren won the election. While it may have been an idle threat at the time, it proved to be remarkably prophetic:

> I have almost given up the Ship as lost. I have gone So far as to declare that if he martin vanburen is elected that I will leave the united States for I never will live under his kingdom. before I will Submit to his Government I will go to the wildes of Texas. I will consider that government a Paridice to what this will be.[26]

Martin Van Buren's one-term presidency was greatly impacted by the

Panic of 1837, an economic downturn that began less than three months after he moved into the White House. Jackson's destruction of the Second Bank of the United States had removed restrictions on the practices of some state banks. Afterwards, wild speculation in lands, based on easy bank credit, swept the West, creating a bubble that was sure to burst. To make matters worse, before he left office, Jackson required that lands be purchased with hard money—gold or silver.

As a result, during Van Buren's presidency, thousands of businesses failed and early settlers lost their land. For the rest of Van Buren's years in office, America experienced the worst depression in the country's history to that point. By the election of 1840, the Whigs had finally gotten themselves organized. Their one candidate, General William Henry Harrison, defeated Martin Van Buren or, as they began calling him, "Martin Van Ruin."

In spite of his great promise as a legislator, the Twenty-fourth Congress would be Adam Huntsman's one and only. In a plot twist that seems more like fiction than reality, he was beaten by Crockett's own son, John Wesley Crockett. Young Crockett followed in his father's footsteps and represented the same Tennessee district for the Twenty-fifth and Twenty-sixth Congresses. He later served as attorney general for Tennessee's Ninth District, then moved to New Orleans where he began a career as a newspaper editor and publisher.

After he was defeated by Van Buren, Hugh Lawson White returned to the Senate but friends noted he was, "much soured and dissatisfied." While the Whigs made headway in Tennessee politics in the latter part of the 1830s, it was not to last. Loyal Democrat James K. Polk was elected the ninth governor of Tennessee in 1839. Polk and other Tennessee legislators put pressure on White to vote as they instructed. White resigned in protest, returned to Tennessee, and died three months later.

In the presidential election of 1844, Polk, who had always remained faithful to Andrew Jackson, was victorious over Whig Henry Clay to become the eleventh president of the United States. It would be Clay's third and final unsuccessful run for that office in spite of his qualifications. During his political career, Clay earned the nickname "The Great Compromiser" because of his ability to negotiate with others in Washington. As a representative, senator, and secretary of state, his actions, including the Missouri Compromise and the Compromise of 1850, balanced states' rights against federal initiatives in a nation teetering on the edge of a civil war over the issue of slavery. The seventy-five-year-old Kentucky statesman died in Washington on June 29, 1852 from tuberculosis. He became the first to lie in state in the Capitol Rotunda.

It would be to recently elected President Polk that Andrew Jackson would write his last letter. On June 6, 1845, he wrote his friend with suggestions relating to the treasury department, corrupt speculators, and Choctaw land claims he called fraudulent. He warned that if Polk didn't follow his advice, it could blow Polk and his administration "sky high." He concluded with, "I can write no more, friendship has aroused me to make this attempt. yr. friend."[27]

Members of Andrew Jackson's family were gathered around his failing body the next day. It was evident that death was near. After he stopped breathing, his friend and physician, Dr. John Esselman, listened for a heartbeat, then declared the seventy-eight-year-old former president dead. His family and friends who had been gathered at the house began comforting each other through their tears of sorrow. Around ten minutes later, Jackson opened his eyes and began to speak again. Even death couldn't beat Old Hickory.

He did die the next day, probably because he chose to.

After a funeral attended by three thousand, he was buried next to Rachel at the Hermitage. In his biography of Jackson, *American Lion*, Jon Meacham relays a Tennessee legend about a conversation between a visitor to the Hermitage and one of Jackson's slaves. The visitor asked if the slave thought Jackson went to heaven. The slave replied, "If the General wants to go, who's going to stop him?"[28]

Rather than mailing that last letter Jackson had written to Polk right away, it was set aside, then misplaced in a stack of letters Jackson had received. When it was finally discovered four months after Jackson's death, the letter was given to President Polk. It must have been quite a surprise for him to receive Jackson's advice about governing the country from beyond the grave.

Polk went on to lead a very productive four years as president, but worked himself into an early grave. As Polk scholar John C. Pinheiro notes:

> Polk accomplished nearly everything that he said he wanted to accomplish as President and everything he had promised in his party's platform: acquisition of the Oregon Territory, California, and the Territory of New Mexico; the positive settlement of the Texas border dispute; lower tariff rates; the establishment of a new federal depository system; and the strengthening of the executive office. He masterfully kept open lines of communication with Congress, established the Department of the Interior, built up an administrative press, and conducted himself as a representative of the whole people.[29]

Polk heartily embraced the concept of manifest destiny and, during his administration, the size of the United States doubled. As he left office, America finally reached from "sea to shining sea." Exausted by years of public service and work as president, he retired after a single term. Polk and his wife, Sarah, left Washington in March for a celebratory tour of the south. It would be a brief tour; likely contracting cholera in New Orleans, he returned home to Nashville where he died on June 15, 1849 at age fifty-three.

What was Crockett's next move after he lost in the election of 1836? It's not certain exactly when and where he said it the first time, but the victories of both Adam "Timber-toe" Huntsman and "Little Van" resulted in a passionate declaration from Crockett that would go down in history as one of the most remembered political quotes of all times:

I told the people of my district that I would serve them faithfully as I had done; but if not, they might go to hell, and I will go to Texas.

And he did.

## Chapter Seventeen Notes

1. Douglass W. Charles, *Bed & Platen Book Printing Machines, American and British Streams of Ingenious Regression in the Quest for Print Quality* (Ketchikan: Plane Surface Press, 2017), iv.
2. Carol Sue Humphrey, *The Press and the Young Republic, 1783-1833* (Westport Connecticut: Greenwood Press, 1996), 155.
3. Seba Smith, *My Thirty Years Out of the Senate* (New York: Derby & Jackson, 1860), 36.
4. Milton Rickels and Patricia Kennedy Rickels, *Seba Smith* (Boston: Twayne Publishers, 1977), 5.
5. Ibid., 5-6.
6. Ibid., 47
7. Ibid.
8. Charles Francis Adams, ed, *Memoirs of John Quincy Adams, Comprising Portions of His Diary from 1795 to 1848* (Philadelphia: J. B. Lippincott & Co., 1874), 39.
9. Shackford, *Crockett*, 198.
10. Ibid., 199.
11. Boylston and Wiener, *Congress*, 266.
12. Edgar Allan Poe. *Southern Literary Messenger* 1, no 8, April 1835, 459.
13. Crockett, *Travels*, 190.
14. David Crockett, *The life of Martin Van Burnen* (Philedelphia: Robert Wright, 1835), 86-87.
15. Paul L. Gresham, "The Public Career of Hugh Lawson White," *Tennessee Historical Quarterly* 3, no. 4 (1944): 294.
16. Ibid., 300.
17. Ibid., 304.
18. Robert V. Remini, *Andrew Jackson: The Course of American Freedom, 1822-1832* (Baltimore and London: The Johns Hopkins University Press, 1981), 43.
19. Nancy Scott, *A Memoir of Hugh Lawson White, Judge of the Supreme Court of Tennessee* (Philedelphia: J.B. Lippincott, & Co., 1856), 243.
20. Shackford, *Crockett*, 175-176.
21. Ibid. 110-111.
22. Shakeford 175-176.
23. Ibid 175-176.
24. Shackford, *Crockett*, 178.
25. Boylston and Wiener, *Congress*, 122.
26. Ibid., 262.
27. Correspondence of Andrew Jackson, edited by John Spencer Bassett. V. 6-7. Washington, D.C., Carnegie Institution of Washington, 1926-35, 414.
28. John Meacham, *American Lion* (Random House: New York, 2008), 346.
29. John C. Pinheiro, Miller Center of Public Affairs, University of Virginia. "James K. Polk." Accessed June 24, 2021. https://millercenter.org/president/polk.

*Touchstone Pictures / Imagine Entertainment*

*The Alamo*, released in 2004, starred Billy Bob Thornton as David Crockett, Dennis Quaid as Sam Houston, and Jason Patric as Jim Bowie. Playing "Davy" as a celebrity struggling to come to terms with the public image he created, some have called it Thornton's greatest performance. In his review, movie critic Roger Ebert wrote that a highlight of the film comes as Crockett is asked about his legendary feats. Ebert wrote, "And then we watch Crockett with a rueful smile as he patiently explains that he did not do and cannot do any of those things, and that his reputation has a life apart from his reality."

Fame is like a shaved pig with a greased tail, and it is only after it has slipped through the hands of some thousands, that some fellow, by mere chance, holds on it.

—David Crockett

Part Three

# Texas

*Library of Congress, Geography and Map Division*

David Crockett represented Tennessee on a map featuring the folklore of the United States created by painter, illustrator, and cartoonist William "Bill" Gropper in 1945. *William Gropper's America, Its Folklore* was a popular teaching tool and promoted American literature, culture, and travel. Joining Crockett are sixty characters including Daniel Boone, Buffalo Bill, Paul Bunyan, Rip Van Winkle, and Calamity Jane. In 1953, Gropper was among artists who were blacklisted when senator Joseph McCarthy accused him of being a Communist. Afterwards, the State Department destroyed all undistributed copies of the map; however, it continued to be a popular tool used in schools and libraries around the country.

**Fame hit me like a ton of bricks.**

**—Eminem**

## Chapter Eighteen

# Sam

David Crockett likely heard a great deal about Texas from his close friend Sam Houston, one of the most colorful political characters to ever call Tennessee home. The two men certainly had a lot in common. Seven years younger than Crockett, Houston was born near Lexington, Virginia in 1793. When Houston was thirteen years old, his father died, and his mother moved with Sam and his siblings to Blount County in East Tennessee. Just as Crockett left his family as a young boy and didn't return for many years, Houston left his family at fifteen years old and made his life among a band of Cherokee across the Tennessee River. The leader, John Jolly, was known among the tribe as Chief Oolooteka which meant "he who puts away the drum." It was a nod to Oolooteka's desire for peace rather than war with the White men. He became like a father to young Houston who was given the Cherokee name Go La Nu or "the Raven" in English.

Like Crockett, Houston was one of those young Tennesseans who volunteered to fight in the Creek War immediately following the massacre at Fort Mims. Fighting in the Seventh Infantry, his bravery impressed

Jackson at the Battle of Horseshoe Bend to such a degree, that Jackson took the young soldier under his wing.

After the war, having Jackson as a mentor paid off, and Houston's political career soared. He served as attorney general for Davidson County, Tennessee, was appointed major general of the state militia, and then represented Tennessee's Seventh District in Congress. In 1827, at just thirty-four years old, he was elected the sixth governor of Tennessee. It would appear nothing could stop his meteoric rise in politics—that is, until he decided it was time to heed Jackson's frequent advice and find a wife.

The young lady who caught his eye was Eliza Allen of Sumner County, Tennessee. On January 22, 1829, the two married, and the handsome, young governor of Tennessee took his even younger bride to live with him at the Nashville Inn.

The marriage lasted eleven weeks. Devastated and embarrassed, Houston hid out and was only willing to talk to a few of his closest friends, one of them being Crockett who was then beginning his second term in Congress. Crockett wrote to a business acquaintance, "I was in Nashville a few days and a Circumstance took place last Saturday which created much excitement. Our Governor Houston has parted with his wife and Resigned the governors appointment he told me he was going to leave the country and go to arkensaw and live with the Indians as he called them his adopted Brothers."[1]

Whatever happened between Sam Houston and Eliza Allen in those eleven weeks of marriage will forever be a mystery. Many amateur sleuths have attempted to figure out the nature of their split since the time it occurred to today; but both Houston and Allen took most of the details to the grave. In fact, Allen went to the extreme; upon her death in 1861, she left instructions to destroy any photos and paintings of her, burn all of her personal letters and other documents, and bury her in an unmarked grave.

From the beginning, the two were certainly not likely to be compatible. He was only one year younger than her mother, so the age difference was against them. Allen may have been immature and spoiled. Houston was likely overbearing, demanding, and jealous and was known to have a temper. It also appeared later she may have been in love with one or more of her other suitors, but married Houston at the urging of her status-seeking father. There was even a theory that she was so repulsed by Houston's old war wound from the Battle of Horseshoe Bend, she let him know on their honeymoon that the marriage would never be consummated.

Regardless of the reason, she returned to her parents' home, and Houston resigned his governorship and fled west to Arkansas where he rejoined Chief Oolooteka and his Cherokee brothers. Houston was quickly granted Cherokee citizenship, grew his hair out, and began dressing as a Native American. Free to nurse his wounds far from the eye of a public that was quick to judge and gossip, Houston buried his sorrow in alcohol and earned a new Cherokee name, "Big Drinker." He also found a wife—exactly what he had been looking for back in Nashville. Although his short marriage to Eliza Allen was not yet officially dissolved, he was able to marry Tiana Rogers Gentry, who was half Cherokee, in a tribal ceremony. Together, they built a trading post called Wigwam Neosho on the Neosho River near Fort Gibson, Oklahoma.

Houston put his skills at negotiation and experience in government to good use. He was part of a tribal delegation that traveled to Washington several times between 1830 and 1832 to negotiate fulfillment of a treaty and to help his tribe obtain a land grant. Although his efforts on behalf of the tribe were ultimately futile at that time, the result was Houston's rebirth in the public eye. He was no longer an abusive, washed-up governor dealing with the weight of scandal with too much alcohol. He was now a colorful, charismatic American, like his friend Crockett, who represented westward expansion.

In 1831, Houston and some of his Cherokee brothers met Alexis de Tocqueville on a steamboat headed to New Orleans. During a question and answer-style interview, Tocqueville asked Houston about the "natural intelligence" of Native Americans. Houston replied,

> I do not think they yield to any race of men on that account. And the same is true of Negroes. The differences between Indians and Negroes are solely from the different education they have received.

> The Indian is born free; he makes use of his freedom from his first steps in life. He is left to look after himself as soon as he can act. As a result, Indian intelligence has a 'development and ingenuity which are often wonderful. The Negro, in contrast, was a slave even before birth. Without pleasures as without needs, and useless to himself, the first notions of existence which he receives make him understand that he is the property of another, that care for his own future is no concern of his, and that the very thought is for him a useless gift of providence.[2]

Houston and Crockett were quite the pair in Washington. While Crockett had grown to despise Jackson, Houston still had great love and respect for his mentor. But it seems the two agreed about more than they disagreed. In April 1834, right before Crockett departed for his book tour, Houston was in Washington, and the two friends enjoyed a night out together. The signatures of both men show up that evening in the guest book of Octavia Walton Le Vert, wealthy granddaughter of George Walton, one of the signers of the Declaration of Independence. Le Vert was a popular socialite who was just at the beginning of her fascinating life that would result in a reputation as a charming hostess and adventurous world traveler. She would also become one of the first nationally recognized southern female writers. Her friendship with Henry Clay and Daniel Webster indicates that her loyalties lay with the growing Whig party. She was fluent in English, French, Italian, and Spanish, but as Clay observed, "Better than all, she has a tongue that speaks no evil."[3]

As the two men with roots in Tennessee parted company that evening, they had no way of knowing the names David Crockett and Sam Houston would one day appear together as heroes of Texas independence. Houston's path led him to service as major general of the Texian Army, president of the Republic of Texas, seantor of Texas, and then governor of Texas—making him the only man to have been a governor of two states.

At some point after he lost that congressional campaign, Crockett realized he was now free to explore Houston's Texas for himself. On October 31, 1835, he wrote to his brother, "I am on the eve of Starting to the Texes—on to morrow morning myself Abner Burgin and Lindsy K Tinkle & our Newphew William Patton from the Lowar Country this will make our Company and we will go through Arkinsaw and I want to explore the Texes well before our return."[4]

The next day, Crockett and his entourage set out to explore "the Texes." The press began reporting on his journey almost immediately, and Crockett was greeted by crowds who wanted to get a look at the frontiersman they had read about. He was wined and dined and given plenty of opportunities to speak to the crowds along the way. As they rode through smaller Tennessee communities, their final destination in the state was Memphis, where they would take a ferry across the river to Arkansas.

As he arrived in the bustling river city, he must have thought back to 1826 and that chance meeting with Marcus Winchester. It had changed the trajectory of Crockett's life when he was at one of his lowest points. At that time, he had failed miserably, and it looked like there was no hope for his future. Perhaps that crossed his mind as he and his crew rode down Poplar Street toward the bluff overlooking the Mississippi River. He likely hoped that launching this next chapter of his life with an evening with Winchester would prove to be just as lucky.

He was not really finished with Washington. If this new Texas frontier had the potential that Sam Houston and others had claimed, there would be many opportunities for cheap land, and Crockett knew better than anyone how it worked. Land led to settlers, which resulted in communities that led to a need for legislation, which led to the need for representatives in Washington. He may have imagined the looks on his enemies' faces if they heard David Crockett was back in town.

Crockett and a few of his Memphis friends, including Winchester, began their evening at the Union Inn at Adams and Third. At some point they may have stopped at the Bell Tavern on Front Street between Jackson and Auction where Paddy Meagher was known for his hospitality. It had been Memphis' first hotel and both Crockett and Sam Houston were known to have visited. As the party began to grow, they moved first to Hart's Saloon on Market Street then next door to Neil McCool's Saloon. The room was now packed with revelers excited they were getting to experience a celebrity in person. Crockett was encouraged to hop up on the bar and give a speech, which of course, he was more than happy to do. He included the "and they can go to hell" talking point that never failed to elicit a response. As if on cue, the crowd erupted in cheers as he finished. He soaked in the response and jumped down.

The alcohol began to take effect, and some in the crowd that had grown to number more than one hundred began to get rowdy. Crockett suggested that he and a smaller group of close friends call it a night. Rather than head back to the hotel, they parted ways to make it appear as though the evening had come to an end, then met up at the door of Jo Cooper's Mercantile Store.

Although his establishment was not a tavern, Cooper sold liquor by the barrel and was known to have the best quality alcohol in Memphis. To get the bachelor to let them in the store where he also lived, one of the men in the group, Bob Lawrence, knew that Cooper had to wake up and go down to the docks anytime, day or night, when a boat arrived with his merchandise. Lawrence banged on the door and shouted, "Freight, Freight!" Cooper made his way downstairs and opened the door, and the group shoved their way in to begin the last part of their evening.

In the words of Memphis historian James Davis, who claimed to have been among the small group of friends that evening, "We all got tight—I might say, yes, very tight…men who never were tight before, and never have been tight since, were certainly VERY TIGHT then." As Crockett and his friends drank, laughed, and swapped stories, no one knew it would be Crockett's last evening in Tennessee. When the men heard of his death only months later, they were no doubt grateful that they were among those from his home state who gave him both a hero's welcome to Memphis and a champion's farewell as he left Tennessee forever. As Davis wrote of the evening, "The best of feeling prevailed to a late hour."[5]

The next morning, a small group made their way down to the ferry where Crockett and his party would cross. Davis also wrote of Crockett's last minutes east of the Mississippi River:

> In the days of which I speak there were no steam ferry-boats, there was simply a ferry-flat, propelled by 'snatch oars,' with a noted old negro, names Limus, as Captain. The ferry landing was then in the mouth of the Wolf river...My recollection of how he looked is as vivid as if it were yesterday...The day I saw him he had been the guest of a few personal friends, Edwin Hickman, C. D. McLean, M. B. Winchester, Robert Lawrence, Gus Young, and others, at the City Hotel. He had left the hotel, accompanied by these gentlemen on foot, for the landing. I followed in silent admiration for the river. He wore that same veritable coonskin cap and hunting shirt, bearing upon his shoulder his ever faithful rifle. No other equipments save his shot-pouch and powder-horn, do I remember seeing.[6]

Davis was known for adding a little color to his history, and his story is impossible to verify now, one way or the other. It is, in some way poetic that the final account of Crockett in Tennessee may or may not be true; the reader gets to decide. According to Davis's account, the friends said their goodbyes, and Crockett and those who remained with him, including his nephew William Patton and friends Abner Burgin and Lindsey Tinkle, stepped into Limus's flatboat. Davis wrote, "The chain was untied from the stob, and thrown with a rattle by old Limus into the bow of the boat, it pushed away from the shore, and floating lazily down the little Wolf, out into the big river, and rowed across to the other side, bearing that remarkable man away from his State and his kindred forever."[7]

**Chapter Eighteen Notes**

1. Boylston and Wiener, *Congress*, 178.
2. Tocqueville, *Journey to America*, 254.
3. "Madame Le Vert and her Friends," *Lexington Herald-Leader*, August 25, 1907, 16.
4. Shackford, *Crockett*, 210.
5. Davis, *Memphis*, 148.
6. Ibid., 139-140.
7. Ibid., 141.

Actor Lane Chandler portrayed David Crockett in *Heroes of the Alamo*, a low-budget film distributed by Columbia Pictures Corporation in 1938. When Lane's Crockett, a minor character in the film, arrives at the Alamo and is asked why he is there, he replies, "The numbskull voters in Tennessee wouldn't send me back to Congress for another term. I figured your little war here was the next best thing to Congress."

**Fame may go by and - so long,**
**I've had you.**
**—Marilyn Monroe**

## Chapter Nineteen

# Endings

Published reports of David Crockett's death on March 6, 1836 at the age of forty-nine did not begin showing up in newspapers around the country until around a month after his death. It likely took even longer for his family to find out. Crockett had been killed by Mexican troops at the Alamo, a half-mile from the town of Béxar, in present-day San Antonio, Texas. The former Misión San Antonio de Valero had been built more than one hundred years earlier by Roman Catholic missionaries, but the name was changed to the Alamo after it made the transition from church to fortress.

Crockett's death came after a thirteen-day battle between Mexican troops led by Antonio López de Santa Anna against early Texian settlers fighting to liberate the region from Mexico. How, just a short time after departing Memphis, did Crockett end up fighting in a revolution to liberate a town he had not even known about weeks earlier?

In *Forget the Alamo: The Rise and Fall of an American Myth*, the authors note that his arrival at the Alamo was "one of history's great juxtapositional flukes." They added, "as if Teddy Roosevelt or Mark Twain had darted onto the *Titanic* at the last minute."[1]

After they arrived in Texas, Crockett and the group had begun exploring the region along the Red River, and he quickly decided that he had found his new home. In January, Crockett wrote a letter to his daughter and son-in-law, Wiley and Margaret Crockett Flowers, a letter in which he called Texas "the garden spot of the world." He also wrote of his plans:

> [Texas has] the best land and the best prospects for health I ever saw and I do believe it is a fortune to any man to come here There is a world of country here to Settle...I have taken the oath of government and have enrolled my name as a volunteer...all volunteers is intitled to a vote for a member to form a Constitution for this province...I am in hopes of making a fortune yet for myself and family bad as my prospects has been"[2]

Ever the optimist, Crockett envisioned cheap land, an opportunity to return to Washington, and finally making that allusive fortune for his family. He arrived at Béxar on February 11 just days before the fighting began. By all accounts, the presence of a well-known celebrity with stories to tell and the ability to play a fiddle greatly boosted the spirits of those preparing to defend the Alamo. In the end, he was as brave as he was entertaining. Although given ample opportunity to see that the odds were not in their favor, he stayed and fought to the end. Once he arrived, there was no turning back. Sadly, Crockett gave his life for a battle that never should have happened, and his memory was forever made part of Texas history.

On April 1, 1836, Crockett's friends in Nashville picked up a copy of the *National Banner and Nashville Whig* and read about the days leading up to the battle that cost their friend his life. A brief glimpse of Crockett was seen in a published letter that had been written to Sam Houston from William Travis on February 25. Travis was requesting that Houston send reinforcements "as rapidly as possible." In the letter, he noted, "The Hon. David Crockett was seen at all points, animating the men to do their duty."[3]

Houston declined to send the help that Travis requested as Houston had never intended that the Alamo be defended in the first place. He planned for a constitution and army to be in place before beginning any military operations. Houston was also skeptical of Travis's reports and misinterpreted them as a vain grab for attention and glory.

James Bowie, a frontiersman with a much-reported reputation for his prowess with a knife, had been sent on a mission to remove cannons from the town, destroy the Alamo, and lead residents out of the path of Santa Anna's army. But once Bowie got there, he ignored Houston's orders and directed his men to further fortify the Alamo rather than destroy it. Colonel William Travis had been sent to follow through on Houston's original orders, but he also became convinced that the town should be defended and the Alamo saved.

Santa Anna arrived in Béxar months earlier than Travis and Bowie expected. Even worse, he brought with him around eighteen hundred soldiers to battle the two hundred men that had had barricaded themselves inside the walls of the Alamo. This ragtag group of soldiers was mostly made up of volunteers with little or no real military experience. Santa Anna had a point to prove, and the Texians were doomed the moment he raised the "blood red flag," meaning no mercy. And no mercy is exactly what was given. With the exception of a small number of women and children and Travis's slave, Joe, all of those fighting to defend the Alamo were slaughtered.

Although the battle was ultimately unnecessary, the bravery of the motley crew fighting for independence from Mexico against all odds—especially Crockett who was the most well-known—provided a public relations victory that spread across the nation. An article in the *New York Sunday News* is only one example of the type of coverage that appeared around the nation:

> Thousands of his countrymen will rise to avenge his death—God speed them. The ashes of Crockett were not given to the winds in vain. A hotter flame than that which consumed his mortal remains, will burn in the hearts of indignant freemen, until the murderer leaves the clench of his dagger, and the bigot, with his fagot and his torch, are stamped to dust.[4]

When Santa Anna and his Mexican troops met Houston's armed forces at San Jacinto the following month, the sacrifice of those at the Alamo played a big role in the victory. "Remember the Alamo" was shouted by Houston's soldiers in a battle against the Mexican troops that lasted a mere eighteen minutes. Santa Anna was captured and held as a prisoner for days until a peace treaty was signed. A big part of what those in battle remembered at the Alamo—and what would fuel passion for Texas independence in years to come—was built on the national popularity of David Crockett. On April 20, the *National Banner and Nashville Whig* reported,

> The end of David Crockett of Tennessee, the great hunter of the west, was as glorious as his career through life had been useful. He and his companions were found surrounded by piles of assailants, whom they had immolated on the altar of Texas' liberties. The countenance of Crockett was unchanged: he had in death that freshness of hue, which his exercise of pursuing beasts of the forest and the prairie had imparted to him, Texas places him, exultingly, amongst the martyrs in her cause.[5]

His dramatic death as a martyr for freedom at the Alamo ensured that his legacy would not only reach epic proportions, but it would also endure forever. The name David Crockett would begin the list of American celebrities who would tragically die long before the end of their natural life. Through the decades, that list would grow to include names like James Dean, Marilyn Monroe, and Elvis Presley. Like Crockett, their tragic deaths contributed to the notoriety that would grow up around their public image keeping them firmly rooted in the public's consciousness generation after generation.

And as with Elvis Presley, there were Crockett sightings for years after his death. Literary critic and biographer Van Wyck Brooks wrote:

> He was said to have feigned death—he had never died at all—and it

> was rumored that he was seen crossing the Cannon Ball River and following the crooked Missouri to the northern prairies. Trappers in the Rockies saw him hunting grizzlies there, and travelers later heard of him on the coast of California and even in the South Sea Islands, searching for pearls.[6]

A May 1836 article in the *Courtland Advocate* included a story that Crockett was found alive among a pile of bodies at the Alamo, and Shackford wrote of a similar 1840 article in the *Niles Weekly Regis*ter. It reported, "The Boston Traveler has been informed that the son of Col. Crockett (a member of Congress from Tennessee) has received information inducing him to believe that the report in relation to his father being in one of the mines of Mexico, is correct. Steps will be taken to ascertain its truth, and procure his liberation."[7] The truth was, a letter had appeared in the *Austin Gazette* in February 1840 from an American who had been living in Mexico named William C. White who claimed that he had encountered an American working in a mine in Guadalajara that he was certain was Crockett. News reached John Wesley Crockett who sent a letter to Secretary of State John Forsyth expressing skepticism but asking him to investigate.

Like many celebrities who die early under tragic circumstances, the details of *exactly how* Crockett died became a source of passionate debate and controversy that continues today. Even while he was living, the facts about his life had become cloaked in misinformation, myth, and tall tales to such a degree that it had become impossible to separate fact from fiction. After his tragic death, it got even worse. Many needed their version of David Crockett to be a swashbuckling hero, shooting the enemy down with "Old Betsy," and then, when out of bullets, using the butt end of his rifle to club scores of the enemy to death. Today, visitors to the Senate chamber at the Texas State Capitol in Austin can't miss the seven-foot by twelve-foot *Dawn at the Alamo* painted in 1905 by Henry Arthur McArdle. The first version of the painting was burned to ash in the fire of 1881 that also destroyed other Crockett paintings. Fortunately, McArdle painted another version. In the lower right corner, he included Crockett with one arm extended protecting a group of women and children against the attackers while swinging "Old Betsy" like a club with the other. Those who are especially observant will notice a slight heavenly glow against his white shirt that lights Crockett up against the darkness, as the violence of the battle rages around him. This is the Crockett that is celebrated in Texas, Tennessee, and around the world.

Of course, this isn't the end of the story. There has been much controversy and disagreement about how his death at the Alamo really happened. Madam Candelaria Villanueva, who may or may not have actually been at the Alamo, claimed that Crockett was one of the first to fall. In 1888, she told a historian, "he advanced from the church building towards the wall… running from the end of the stockade…when suddenly, a volley was fired by the Mexicans causing him to fall forward on his face, dead."[8] One witness that we know for certain was at the Alamo when Crockett was killed was Susanna Wilkerson Dickinson of Bolivar, Tennessee. Although her husband, Almaron, was one of the Texians who was killed during the siege, she and her fifteen-month-old daughter survived by hiding while the battle raged around them. She did not claim to see Crockett struck down but reported, "I recognized Col. Crockett lying dead and mutilated between the church and two-story barrack building, and even remember seeing his particular cap lying by his side."[9]

William Travis's slave, Joe, also survived the battle and gave a similar report. He later testified before cabinet members of the new Republic of Texas that "the kind-hearted, brave David Crockett, and a few of the devoted friends who entered the Fort with him, were found lying together, with 24 of the slain enemy around him."[10]

Others claimed to have seen something different. D. N. Labadie, a doctor who treated wounded Mexicans after the battle, later claimed that one of Santa Anna's aides told him he had seen Crockett shortly before he was killed. The patient described the person he saw as an old man with a red face who stooped forward as he walked. He was certain that he heard others calling him "Coket," so it must have been him? It was likely not.

In October 1975, Texas A&M University created perhaps the biggest controversy when they published the diary of one of Santa Anna's officers,

Lieutenant Colonel José Enrique de la Peña. The diary had been translated into English by Carmen Perry special collections librarian at the University of Texas at San Antonio. De la Peña's version of what happened to Crockett was very different than what you see in McArdle's painting in Austin. He wrote,

> Some seven men survived the general massacre and guided by General Castrillon, who protected them, were presented to Santa Anna. Among them was one of great stature, well-formed and with regular features, in whose face was stamped the pain of adversity. He was the naturalist David Croket [sic]... Santa Anna answered the intervention of Castrillon as a gesture of indignation, and addressing himself immediately to the sappers, which was the soldiery he had nearest, ordered that they shoot them. The junior and senior officers became indignant at this action and did not repeat the command, hoping that with the passing of the first moment of fury, those men would be saved; but different officers who were around the President and who perhaps had not been there in the moment of danger, made themselves conspicuous by a despicable act; surpassing the soldiers cruelty, they pushed themselves forward to them, in order to flatter the [cruelty] of their commander, and sword in hand they threw themselves on those unhappy defenseless men, in the same way that a tiger leaps upon its prey. They tortured them before they killed them, and these miserable ones died moaning, but without humbling themselves before their executioners.[11]

To say Perry's published translation of de la Peña's diary created controversy would be an understatement. The seventy-year-old librarian certainly didn't anticipate death threats, hate mail, and an article in *People* magazine with the headline "Did Crockett Die at the Alamo? Historian Carmen Perry Says No." In the article, she is even quoted as saying she thinks "we have to face facts and rewrite the textbooks."[12] Those were fighting words in Texas.

Some historians believe the de la Peña account rings true, while others believe the evidence shows de la Peña was mistaken and Crockett went down fighting like the superhero of the painting. Popular historian Walter Lord, best known for his 1955 account of the sinking of the RMS *Titanic*, *A Night to Remember* also wrote *A Time to Stand*, a book about the Alamo that was released in 1961. Lord's account of Crockett's death came from two of the soldiers standing near Santa Anna when he gave the order to kill the "six Texans found still alive, hidden under some mattresses."[13] Lord noted that the soldiers always remembered the scene "partly because it seemed so unnecessary; partly because they both were told one of the victims was the famous David Crockett."[14] However, Lord also left room for the account of Crockett's death in which he fell in battle "fighting like a tiger."

> So there's a good chance Crockett lived up to his legend, and in some circles it remains dangerous even to question the matter. A few years ago when *The Columbia Encyclopedia* ventured the opinion that Crockett surrendered, an angry retort in the *Southwestern Historically Quarterly* declared that Texas would need better authority than "a New York publication." Next edition, the New York editors meekly changed their copy.[15]

The specifics of exactly how Crockett died will never be known for certain. What is proven is that he fought at the Alamo, was killed, and his body ended up on a funeral pyre in San Antonio, Texas. He died as lived—with passion, bravery, and a bit of controversy tossed in to keep things interesting.

## Chapter Nineteen Notes

1 Bryan Burrough, Chris Tomlinson, and Jason Stanford, *Forget the Alamo: The Rise and Fall of an American Myth* (New York, Penguin Press, 2021).
2. Boylston and Wiener, *Congress*, 287.
3. *National Banner and Nashville Whig*, April 1, 1936, 3.
4. "David Crockett," *New York Sunday News* reprinted in *Huron Reflector*, "David Crockett" May 31, 1836, 1.
5. *National Banner and Nashville Whig*, April 20, 1836, 3.
6. Van Wyck Brooks, *The World of Washington Irving* (New York: E.P. Dutton & Company, Inc., 1944), 299.
7. Shakeford, *Crockett*, 239.
8. Ibid., 230-231.
9. J. M. Morphis, *History of Texas from its Discovery and Settlement* (New York: United States Publishing Company, 1875), 177.
10. Dan Kilgore and James E. Crisp, *How did Davy Die? And Why Do We Care So Much?* (College Station, Texas: A&M University Press, 2010), 41.
11. José Enrique de la Peña, *With Santa Anna in Texas: A Personal Narrative of the Revolution*, trans. and ed. by Carmen Perry (College Station, Texas), 52-53.
12. "Did Crockett Die at the Alamo? Historian Carmen Perry Says No," *People Magazine*, October 13, 1975.
13. Walter A. Lord, *A Time to Stand: A Chronicle of the Valiant Battle at the Alamo* (New York: Bonanza Books, 1987), 174.
14. Ibid., 175.

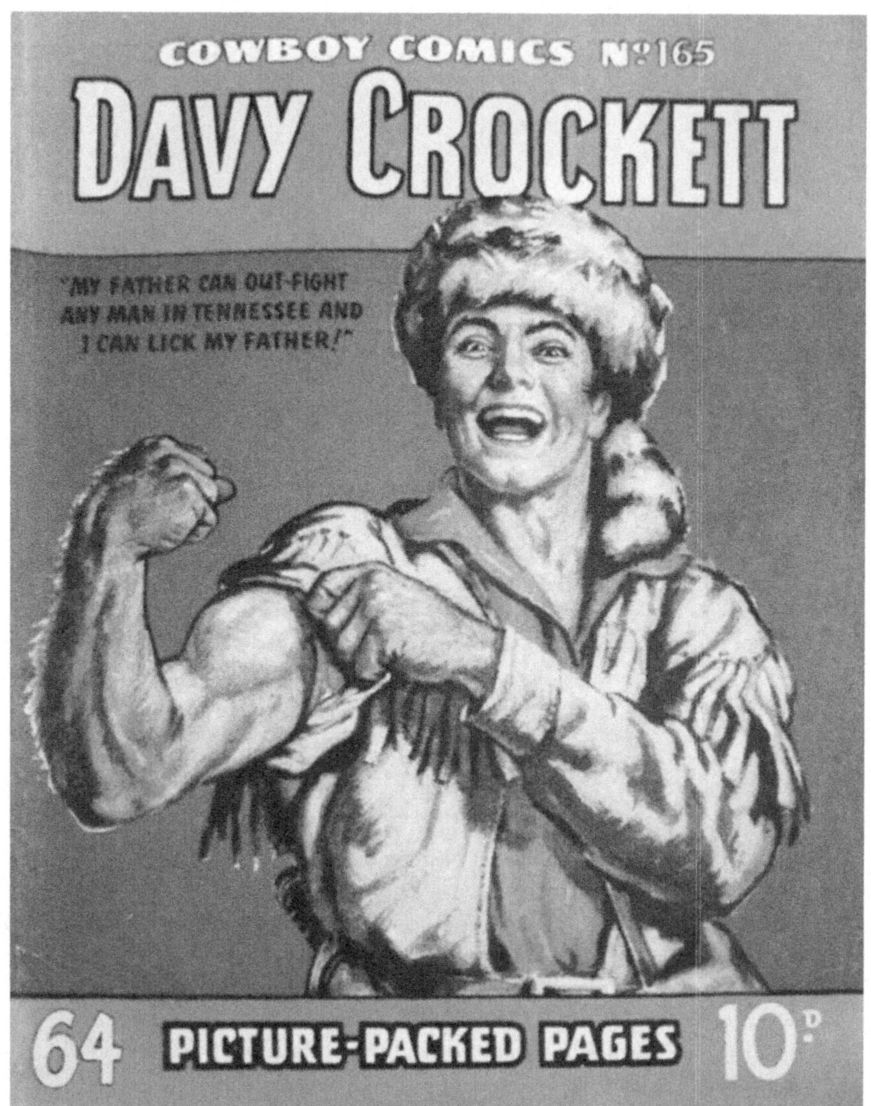


*Fleetway Publications*

Crockettmania spread far and wide in the mid-1950s and coincided with the popularity of comics and interest in "Cowboys and Indians" from consumers around the world. The Davy Crockett comic seen here was produced by Amalagamated Press of Farringdon Street, London with cover art likely from illustrator James E. McConnell.

**Fame is like the dessert that comes with your achievements.**

**— Adam Clayton**

## Epilogue

While David Crockett's life ended at the Alamo, it did not bring to an end the character he helped create. His name and image became commercially viable while he was alive; after his death, it become solid gold. In the months before he departed for Texas, the last two books published with Crockett listed as the author had not performed as well as he and the publishers had hoped. How surprised he would have been to know that after his death, those two books sold out around the country, and another popular book with his name on the cover as the author was still to come. Supposedly written by Crockett on his way to Texas, it was published by Carey and Hart *after* his death and became a bestseller with reprints occurring for more than a decade. *Col. Crockett's Exploits and Adventures in Texas, Written by Himself* was supposedly taken directly from a diary that was "discovered among Crockett's belongings" after his death at the Alamo. It was actually copied from newspaper accounts and in some cases, completely fabricated by Richard Penn Smith. A Philadelphia novelist and playwright, Smith wrote the book in less than twenty-four hours. There's no doubt it was a work of fiction and included melodramatic scenes conjured up from Smith's imagination. Of Crockett's death, he wrote,

> The battle was desperate until daylight, when only six men belonging to the Texian garrison were found alive…Colonel Crockett was of the number. He stood alone in an angle of the fort, the barrel of his shattered rifle in his right hand, in his left his huge Bowie knife dripping blood. There was a frightful gash across his forehead, while around him there was a complete barrier of about twenty Mexicans, lying pell-mell, dead, and dying.[1]

In Smith's account of the Tennessee hero's last minutes, Crockett sees Santa Anna's order for "no quarter" become a reality as soldiers began stabbing their swords into the chests of the other five survivors. Crockett "sprang like a tiger" at Santa Anna and "a dozen swords were sheathed in his indomitable heart; and he fell, and died without a groan, a frown on his brow, and a smile of scorn and defiance on his lips."[2]

Although Crockett was gone, he was not forgotten. In the coming years, the "Davy" Crockett of literature continued its transformation to "King of the Wild Frontier" with the release of more than fifty Davy Crockett almanacs between 1835 and 1856. The almanacs were first published in Nashville, but sales grew and the potential became quickly evident. The Davy Crockett of the almanacs was especially popular in the major metropolitan areas like the ones where David Crockett the author had been so popular during his book tour. Eventually, there were versions published out of New York, Boston, and Philadelphia, among other cities.

David Crockett left Northwest Tennessee for Washington at the exact moment that his unique combination of charisma, confidence, and sense of humor, would enhance his status as a "common man of the people." As a result, he became one of the biggest celebrities of that time. Along the same lines, the *character* of "Davy" Crockett that he created during his lifetime could not have been any more perfect to represent the growing genre of southwestern humor that became popular after his death. Davy breathed life into this entirely new genre of entertainment

Professor Richard M. Dorson, known as "the father of American folklore," wrote, "There are a number of conventions that readily mark this frontier humor, and give it its most agreeable features. The most obvious ones are the frontier boasts, backwoods invective and imagery, racy dialect, ugly people, [and] earthiness."[3]

Those elements are abundant in the Crockett almanacs. Dorson notes,

> They are a virtually untapped magic source of frontier lore in all its varied aspects—realistic stories of Indian fighting and pioneer heroes; fantastic adventures of legendary characters; descriptions of wildlife and nature sketches; anecdotes of the far-flung frontier from Kentucky to California. The uniquely American figure that emerged [from Crockett's earlier books] grows to bizarre proportions in the series of Crockett Almanacs; from the cumulative myth is shaped the outlines of America's first superman, grinning with the silent humor of the day.[4]

Along with the success of the almanacs came other books, publications, and even music. In 1860, publishers Erastus and Irwin Beadle published a series of inexpensive paperback books called *Beadle's Dime Novels*. From 1871-1896, they produced a popular series based on David Crockett that brought the frontiersman to life for a whole new generation of readers.

The English took notice of the evolution of literature that was taking place in America that was thanks, in part, to the inspiration provided by adventurers like David Crockett. Ralph Waldo Emerson observed in 1843, "Our eyes will be turned westward, and a new and stronger tone in literature will be the result. The Kentucky stump-oratory, the exploits of Boon and David Crockett, the journals of western pioneers, agriculturalist, and socialist, and the letters of Jack Downing, are genuine growths, which are sought with avidity in Europe, where our European-like books are of no value."[5]

Crockett's prowess with a gun and hunting skills remained a memorable part of his legacy. President Theodore Roosevelt's admiration became evident in 1887 when he announced he was forming the Boone and Crockett Club.

Roosevelt, a skilled hunter and passionate outdoorsman, came to realize that without regulation and conservation, America would soon be without its natural beauty and wildlife. Unrestricted hunting, irresponsible land-use practices, and settlers removing natural habitat had decimated North America's big game populations. The club was organized "to promote manly sport with the rifle among the large game of the wilderness, to encourage travel and exploration in little-known regions of our country, and to work for game and forest preservation by the State."

*American Big-Game Hunting, The Book of the Boone and Crockett Club* was published in 1893. Edited by Roosevelt and anthropologist and naturalist George Bird Grinnell, Crockett's status as a true legendary hunter and explorer was celebrated:

> Throughout the pioneer stages of American history, big-game hunting was not merely a pleasure, but a business, and often a very important and in fact vital business. At different times many of the men who rose to great distinction in our after history took part in it as such: men like Andrew Jackson and Sam Houston, for instance. Moreover, aside from these pioneers who afterward won distinction purely as statesmen or soldiers, there were other members of the class of professional hunters—men who never became eminent in the complex life of the old civilized regions, who always remained hunters, and gloried in the title—who, nevertheless, through and because of their life in the wilderness, rose to national fame and left their mark on our history. The three most famous instances of this class are Daniel Boone, David Crockett, and Kit Carson: men who were renowned in every quarter of the Union for their skill as game-hunters, Indian-fighters, and wilderness explorers, and whose deeds are still stock themes in the floating legendary lore of the border. They stand for all time as types of the pioneer settlers who won our land: the bridge-builders, the road-makers, the forest-fellers, the explorers, the land-tillers, the mighty men of their hands, who laid

the foundations of this great commonwealth.[6]

Today, the Boone and Crockett Club is North America's oldest wildlife and habitat conservation organization and continues its role as a think tank. It is known primarily for maintaining a scoring and data collection system by which native North American big-game animals are measured and tracked as a gauge of successful wildlife management.

Crockett's catchphrase continued to be used in popular culture for a number of years. While on a visit to London in 1844, little person Charles Sherwood Stratton, better known by his stage name, General Tom Thumb, had a miniature coach built. On the door panels were emblazoned his family coat of arms, illustrations of Britannia, the Goddess of Liberty, the British Lion, an American eagle, the Rising Sun, an American flag, and the Crockett catchphrase, "Go-a-head!"[7]

That wasn't the only Crockett-inspired maxim. As historian and biographer Van Wyck Brooks noted, his mythical status was even memorialized in the form of an American saying that has long since disappeared. He wrote, "People were in the habit of saying, when anything out of the way occurred, 'Just the same, I can tell you it's nothing to Crockett.'"[8]

James Hackett had discovered that David Crockett was a name that would sell tickets at the theater when he opened in *The Lion of the West* in 1831. Actor and comedian Frank Mayo discovered the same thing more than forty years later when he introduced *David Crockett; Or, Be Sure You're Right, Then Go Ahead* in 1872. The popularity of the play meant that Mayo would represent Crockett on stage in more than two thousand performances. After his death in 1896, Mayo's obituary in *The New York Times* noted, "his perfectly sympathetic and pictorially striking embodiment of this hero of the forest proved a bar to his ambition when he tired of the play. For ten years he was Davy Crockett and as Davy only the public recognized him."[9]

Crockett's first appearance as a character on the silver screen came on June 4, 1909 in *Davy Crockett – in Hearts United.* Actor Charles K. French portrayed the frontiersman, as did numerous other silent-film actors through the early years of film. Lance Chandler would be the first actor to portray

Crockett in a "talkie" in the 1926 film *Heroes of the Alamo*. Through the years, audiences would go on to cheer for and then mourn other "on-screen Davys" including Fess Parker, John Wayne, Johnny Cash, Billy Bob Thornton, and even cartoon character Bugs Bunny.

The biggest boost to Crockett's visibility in more modern popular culture came courtesy Walt Disney and comic author, film producer, and screenwriter Bill Walsh in 1955. Walsh brought the concept to Disney, who was looking for a hook for a segment of his *Disneyland* series on the ABC network that would also promote the theme park he was building. The episodes were filmed on location in the Great Smoky Mountains and in North Carolina. Disney spared no expense in producing the five episodes, the first of which premiered on December 15, 1954.

*Davy Crockett, Indian Fighter* aired to an audience of forty million. That means more than 70 percent of American households that owned a television that evening experienced the adventures of a frontier hero that took place more than a century earlier. As one would expect, liberties were taken with the historic story of David Crockett to package a "Technicolored-and-Disneyfied-Davy," ready for public consumption.

Fortunately, the authenticity of the props and costumes were taken into consideration as they produced the episodes. No doubt the costume designer took inspiration for Davy from the engraving of James Hackett as Nimrod Wildfire wearing a wildcat as a hat in *Lion of the West*. When they put the actor portraying Davy, Fess Parker, in a coonskin hat similar to Nimrod's, a product endorsement phenomenon was born.

After the enormous popularity of the episodes, children's coonskin caps sold at an average of five thousand per day. Journalist Mike Flanagan wrote about what happened next. "Merchandising not being the well-oiled animal it is today, retailers were at a loss when customers came in waving dollars, desperately seeking non-existent coonskin hats. In the ensuing madness, raccoon tails soared from 25 cents a pound to $8 and more. When the country's raccoon population couldn't meet the demand, hunters went after foxes and skunks."[10]

Suddenly, products bearing the likeness of Davy Crockett in his now-trademark coonskin cap, flooded the market. From wallets and action figures to purses and costumes, the children of the 1950s couldn't get enough.

Disney had only one problem; he only had five episodes of this hit show and his main character died in the end. So, he simply repackaged the episodes into a couple of feature-length films starring Fess Parker and Buddy Ebsen. Ebsen, who played Crockett's friend and sidekick Georgie Russell, would later find his own fame and fortune playing Jed Clampett on *The Beverly Hillbillies*. The two men even attended the opening of Disneyland where Walt Disney himself read aloud the plaque that appeared in front of Frontierland for the news cameras. It included the dedication, "… Frontierland is a tribute to the faith, courage and ingenuity of the pioneers who blazed the trails across America." In the grainy black-and-white footage from that day, you can see Parker and Ebsen making a dramatic entrance in character on horseback and being welcomed by Art Linkletter. After a sappy song and dance number that celebrated "Old Betsy," Parker and Ebsen departed and set off on a Davy Crockett promotional world tour through Europe, Japan, and the United States.

During Crockett's lifetime, blackface performers like Thomas Dartmouth Rice incorporated the frontiersman into their minstrel shows performances. Nearly 120 years after Crockett's death, on March 26, 1955, Bill Hayes's version of the *The Ballad of Davy Crockett* hit number one on the Billboard chart and stayed there for four weeks. Billboard later reported that the total sales of versions recorded by entertainers like Steve Allen, Burl Ives, Tennessee Ernie Ford, and others added up to eighteen million records sold in six months.

Today, David Crockett sightings take place mostly in history books or at various Texas or Tennessee memorials and tourist attractions. For now, at least, the Davy Crockett brand has lost most of the commercial power it had in the 1950s—with an occasional exception. Since Disneyland Paris opened in April 1992, guests can opt to stay in one of the 595 cabins at Disney's Davy Crockett Ranch where they can dine in Crockett's Tavern, shop at the Alamo Trading Post, and even try their hand in the arcade named the Lucky Racoon.

Those visiting Northwest Tennessee can follow in Crockett's footsteps, if they can find them. In *The Historic Reelfoot Lake Region*, David G. Hayes writes that Crockett's first home in Northwest Tennessee was neither in Carroll or Gibson Counties as many biographers claim.[11] Although initially part of Henry County when he moved there, parts of Crockett's eight hundred acres and the numerous cabins that he and his family lived in were in various counties at different times as boundaries were redrawn and new counties created. His eight hundred acres were in Henry County until boundaries were redrawn in October 1823, and it became part of Weakley County, which it remained until after his death. That area became Gibson County in 1837. Today, the site of his first cabin sits close to the intersections of Weakley, Obion, and Gibson Counties, near Rutherford, Tennessee.

In 1934, the president of the Rutherford Bank, Fred P. Elrod, heard that a farmer was making plans to tear down the last cabin that Crockett lived in before he departed Tennessee for the final time. Elrod and his friend, C. H. Sharp, paid twenty-five dollars for the cabin and moved the logs about four miles west to Rutherford, where they were stored until a suitable location could be found and funds raised to rebuild David Crockett's last cabin.

It took a couple of decades, but on March 6, 1956, then Tennessee Governor Frank Clement, known for his passionate, sermon-like speeches, was the keynote speaker at a dedication ceremony for a new cabin. The date was selected to coincide with the 120th anniversary of Crockett's death at the Alamo. The cabin they dedicated was similar to the homes early settlers built during Crockett's time and included some of those logs that Elrod and Sharp rescued twenty years earlier. National Guardsmen were on hand to fire a twenty-one-gun salute, and an American flag was raised by Crockett's great-great-grandson, J. D. Tate. Many other descendants from around the country also attended.

During another ceremony that day, a tombstone was unveiled for the fresh grave of Crockett's mother, Rebecca Hawkins Crockett. Her remains, previously in an unmarked grave on a nearby farm, had been reinterred next to the cabin.

Today, that cabin has been decorated with period furniture and memorabilia from many decades of Crockett celebrations and can still be visited by those curious about the frontiersman's final days in Tennessee.

Those who want to experience even more about his life and career will find Crockett well represented at Discovery Park of America just a few miles up the road in Union City, Tennessee. The museum and heritage park, opened in 2013 by philanthropists Robert and Jenny Kirkland, includes a statue of Crockett, reproductions of artifacts like "Old Betsy," an entire 1800s frontier cabin community, an exhibit on Crockett, and more.

The living legacy of Crockett himself can be found around the world through the descendants of of his six children and two stepchildren. All eight were living at the time of death at the Alamo.

John Wesley Crockett, his oldest son who had followed in his father's political footsteps, was twenty-eight at the time. He studied law with John C. Hamilton, the first circuit judge of Paris, Tennessee. In 1828, John Wesley married the judge's daughter, Martha, and began practicing law there himself. They would go on to have fourteen children together. John Wesley ran as a Whig in 1837 and defeated Adam Huntsman to represented the Twelfth District of West Tennessee in both the twenty-fifth and twenty-sixth sessions of Congress. Under his leadership, on February 18, 1841, a Tennessee land bill with concessions for squatters passed the House and the Senate and became law. After his congressional career ended in 1843, he moved his large family to New Orleans, where he held a position as Superintendent of Construction of Public Buildings and worked as editor of the *National* newspaper.

In 1850, John Wesley Crockett purchased the *Daily Crescent* and in 1851, began publishing it as the *New Orleans Daily Crescent.* It was noted by a minister who visited with John Wesley in New Orleans that he was not eager to discuss the myths that had grown up around his father. The minister wrote, "The son was sensitive about those caricatures that made his father the type of the western frontiersman; that had been pamphletted and circulated to the old gentleman's annoyance in his lifetime."

After nearly a decade in New Orleans, John Wesley Crockett moved to Memphis in 1852, where he died at the young age of forty-five on the day before Thanksgiving. He was buried in the Old City Cemetery in Paris,

Tennessee. Today, it is known as the Paris City Cemetery.

Crockett's next-to-oldest son, William Finley Crockett, was twenty-six years old when his father died. He married Clorinda Boyett in 1830. William died in Saline County, Arkansas in 1846 at age thirty-six.

Oldest daughter, Margaret Finley Crockett Flowers, to whom Crockett wrote his last letter, was twenty-three years old at the time of her father's death. She married Wiley Flowers in Gibson County on March 22, 1830 and made that her home. She died in the town of Kenton in 1860 at the age of forty-eight.

Robert Patton Crockett was nineteen years old when his father died. As the first-born son of the union between David Crockett and his second wife, Elizabeth Patton Crockett, Robert not only avenged his father's death, but he also remained close to and cared for his mother until her death. After David Crockett was killed at the Alamo, Robert joined the Texas Revolution and fought until Texas won its independence. He returned to Tennessee and married Matilda Porter in 1841, then, then married Louisa Wohlford after Matilda's death in 1864.

Rebecca Elvira Crockett, who went by the nickname "Sissy," was seventeen years old when her father died. She married George Kimbrough in 1839 in Gibson County, Tennessee and later married Baptist minister James Halford.

Matilda Crockett, the youngest of Crockett's children, was fourteen years old when he died. Many years later, she shared with a reporter her memories of her father's departure for Texas. She said, "He seemed very confident the morning he went away that he would soon have us all join him in Texas." During her life, she married three men: Thomas Tyson, James Wilson, and Redden Fields. She never joined her family in Texas and died in 1890 at the age of sixty-eight in Gibson County, Tennessee.

When David Crockett married Elizabeth Patton, he became a step-father to her two young children, George Patton and Margaret, who was nicknamed "Peggy Ann." George was twenty-six years old when his stepfather died at the Alamo. He married his cousin, Rhoda Ann McWhorter. She was a daughter of his mother's sister, Anna Catherine Patton McWhorter, who had joined the Crocketts in Northwest Tennessee. George Patton died in 1880 at the age of seventy. His sister, Peggy Ann, also married one of the McWhorter cousins, Hance Alexander McWhorter III. He was Rhoda Ann McWhorter Patton's brother. Peggy Ann McWhorter died in 1884 at age seventy-three in Carroll County, Tennessee.

In his quest for fame and fortune, David Crockett was absent for much of his children's lives, and while he certainly found fame, the fortune proved to be more elusive. Perhaps hoping to make up for his shortcomings, in his last letter he wrote that he hoped Texas would provide "a fortune" for his family. Ironically, because of his death at the Alamo, Texas would eventually do just that.

Several members of the Crockett and Patton families joined 65-year-old matriarch Elizabeth Crockett in migrating west to Texas in the mid-1850s. Included in the group were sons Robert Crockett and George Patton and daughter Rebecca Crockett Halford and their immediate families.

Once they arrived to what David Crockett had described in the letter to his daughter Margaret as "the garden spot of the world," they settled in Ellis County, Texas. They then moved eighty-five miles west and built cabins on Rucker's Creek in Johnson County, Texas (later known as Hood County) near a town called Action, just thirty-four miles southwest of present-day Fort Worth. Rebecca's husband, James Halford, became minister of the Harmony Baptist Church in that community, a position he held until he died fighting in the Civil War.

On February 2, 1856, the Texas state legislature passed an act giving Elizabeth 4,428 acres of land to honor her late husband's sacrifice. They also allowed her to claim 320 of those acres in Johnson County where she was living. She sold the remainder of the land for $1,000. David Crockett had finally provided a fortune for his family, albeit a small one. Today, that would be the equivalent of around $35,000.

Harmony Baptist Church later became the Action Baptist Church, and many Crockett and Patton family members, including Elizabeth, are buried in the church's cemetery. By 1889, Robert was the last of David Crockett's children still living when he died of injuries sustained after a team of runaway horses caused him to be thrown from a wagon. He was buried in the cemetery with his mother and sister. In 1913, the state of Texas placed a large granite monument dedicated to pioneer women at Elizabeth Crockett's grave.

Long ago, the mythical Davy Crockett of fiction replaced the real David Crockett of history for many. But would it even matter to him? Probably not. Of course, it's impossible to know exactly how David Crockett himself would want to be remembered or how he would have answered the question from Bart Simpson that began this book. Perhaps the best way to remember David Crockett is with his own words included at the end of that last known letter, written to his family on January 9, 1836, only months before his death:

> I am rejoiced at my fate. I had rather be in my present situation than to be elected to a seat in Congress for life. I hope you will all do the best you can and I will do the same. Do not be uneasy about me. I am among friends.

**Epilogue Notes**

1. Richard Penn Smith, *Col. Crockett's Exploits and Adventures in Texas* (Nafis & Cornish: New York, 1845), 204.
2. Ibid., 205.
3. Richard M. Dorson, *Davy Crockett, American Comic Legend* (Rockland Editions: New York ,1939), xiii.
4. Ibid., Editor's note
5. Harry J. Owens and Franklin Julius Meine, The Crockett Almanacks (Chicago: Caxton Club, 1955), vi.
6. George Bird Grinnell and Theodore Roosevelt, *American Big-Game Hunting, The Book of the Boone and Crockett Club* (Edinburgh: David Douglass, 1893), 320.
7. Vizetelly, Arthur. "Some Notable Dwarfs." The English Illustrated Magazine, v. 22 (1900): 487.
8. Van Wyck Brooks, *The World of Washington Irving* (Boston: E. P. Duttong & Company, Inc., 1944), 298.
9. "Death of Frank Mayo," *The New York Times*. June 9, 1896, 5.
10. Mike Flanagan, "Kids Went Davy Crockett Crazy," *South Florida Sun Sentinel*, June 23, 1985.
11. David G. Hayes, *The Historic Reelfoot Lake Region: An Early History of the People and Places of Western Obion County and Present Day Lake County* (Collierville, Tennessee: InstantPublisher.com, 2017), 48-50.

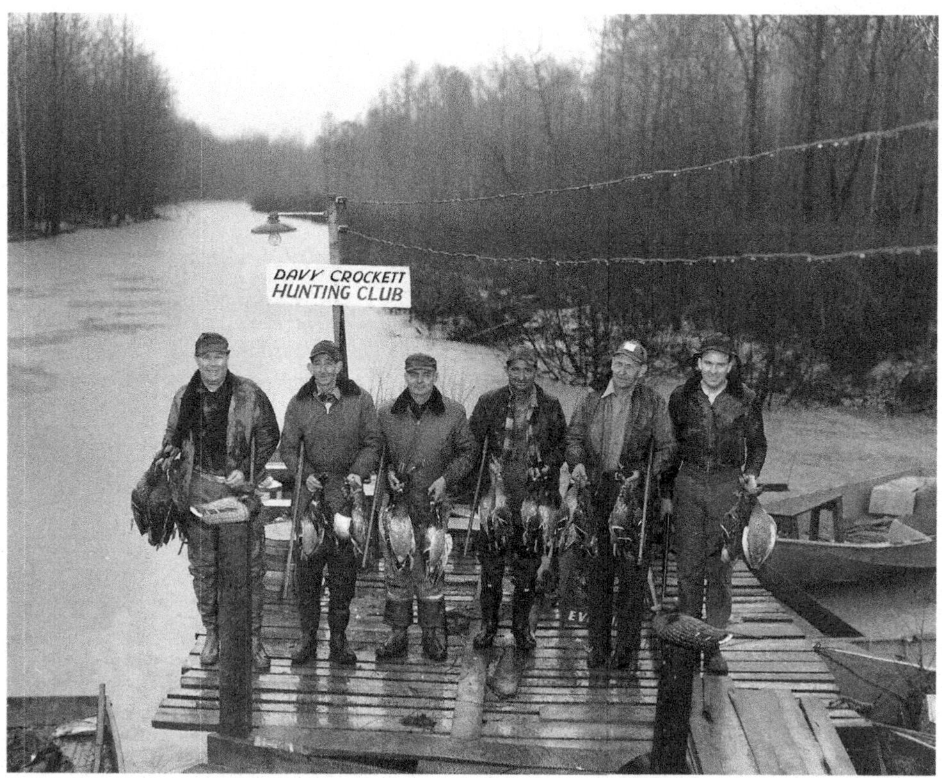


*Courtesy Tennessee State Library and Archives*

The Davy Crockett Hunting Club was established in 1947 by Ralph Morton and Earl Houston on a 2,000-acre tract in the Obion River bottom. At the time, Morton was the owner of the Davy Crockett Hotel in Union City, Tennessee. Pictured on the Obion River in 1948 is, left to right, Gordon Browning who served as the Governor of Tennessee from 1937 to 1939 and again from 1949 to 1953; Sharpie Shaw, celebrated Reelfoot Lake guide; Ralph Morton; Grady Hardin; and two unidentified duck hunters. Today, the Davy Crockett Hunting Club remains one of the most prestigious clubs in the sport.

# Addendum

# Images of David Crockett

This mezzotint was produced in 1839 by Charles Gilbert Stuart. It was based on the life-size portrait painted by John Gadsby Chapman in 1834. While the original painting was destroyed in a fire in 1881 in the Texas State Capitol in Austin, a small version also painted by Chapman exists.

*National Portrait Gallery*

James Hamilton Shegogue painted this watercolor of Crockett in 1831.

*Log Cabin Village*

This photograph is of a portrait painted in oil by an unkown artist around 1830. The original was owned by Crockett's son, Robert Patton Crockett, but was lost in the same 1881 fire that destroyed the Chapman painting. This photograph was discovered in 2016 in the collection of Log Cabin Village, a museum in Ft. Worth, Texas.

*Library of Congress*

This 1834 lithograph by Albert Newsam was based on a portrait by Samuel Stillman Osgood. An engraving of the portrait was used as the frontispiece in Crockett's book about his tour of the East. The lithograph was widely circulated and included Crockett's "Go Ahead" catchphrase.

*The Ernst Wilhelm Raba Photograph Collection*

This was the first portrait of Crockett painted by John Gadsby Chapman in 1834.

*Library of Congress*

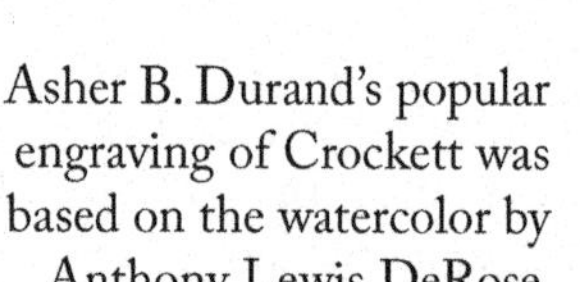

Asher B. Durand's popular engraving of Crockett was based on the watercolor by Anthony Lewis DeRose.

*Dallas Museum of Art*

William Henry Huddle painted this oil painting of Crockett in 1889. It currently hangs in the Texas State Capitol.

*National Portrait Gallery*

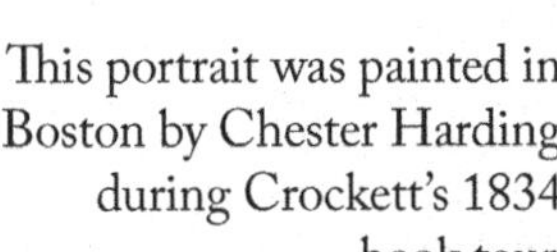

This portrait was painted in Boston by Chester Harding during Crockett's 1834 book tour.

## The Ballad of Davy Crockett

Music by George Bruns, lyrics by Thomas W. Blackburn

Born on a mountain top in Tennessee,
Greenest state in the land of the free.
Raised in the woods so's he knew every tree,
Killed him a bear when he was only three.
Davy, Davy Crockett King of the Wild Frontier.

He fought single handed through the Injun war,
Till the Creeks was whipped and peace was restored.
And while he was handling this risky chore,
Made himself a legend, forevermore.
Davy, Davy Crockett the man who don't know fear.

When he lost his love, and his grief was gall,
In his heart he wanted to leave it all,
And lose himself in the forest tall,
But he answered instead, his country's call.
Davy, Davy Crockett, the choice of the whole frontier.

He went off to Congress and served a spell
Fixin' up the government and laws as well.
Took over Washington, so we hear tell,
And patched up the crack in the Liberty Bell.
Davy, Davy Crockett, seein' his duty clear. (Serving his country well)

When he come home, his politickin' done,
The western march had just begun.
So he packed his gear, and his trusty gun
And lit out a grinnin' to follow the sun.
Davy, Davy Crockett, Leadin the Pioneers.

His land is biggest, and his land is best
From grassy plains to the mountain crest
He's ahead of us all in meeting the test
Followin' his legend right into the West
Davy, Davy Crockett, King of the Wide Frontier
King of the Wild Frontier.

Introduced on ABC's television series *Disneyland* in the premiere episode on October 27, 1954.

*Davy Crockett* was a five-part series staring Fess Parker that first aired on ABC from 1954–1955 as part of the *Disneyland* series. Crockett's explosion of popularity surprised even Walt Disney. He capitalized on the success of the series and the "coonskin cap" fad it inspired by launching a licensed product campaign that featured more than three thousand products in every category imaginable.

## The Book of Chronicles, West of Tennessee, and East of the Mississippi Rivers

By Adam Huntsman, 1786-1849

1. And it came to pass in those days, when Andrew was chief ruler over the children of Columbia, that there arose a mighty man in the river country, whose name was David; he belonged to the tribe of Tennessee, which lay upon the border of the Mississippi and over against Kentucky.

2. Now David was chief of the hosts of Forked Deer, and Obion, and round about the Hatchee and the Mississippi Rivers; and behold his fame had spread abroad throughout all the land of Columbia, insomuch that there were none to be found like unto him for wisdom and valor; no, not one in all the land.

3. David was a man wise in council, smooth in speech, valiant in war, and of fair countenance and goodly stature; such was the terror of his exploits, that thousands of wild cats and panthers did quake and tremble at his name.

4. And it came to pass that David was chosen by the people in the river country, to go with the wise men of the tribe of Tennessee to the grand Sanhedrim, held yearly in the twelfth month, and on the first Monday in the month, at the city of Washington, where the wise men from the east, from the west, from the north, and from the south, gathered themselves together to consult on the welfare of Columbia and her twenty-four tribes.

5. In those days there were many occupants spread abroad throughout the river country: these men loved David exceedingly, because he promised to give them lands flowing with milk and honey.

6. And it came to pass in the 54th year after the children of Columbia had escaped from British bondage, and on the first month, when Andrew and the wise men and rulers of the people were assembled in the great Sanhedrim, that David, arose in the midst of them, saying, Men and brethren, wot ye not

that there are many occupants in the river country on the west border of the tribe of Tennessee, who are settled down upon lands belonging to Columbia; now I beseech you give unto these men each a portion for his inheritance, so that his soul may be glad, and he will bless you and your posterity.

7. But the wise men from the South, the Southeast, the West, and the middle country, arose with one accord, and said, Lo! Brethren, this cannot be done. The thing which our brother David asketh is unjust; the like never hath been done in the land of Columbia. If we give the lands away, it must be to the tribe of Tennessee; so that they may deal with the occupants as it may seem good in their sight. This has been the practice in old times, and with our fathers, and we will not depart therefrom. Furthermore, we cannot give this land away until the warrants are satisfied.

8. Behold, when David heard these sayings, he was exceeding wroth against the wise men and the rulers of the congregation, and against Andrew, and made a vow unto the Lord that he would be avenged of them. Then John, one of the wise men of the tribe of Tennessee, who lived at the rocky city, arose in the midst, and said. If we give this land unto the occupants instead of the tribe, all the occupants in the land of Columbia will beseech us for lands, and there will be none left to pay the debt which redeemed us from bondage; no, not an acre: and this saying pleased the wise men and the rulers, and they did accordingly.

9. Now there were in these days wicked men, sons of Belial, to wit: the Claytonites, the Holmesites, Burgessites, the Everettites, the Chiltonites, and the Bartonites, who were of the tribes of Maine, Massachusetts, Rhode Island, Kentucky and Missouri, and who hated Andrew and his friends of old times, because the children of Columbia had chosen him to rule over them instead of Henry, whose surname was Clay, whom they desired for their chief ruler.

10. And lo, when those men saw that David was sorely troubled in spirit, they communed one with another, and said, Is this not David from the river country

in the west, who of old times was very valiant for Andrew to be ruler, and who perplexed our ranks in the Sanhedrim, and who was foremost in battle against our great chiefs Henry and John Q. when they were defeated by Andrew? Now Tristram, whose surname was Burgess, answered and said, Men and brethren, as the Lord liveth it is he.

11. Then Daniel, whose surname was Webster, and who was a prophet of the order of Balaam, said. Let us comfort David in his afflictions; his wrath is kindled against Andrew and his friends, and against the wise men of Tennessee; peradventure he will come over to us at the next election to fight for Henry against Andrew; and Thomas, whose surname was Chilton, said, Thou speaketh wisely; let what thou sayest be done according to thy words.

12. Then Daniel drew nigh unto David and said unto him, Wherefore, O my brother, dost thou seem sad and sorrowful? Why is thy soul bowed down with affliction? Hath the hand of the Lord smote heavily upon thee? Have famine and pestilence destroyed thy land and all thy beloved occupants? Or have the wise men and rulers been unkind to thee? I pray thee tell me, and I will comfort thee.

13. And David lifted up his eyes and wept, and said, O, Daniel! Live forever. If the wise men and rulers had given my occupants the lands according to the manner I beseeched them, I could have been wise man and chief ruler in the river country for life. But if I join the wise men and give it to the state of Tennessee, then they will share the honor with me, and the council of the state of Tennessee will give it to the occupants at twelve and one-half cents per acre, and they will receive the honor instead of me; then the people of the river country will not have me for their wise man and chief ruler forever, and it grieveth me sore,

14. And Daniel answered and said unto David, Swear unto me that thou and all thy people in the river country will come over unto me and fight with me at the next election against Andrew and his people, in favor of Henry for chief

ruler of Columbia; then I will help thee to get the land, for thine occupants; and David swore accordingly, and there is a league existing between them even unto this day.

15. Now there was a man in the river country, about the centre way thereof, whose name was William. He loved David as he loved his own soul; his soul and David's were knit as though they were but one; he was David's chief counsellor. When David wept, he wept; when David rejoiced, he rejoiced; if David bade him go, he went; if David bade him come, he came.

16. So it came to pass when David returned from the great Sanhedrim, that William ran and fell upon his neck and wept for joy; then David said unto him, I have been discomfited in all my plans; I could not get my beloved occupants their lands without dividing the honor with the wise men of my state, and giving it to the whole tribe of the Tennessee; I wot not but the council would give it to them as cheap as I, but it would rob me of the honor, and then I cannot be wise man and chief ruler for life; I have therefore engaged to forsake Andrew and join the ranks of Henry, for the chief ruler over the children of Columbia----for the wise men of my tribe and the friends of Andrew have forsaken me. Wilt thou, in whom my soul delighteth, go with me in these things?

17. And William answered, and said, Where thou goest, I will go; where thou stayest, I will stay; what thou doest, I will do; and I will have none other God but thee----when I forsake thee, let the Lord forsake me, do as thou wilt.

18. And David said unto William, Draw near unto me; I will counsel thee, for thou art my beloved disciple, in whom I am well pleased. Go thou through all the river country, and every neighborhood thereof; tell the people I will be elected by five thousand votes. As thou art a Baptist, they will put trust in thee.

19. If thou dost come to a people who knoweth thee not, if they are for me, say unto them, be strong and valiant on the day of the election;----if they

are against me, say unto them thou art against me also----but that thou hast been all through the river country, and I will be elected by a mighty host: this will terrify them, and they will join me. If thou shalt come to an ignorant people, say unto them my adversary is guilty of corruption. If a Jackson man approaches thee, say unto him I have always been for Jackson.

20. If a Clay man encounter thee, then mayest thou tell him of the bargain with Daniel. If a Baptist greet thee, say unto him I am religiously disposed and think highly of the Baptists. If a Methodist shall enquire of thee, say unto him I always attend their camp-meetings. If a Cumberland Presbyterian shall call upon thee, say unto him I have joined his society.

21. But be thou circumspect in all things, and do not say unto the people that I have franked sack-bags full of books into the river country, against Andrew, at their expense. Thou shalt not say unto the people that I have franked Hume's History of England, or a sack of feathers; be careful to inform Roland, the High Priest, of all these things, so that he may direct the congregation accordingly.

22. Remember now, my beloved disciple, that I am thy light and thy life; I have sent thee big coats, bibles, hymn books, and many articles from the great Sanhedrim, for thyself and family. I will send thee many other things if thou art faithful unto the end. Go forth, and the Lord prosper thee.

23. And William went unto all the river country and did according to all that David commanded him; but the people were a stiff-necked generation, and would not agree that David should bring Henry to be chief ruler over the children of Columbia instead of Andrew; but with one accord said unto William, David hath beguiled us, we will desert him and stick to Andrew, who hath brought us out of British bondage----and we will vote for William, whose surname is Fitzgerald----and the people all said, Amen!

COMMUNICATIONS.

For the Southern Statesman.

*The Book of Chronicles, West of the Tennessee and East of the Mississippi rivers.*

1. And it came to pass in those days when Andrew was chief ruler over the children of Columbia, that there arose a mighty man in the river country, whose name was David; he belonged to the tribe of Tennessee, which lay upon the border of the Mississippi and over against Kentucky.

2. Now David was chief of the hosts of Forked Deer, and Obion, and around about the Hachie, and the Mississippi rivers, and behold his fame had spread abroad throughout all the land of Columbia, insomuch, that there was none to be found like unto him, for wisdom and valour; no, not one in all the land.

3. David was a man wise in council, smooth in speech, valiant in war, and of fair countenance and goodly stature, such was the terror of his exploits, that thousands of wild cats and panthers did quake and tremble at his name.

4. And it came to pass that David was chosen by the people in the river country, to go with the wise men of the tribe of Tennessee to the grand Sanhedrim held yearly in the twelth month, and on the first Monday in the month, at the city of Washington, where the wise men from the east, from the west, from the north and from the south, gathered themselves together to consult on the welfare of Columbia and her twenty four tribes.

5. In those days there were many occupants spread abroad throughout the river country; these men loved David exceedingly, because he promised to give them lands flowing with milk and honey.

6. And it came to pass in the 54th year after the children of Columbia had escaped from British bondage, and on the first month, when Andrew and the wise men and rulers of the people were assembled in the great Sanhedrim, that David arose in the midst of them saying, *Men and brethren, wot ye not that there are ma-*

17. And William answered, and said, Where thou goest I will go; where thou stayest, I will stay, what thou doest, I will do; and will have none other God but thee—when I forsake thee, let the Lord forsake me, do as thou wilt.

18. And David said unto William, draw near unto me, I will counsel thee, for thou art my beloved disciple, in whom I am well pleased. Go thou through all the river country, and every neighborhood thereof, tell the people I will be elected by five thousand votes, as though art a baptist, they will put trust in thee.

19. If thou dost come to a people who knoweth thee not, if they are for me, say unto them be strong and valiant on the day of the election; if they are against me, say unto them thou art against me also, but thou hast been all through the river country and I will be elected by a mighty host, this will terrify them and they will join me; If thou shalt come to an ignorant people, say unto them my adversary is guilty of corruption; If a Jackson man approach thee say unto him, I have always been for Jackson.

20. If a Clay man encounter thee then mayest thou tell him of the bargain with Daniel; If a baptist greet thee, say unto him, I am religiously disposed and think highly of the baptists; If a methodist shall enquire of thee, say unto him I always attend their camp-meetings; If cumberland Presbyterian shall call upon thee say unto him I have joined his society.

21. But be thou circumspect in all things, and do not say unto the people that I have franked sack bags full of books into the river country against Andrew at their expense. Thou shalt not say unto the people that I have franked Humes' history of England or a sack of feathers; be careful to inform Roland, the High Priest, of all these things, so that he may direct his congregation accordingly.

22. Remember now, my beloved disciple, that I am thy light and thy life; I have sent thee big coats, bibles, hymn books, and many articles from the great Sanhedrim, for thyself and family; I will send thee many other things if thou art faithful unto the end; go forth, and the lord prosper thee.

A section of "The Book of Chronicles, West of Tennessee, and East of the Mississippi River" by Adam Huntsman as it appeared in the *Southern Statesman* of Jackson, Tennessee on June 25, 1831.

## President Andrew Jackson's 1830 Message to Congress 'On Indian Removal'

*On December 6, 1830, in his annual message to Congress, President Andrew Jackson updated Congress on the staus of his plan for the removal of Indian tribes living east of the Mississippi River to unsettled land in the west.*

It gives me pleasure to announce to Congress that the benevolent policy of the Government, steadily pursued for nearly thirty years, in relation to the removal of the Indians beyond the white settlements is approaching to a happy consummation. Two important tribes have accepted the provision made for their removal at the last session of Congress, and it is believed that their example will induce the remaining tribes also to seek the same obvious advantages.

The consequences of a speedy removal will be important to the United States, to individual States, and to the Indians themselves. The pecuniary advantages which it promises to the Government are the least of its recommendations. It puts an end to all possible danger of collision between the authorities of the General and State Governments on account of the Indians. It will place a dense and civilized population in large tracts of country now occupied by a few savage hunters. By opening the whole territory between Tennessee on the north and Louisiana on the south to the settlement of the whites it will incalculably strengthen the southwestern frontier and render the adjacent States strong enough to repel future invasions without remote aid. It will relieve the whole State of Mississippi and the western part of Alabama of Indian occupancy, and enable those States to advance rapidly in population, wealth, and power. It will separate the Indians from immediate contact with settlements of whites; free them from the power of the States; enable them to pursue happiness in their own way and under their own rude institutions; will retard the progress of decay, which is lessening their numbers, and perhaps cause them gradually, under the protection of the Government and through the influence of good counsels, to cast off their savage habits and become an interesting, civilized, and Christian community.

What good man would prefer a country covered with forests and ranged by a few thousand savages to our extensive Republic, studded with cities, towns, and prosperous farms embellished with all the improvements which art can devise or industry execute, occupied by more than 12,000,000 happy people, and filled with all the blessings of liberty, civilization and religion?

The present policy of the Government is but a continuation of the same progressive change by a milder process. The tribes which occupied the countries now constituting the Eastern States were annihilated or have melted away to make room for the whites. The waves of population and civilization are rolling to the westward, and we now propose to acquire the countries occupied by the red men of the South and West by a fair exchange, and, at the expense of the United States, to send them to land where their existence may be prolonged and perhaps made perpetual.

Doubtless it will be painful to leave the graves of their fathers; but what do they more than our ancestors did or than our children are now doing? To better their condition in an unknown land our forefathers left all that was dear in earthly objects. Our children by thousands yearly leave the land of their birth to seek new homes in distant regions. Does Humanity weep at these painful separations from everything, animate and inanimate, with which the young heart has become entwined? Far from it. It is rather a source of joy that our country affords scope where our young population may range unconstrained in body or in mind, developing the power and facilities of man in their highest perfection. These remove hundreds and almost thousands of miles at their own expense, purchase the lands they occupy, and support themselves at their new homes from the moment of their arrival. Can it be cruel in this Government when, by events which it cannot control, the Indian is made discontented in his ancient home to purchase his lands, to give him a new and extensive territory, to pay the expense of his removal, and support him a year in his new abode? How many thousands of our own people would gladly embrace the opportunity of removing to the West on such conditions! If the offers made to the Indians were extended to them, they would be hailed with gratitude and joy.

And is it supposed that the wandering savage has a stronger attachment to his home than the settled, civilized Christian? Is it more afflicting to him to leave the graves of his fathers than it is to our brothers and children? Rightly considered, the policy of the General Government toward the red man is not only liberal, but generous. He is unwilling to submit to the laws of the States and mingle with their population. To save him from this alternative, or perhaps utter annihilation, the General Government kindly offers him a new home, and proposes to pay the whole expense of his removal and settlement.

## A Sketch of the Remarks of the Hon. David Crockett, Representative From Tennessee, on the Bill for the Removal of the Indians

*Made in the House of Representatives, Wednesday, May 19, 1830*

Mr. Crockett said, that, considering his very humble abilities, it might be expected that he should content himself with a silent vote; but, situated as he was, in relation to his colleagues, he felt it to be a duty to himself to explain the motives which governed him in the vote he should give on this bill. Gentlemen had already discussed the treaty-making power; and had done it much more ably than he could pretend to do. He should not therefore enter on that subject, but would merely make an explanation as to the reasons of his vote, He did not know whether a man (that is, a member of Congress) within 500 miles of his residence would give a similar vote; but he knew, at the same time, that he should give that vote with a clear conscience. He had his constituents to settle with, he was aware; and should like to please them as well as other gentlemen; but he had also a settlement to make at the bar of his God; and what his conscience dictated to be just and right he would do, be the consequences what they might. He believed that the people who had been kind enough to give him their suffrages, supposed him to be an honest man, or they would not have chosen him.

If so, they could not but expect that he should act in the way he thought honest and right. He had always viewed the native Indian tribes of this country as a sovereign people. He believed they had been recognised as such from the very foundation of this government, and the United States were bound by treaty to protect them; it was their duty to do so.

And as to giving the money of the American people for the purpose of removing them in the manner proposed, he would not do it. He would do that only for which he could answer to his God. Whether he could answer it before the people was comparatively nothing, though it was a great satisfaction to him to have the approbation of his constituents.

Mr. C. said he had served for seven years in a legislative body. But from the first hour he had entered a legislative hall, he had never known what party was in legislation; and God forbid he ever should. He went for the good of the country, and for that only. What he did as a legislator, he did conscientiously. He should love to go with his colleagues, and with the West and the South generally, if he could; but he never would let party govern him in a question of this great consequence.

He had many objections to the bill—some of them of a very serious character. One was, that he did not like to put half a million of money into the hands of the Executive, to be used in a manner which nobody could foresee, and which Congress was not to control. Another objection was, he did not wish to depart from from the foundation of the government. He considered the present application as the last alternative for these poor remnants of a once powerful people. Their only chance of aid was at the hands of Congress. Should its members turn a deaf ear to their cries, misery must be their fate. That was his candid opinion.

Mr. C. said he was often forcibly reminded of the remark made by the famous Red Jacket, in the rotundo of this building, where he was shown the pannel which represented in sculpture the first landing of the Pilgrims, with an Indian chief presenting to them an ear of corn, in token of friendly welcome. The aged Indian said "that was good." The Indian said, he knew that they came from the Great Spirit, and he was willing to share the soil with his brothers from over the great water. But when he turned round to another pannel representing Penn's treaty, he said "Ah! all's gone now." There was a great deal of truth in this short saying; and the present bill was a strong commentary upon it.

Mr. C. said that four counties of his district bordered on the Chickasaw country. He knew many of their tribe; and nothing should ever induce him to vote to drive them west of the Mississippi. He did not know what sort of a country it was in which they were to be settled. He would willingly appropriate money in order to send proper persons to examine the country. And when this had been done, and a fair and free treaty had been made with the tribes if they were desirous of removing, he would vote an appropriation of any sum necessary; but till this had been done, he would not vote one cent. He could not clearly understand the extent of this bill. It seemed to go to the removal of all the Indians, in any State east of the Mississippi river, in which the United States owned any land; Now, there was a considerable number of them still neglected; there was a considerable number of them in Tennessee, and the United States' government owned no land in that State, north and east of the congressional reservation line. No man could be more willing to see them remove than he was if it could be done in a manner agreeable to themselves; but not otherwise. He knew personally that a part of the tribe of the Cherokees were unwilling to go.

When the proposal was made to them, they said, ``No; we will take death here at our homes. Let them come and tomahawk us here at home: we are willing to die, but never to remove." He had heard them use this language. Many different constructions might be put upon this bill. One of the first things which had set him against the bill, was the letter from the secretary of war to colonel Montgomery--from which it appeared that the Indians had been intruded upon. Orders had been issued to turn them all off except the heads of the Indian families, or such as possessed improvements Government had taken measures to purchase land from the Indians who had gone to Arkansas. If this bill should pass, the same plan would be carried further; they would send and buy them out, and put white men upon their land. It had never been known that white men and Indians could live together; and in this case, the Indians were to have no privileges allowed them, while the white men were to have all. Now, if this was not oppression with a vengeance, he did not know what was.

It was the language of the bill, and of its friends, that the Indians were not to be driven off against their will. He knew the Indians were unwilling to go: and therefore he could not consent to place them in a situation where they would be obliged to go. He could not stand that. He knew that he stood alone, having, perhaps, none of his colleagues from his state agreeing in sentiment. He could not help that. He knew that he should return to his home glad and light in heart, if he voted against the bill. He felt that it was his wish and purpose to serve his constituents honestly, according to the light of his conscience. The moment he should exchange his conscience for mere party views, he hoped his Maker would no longer suffer him to exist. He spoke the truth in saying so.

If he should be the only member of that House who voted against the bill, and the only man in the United States who disapproved it, he would still vote against it; and it would be matter of rejoicing to him till the day he died, that he had given the vote. He had been told that he should be prostrated; but if so, he would have the consolation of conscience. He would obey that power, and gloried in the deed. He cared not for popularity, unless it could be obtained by upright means. He had seen much to disgust him here; and he did not wish to represent his fellow citizens, unless he could be permitted to act conscientiously. He had been told that he did not understand English grammar. That was very true. He had never been six months at school in his life; he had raised himself by the labor of his hands. But he did not, on that account, yield upon his privilege as the representative of freemen on this floor. Humble as he was, he meant to exercise his privilege. He had been charged with not representing his constituents. If the fact was so, the error (said Mr. C.) is here, (touching his head) not here (laying his hand upon his heart). He never had possessed wealth or education, but he had ever been animated by an independent spirit; and he trusted to prove it on the present occasion.

*Speeches on the Passage of the Bill for the Removal of the Indians*
Perkins and Marvin, 1830

## Northwest Tennessee Bear Hunting in 1834

*Except from "David Crockett, A Narrative of the Life of David Crockett of the State of Tennessee"*

I worked on with my hands till the bears got fat, and then I turned out to hunting, to lay in a supply of meat. I soon killed and salted down as many as were necessary for my family; but about this time one of my old neighbours, who had settled down on the lake about twenty-five miles from me, came to my house and told me he wanted me to go down and kill some bears about in his parts. He said they were extremely fat, and very plenty. I know'd that when they were fat, they were easily taken, for a fat bear can't run fast or long. But I asked a bear no favours, no way, further than civility, for I now had eight large dogs, and as fierce as painters; so that a bear stood no chance at all to get away from them.

So I went home with him, and then went on down towards the Mississippi, and commenced hunting. We were out two weeks, and in that time killed fifteen bears. Having now supplied my friend with plenty of meat, I engaged occasionally again with my hands in our boat building and getting staves. But I at length couldn't stand it any longer without another hunt. So I concluded to take my little son, and cross over the lake, and take a hunt there. We got over, and that evening turned out and killed three bears, in little or no time. The next morning we drove up four forks, and made a sort of scaffold, on which we salted up our meat, so as to have it out of the reach of the wolves, for as soon as we would leave our camp, they would take possession.

We had just eat our breakfast, when a company of hunters came to our camp, who had fourteen dogs, but all so poor, that when they would bark they would almost have to lean up against a tree and take a rest. I told them their dogs couldn't run in smell of a bear, and they had better stay at my camp, and feed them on the bones I had cut out of my meat. I left them there, and cut out; but I hadn't gone far, when my dogs took a first-rate start after a very large fat old he-bear, which run right plump towards my camp.

I pursued on, but my other hunters had heard my dogs coming, and met them, and killed the bear before I got up with him. I gave him to them, and cut out again for a creek called Big Clover, which wa'n't very far off. Just as I got there, and was entering a cane brake, my dogs all broke and went ahead, and, in a little time, they raised a fuss in the cane, and seemed to be going every way. I listened a while, and found my dogs was in two companies, and that both was in a snorting fight. I sent my little son to one, and I broke for t'other. I got to mine first, and found my dogs had a two-year-old bear down, a-wooling away on him; so I just took out my big butcher, and went up and slap'd it into him, and killed him without shooting.

There was five of the dogs in my company. In a short time, I heard my little son fire at his bear; when I went to him he had killed it too. He had two dogs in his team. Just at this moment we heard my other dog barking a short distance off, and all the rest immediately broke to him. We pushed on too, and when we got there, we found he had still a larger bear than either of them we had killed, treed by himself. We killed that one also, which made three we had killed in less than half an hour. We turned in and butchered them, and then started to hunt for water, and a good place to camp.

But we had no sooner started, than our dogs took a start after another one, and away they went like a thunder-gust, and was out of hearing in a minute. We followed the way they had gone for some time, but at length we gave up the hope of finding them, and turned back. As we were going back, I came to where a poor fellow was grubbing, and he looked like the very picture of hard times. I asked him what he was doing away there in the woods by himself? He said he was grubbing for a man who intended to settle there; and the reason why he did it was, that he had no meat for his family, and he was working for a little.

I was mighty sorry for the poor fellow, for it was not only a hard, but a very slow way to get meat for a hungry family; so I told him if he would go with me, I would give him more meat than he could get by grubbing in a month. I intended to supply him with meat, and also to get him to assist my little boy in packing in and salting up my bears. He had never seen a bear killed in his life. I told him I had six killed then, and my dogs were hard after another. He went off to his little cabin, which was a short distance in the brush, and his wife was very anxious he should go with me. So we started and went to where I had left my three bears, and made a camp. We then gathered my meat and salted, and scuffled it, as I had done the other. Night now came on, but no word from my dogs yet. I afterwards found they had treed the bear about five miles off, near to a man's house, and had barked at it the whole enduring night. Poor fellows! many a time they looked for me, and wondered why I didn't come, for they knowed there was no mistake in me, and I know i they were as good as ever fluttered. In the morning, as soon as it was light enough to see, the man took his gun and went to them, and shot the bear, and killed it. My dogs, however, wouldn't have anything to say to this stranger; so they left him, and came early in the morning back to me.

We got our breakfast, and cut out again; and we killed four large and very fat bears that day. We hunted out the week, and in that time we killed seventeen, all of them first-rate. When we closed our hunt, I gave the man over a thousand weight of fine fat bear-meat, which pleased him mightily, and made him feel as rich as a Jew. I saw him the next fall, and he told me he had plenty of meat to do him the whole year from his week's hunt. My son and me now went home. This was the week between Christmas and New-year that we made this hunt.

When I got home, one of my neighbours was out of meat, and wanted me to go back, and let him go with me, to take another hunt. I couldn't refuse; but I told him I was afraid the bear had taken to house by that time, for after they get very fat in the fall and early part of the winter, they go into their holes, in large hollow trees, or into hollow logs, or their cane-houses, or the hurricanes; and lie there till spring, like frozen snakes. And one thing about this will seem mighty strange to many people. From about the first of January to about the last of April, these varments lie in their holes altogether. In all that time they have no food to eat; and yet when they come out, they are not an ounce lighter than when they went to house.

I don't know the cause of this, and still I know it is a fact; and I leave it for others who have more learning than myself to account for it. They have not a particle of food with them, but they just lie and suck the bottom of their paw all the time. I have killed many of them in their trees, which enables me to speak positively on this subject. However, my neighbour, whose name was McDaniel, and my little son and me, went on down to the lake to my second camp, where I had killed my seventeen bears the week before, and turned out to hunting. But we hunted hard all day without getting a single start. We had carried but little provisions with us, and the next morning was entirely out of meat. I sent my son about three miles off, to the house of an old friend, to get some. The old gentle- man was much pleased to hear I was hunting in those parts, for the year before the bears had killed a great many of his hags. He was that day killing his bacon hogs, and so he gave my son some meat, and sent word to me that I must come in to his house that evening that he would have plenty of feed for my dogs, and some accommodations for ourselves; but before my son got back, we had gone out hunting, and in a large cane brake my dogs found a big bear in a cane-house, which he had fixed for his winter-quarters, as they some times do.

When my lead dog found him, and raised the yell, all the rest broke to him, but none of them entered his house until we got up. I encouraged my dogs, and they knowed me so well, that I could have made them seize the old serpent himself, with all his horns and heads, and cloven foot and ugliness into the bargain, if he would only have come to light, so that they could have seen him. They bulged in, and in an instant the bear followed them out, and I told my friend to shoot him, as he was mighty wrathy to kill a bear. He did so, and killed him prime. We carried him to our camp, by which time my son had returned; and after we got our dinners we packed up, and cut for the house of my old friend, whose name was Davidson.

We got there, and staid with him that night; and the next morning having salted up our meat, we left it with him, and started to take a hunt between the Obion lake and the Red-foot lake; as there had been a dreadful hurricane, which passed between them, and I was sure there must be a heap of bears in the fallen timber. We had gone about five miles without seeing any sign at all; but at length we got on some high cony ridges, and, as we rode along, I saw a hole in a large black oak, and on examining more closely, I discovered that a bear had clomb the tree. I could see his tracks going up, but none coming down, and so I was sure he was in there. A person who is acquainted with bear-hunting, can tell easy enough when the varment is in the hollow; for as they go up they don't slip a bit, but as they come down they make long scratches with their nails.

My friend was a little ahead of me, but I called him back, and told him there was a bear in that tree, and I must have him out. So we lit from our horses, and I found a small tree which I thought I could fall so as to lodge against my bear tree, and we fell to work chopping it with our tomahawks. I intended, when we lodged the tree against the other, to let my little son go up, and look into the hole, for he could climb like a squirrel. We had chop'd on a little time and stop'd to rest, when I heard my dogs barking mighty severe at some distance from us, and I told my friend I knowed they had a bear, for it is the nature of a dog, when he finds you are hunting bears, to hunt for nothing else; he becomes fond of the meat, and considers other game as "not worth a notice," as old Johnson said of the devil.

We concluded to leave our tree a bit, and went to my dogs, and when we got there, sure enough they had an eternal great big fat bear up a tree, just ready for shooting. My friend again petitioned me for liberty to shoot this one also. I had a little rather not, as the bear was so big, but I couldn't refuse; and so he blazed away, and down came the old fellow like some great log had fell. I now missed one of my dogs, the same that I before spoke of as having treed the bear by himself sometime before, when I had started the three in the cane break. I told my friend that my missing dog had a bear somewhere, just as sure as fate; so I left them to butcher the one we had just killed, and I went up on a piece of high ground to listen for my dog. I heard him barking with all his might some distance off, and I pushed ahead for him.

My other dogs hearing him broke to him, and when I got there, sure enough again he had another bear ready treed; if he hadn't, I wish I may be shot. I fired on him, and brought him down; and then went back, and help'd finish butchering the one at which I had left my friend. We then packed both to our tree where we had left my boy. By this time, the little fellow had cut the tree down that we intended to lodge, but it fell the wrong way; he had then feather'd in on the big tree, to cut that, and had found that it was nothing but a shell on the outside, and all doted in the middle, as too many of our big men are in these days, having only an outside appearance. My friend and my son cut away on it, and I went off about a hundred yards with my dogs to keep them from running under the tree when it should fall. On looking back at the hole, I saw the bear's head out of it, looking down at them as they were cutting. I hollered to them to look up, and they did so; and McDaniel catched up his gun, but by this time the bear was out, and coming down the tree. He fired at it, and as soon as it touch'd ground the dogs were all round it, and they had a roll-and-tumble fight to the fact of the hill, where they stop'd him. I ran up, and putting my gun against the bear, fired and killed him. We now had three, and so we made our scaffold and salted them up.

In the morning I left my son at the camp, and we started on towards the harricane; and when we had went about a mile, we started a very large bear, but we got along mighty slow on account of the cracks in the earth occasioned by the earthquakes. We, however, made out to keep in hearing of the dogs for about three miles, and then we came to the harricane. Here we had to quit our horses, as old Nick himself couldn't have got through it without sneaking it along in the form that he put on, to make a fool of our old grandmother Eve. By this time several of my dogs had got tired and come back; but we went ahead on fact for some little time in the hurricane, when we met a bear coming straight to us, and not more than twenty or thirty yards off. I started my tired dogs after him, and McDaniel pursued them, and I went on to where my other dogs were. I had seen the track of the bear they were after, and I knowed he was a screamer. I followed on to about the middle of the harricane; but my dogs pursued him so close, that they made him climb an old stump about twenty feet high.

I got in shooting distance of him and fired, but I was all over in such a flutter from fatigue and running, that I couldn't hold steady; but, however, I broke his shoulder, and he fell. I run up and loaded my gun as quick as possible, and shot him again and killed him. When I went to take out my knife to butcher him, I I found I had lost it in coming through the harricane. The vines and briars was so thick that I would sometimes have to get down and crawl like a varment to get through at all; and a vine had, as I sup- posed, caught in the handle and pulled it out. While I was standing and studying what to do my friend came to me. He had followed my trail through the harricane, and had found my knife, which was mighty good news to me; as a hunter hates the worst in the world to lose a good dog, or any part of his hunting-tools. I now left McDaniel to butcher the bear, and I went after our horses, and brought them as near as the nature of case would allow. I then took our bags, and went back to where he was; and when we had skin'd the bear, we fleeced off the fat and carried it to our horses at several loads. We then packed it up on our horses, and had a heavy pack of it on each one. We now started and went on till about sunset, when I concluded we must be near our camp; so I hollered and my son answered me, and we moved on in the direction to the camp. We had gone but a little way when I heard my dogs make a warm start again; and I jumped down from my horse and gave him up to my friend, and told him I would follow them. He went on to the camp, and I went ahead after my dogs with all my might for a considerable distance, till at last night came on. The woods were very rough and hilly, and all covered over with cane.

I now was compel'd to move on more slowly; and was frequently falling over logs, and into the cracks made by the earthquakes, so that I was very much afraid I would break my gun. However I went on about three miles, when I came to a good big creek, which I waded. It was very cold, and the creek was about knee-deep; but I felt no great inconvenience from it just then, as I was all over wet with sweat from running, and I felt hot enough. After I got over this creek and out of the cane, which was very thick on all our creeks, I listened for my dogs. I found they had either treed or brought the bear to a stop, as they continued barking in the same place. I pushed on as near in the direction to the noise as I could, till I found the hill was too steep for me to climb, and so I backed and went down the creek some distance till I came to a hollow, and then took up that, till I come to a place where I could climb up the hill. It was mighty dark, and was difficult to see my way or anything else. When I got up the hill, I found I had passed the dogs; and so I turned and went to them. I found, when I got there, they had treed the bear in a large forked poplar, and it was setting in the fork.

I could see the lump, but not plain enough to shoot with any certainty, as there was no moonlight; and so I set in to hunting for some dry brush to make me a light; but I could find none, though I could find that the ground was torn mightily to pieces by the cracks.

At last I thought I could shoot by guess, and kill him; so I pointed as near the lump as I could, and fired away. But the bear didn't come, he only clomb up higher, and got out on a limb, which helped me to see him better. I now loaded up again and fired, but this time he didn't move at all. I commenced loading for a third fire, but the first thing I knowed, the bear was down among my dogs, and they were fighting all around me. I had my big butcher in my belt, and I had a pair of dressed buckskin breeches on. So I took out my knife, and stood, determined, if he should get hold of me, to defend myself in the best way I could. I stood there for some time, and could now and then see a white dog I had, but the rest of them, and the bear, which were dark coloured, I couldn't see at all, it was so miserable dark. They still fought around me, and sometimes within three feet of me; but, at last, the bear got down into one of the cracks, that the earthquakes had made in the ground, about four feet deep, and I could tell the biting end of him by the hollering of my dogs. So I took my gun and pushed the muzzle of it about, till I thought I had it against the main part of his body, and fired; but it happened to be only the fleshy part of his foreleg. With this, he jumped out of the crack, and he and the dogs had another hard fight around me, as before. At last, however, they forced him back into the crack again, as he was when I had shot.

I had laid down my gun in the dark, and I now began to hunt for it; and, while hunting, I got hold of a pole, and I concluded I would punch him awhile with that. I did so, and when I would punch him, the dogs would jump in on him, when he would bite them badly, and they would jump out again. I concluded, as he would take punching so patiently, it might be that he would lie still enough for me to get down in the crack, and feel slowly along till I could find the right place to give him a dig with my butcher. So I got down, and my dogs got in before him and kept his head towards them, till I got along easily up to him; and placing my hand on his rump, felt for his shoulder, just behind which I intended to stick him. I made a lounge with my long knife, and fortunately stock him right through the heart; at which he just sank down, and I crawled out in a hurry. In a little time my dogs all come out too, and seemed satisfied, which was the way they always had of telling me that they had finished him.

I suffered very much that night with cold, as my leather breeches, and every thing else I had on, was wet and frozen. But I managed to get my bear out of this crack after several hard trials, and so I butchered him, and laid down to try to sleep. But my fire was very bad, and I couldn't find any thing that would burn well to make it any better; and I concluded I should freeze, if I didn't warm myself in some way by exercise. So I got up, and hollered a while, and then I would just jump up and down with all my might, and throw myself into all sorts of motions. But all this wouldn't do; for my blood was now getting cold, and the chills coming all over me. I was so tired, too, that I could hardly walk; but I thought I would do the best I could to save my life, and then, if I died, nobody would be to blame. So I went to a tree about two feet through, and not a limb on it for thirty feet, and I would climb up it to the limbs, and then lock my arms together around it, and slide down to the bottom again. This would make the insides of my legs and arms feel mighty warm and good. I continued this till daylight in the morning, and how often I clomb up my tree and slid down I don't know, but I reckon at least a hundred times.

In the morning I got my bear hong up so as to be safe, and then set out to hunt for my camp. I found it after a while, and McDaniel and my son were very much rejoiced to see me get back, for they were about to give me up for lost. We got our breakfasts, and then secured our meat by building a high scaffold, and covering it over. We had no fear of its spoiling, for the weather was so cold that it couldn't.

We now started after my other bear, which had caused me so much trouble and suffering; and before we got him, we got a start after another, and took him also. We went on to the creek I had crossed the night before and camped, and then went to where my bear was, that I had killed in the crack. When we examined the place, McDaniel said he wouldn't have gone into it, as I did, for all the bears in the woods.

We took the meat down to our camp and salted it, and also the last one we had killed; intending, in the morning, to make a hunt in the harricane again.

We prepared for resting that night, and I can assure the reader I was in need of it. We had laid down by our fire, and about ten o'clock there came a most terrible earthquake, which shook the earth so, that we were rocked about like we had been in a cradle. We were very much alarmed; for though we were accustomed to feel earthquakes, we were now right in the region which had been torn to pieces by them in 1812, and we thought it might take a notion and swallow us up, like the big fish did Jonah.

In the morning we packed up and moved to the harricane, where we made another camp, and turned out that evening and killed a very large bear, which made eight we had now killed in this hunt.

The next morning we entered the harricane again, and in little or no time my dogs were in full cry. We pursued them, and soon came to a thick cane brake, in which they had stop'd their bear. We got up close to him, as the cane was so thick that we couldn't see more than a few feet. Here I made my friend hold the cane a little open with his gun till I shot the bear, which was a mighty large one. I killed him dead in his tracks. We got him out and butchered him, and in a little time started another and killed him, which now made ten we had killed; and we know'd we couldn't pack any more home, as we had only five horses along; therefore we returned to the camp and salted up all our meat, to be ready for a start homeward next morning.

The morning came, and we packed our horses with the meat, and had as much as they could possibly carry, and sure enough cut out for home. It was about thirty miles, and we reached home the second day. I had now accommodated my neighbour with meat enough to do him, and had killed in all, up to that time, fifty-eight bears, during the fall and winter.

As soon as the time come for them to quit their houses and come out again in the spring, I took a notion to hunt a little more, and in about one month I killed forty-seven more, which made one hundred and five bears I had killed in less than one year from that time.

*David Crockett, A Narrative of the Life of David Crockett of the State of Tennessee* (Philadelphia: E.L. Carey and A. Hart, 1834), 174–194.

# Index of Key Names

## T



## V



## W



## Z

# Selected Bibliography


### Newspapers

"A True Account of the Life and Surroundings of Davy Crockett as Viewed on the Grounds by an Enterprise Reporter." *Sheffield Daily Enterprise*, August 17, 1890.

Barry, Virginia. "On The Aisle With the Press." Asbury Park Press, May 23, 1948.

Armstrong, Zella. "Three Tennesseans Impeached." *Daily Times*, April 26, 1936.

"Carmen Perry Was One of a Kind." *Laredo Morning Times*, February 25, 2017.

"Col. Crockett Alive." *The Lorain Standard*, 09 June 9, 1840.

"Col. Crockett and his Course in Congress." *Southern Statesman*, May 14, 1831.

"Col. David Crockett." *York Gazette*, December 17, 1833, 2.

"Crockett's Death at Alamo Doubted." *The New York Times*, September 21, 1975.

"David Crockett's Family." *Spirit of the Times*, January 23, 1855.

Flanagan, Mike. "Kids Went Davy Crockett Crazy." *South Florida Sun Sentinel*, June 23, 1985.

Fund, John. "Davy Crockett, Libertarian." *Wall Street Journal*, April 12, 2004.

"Going! Going! Gone!" *North Carolina Spectator and Western Advertiser*, April 30, 1831.

Green, Robert. "Identity Crisis: David Crockett Tried to Trim his Myth, but it Grew Back." *The Texas Observer,* August *3, 2010.*

Johnson, Seale. "Doctor William Edward Butler, Founder of the City of Jackson." *The Jackson Sun*, September 16, 1943.

Jones, Cecil. "Crockett in Lawrence." *The Tennessean,* November 3, 1946.

Lewis, W. B. "General Jackson and Governor Shelby." *The Argus of Western America*, July 30, 1826.

"Letter from Major Jack Downing." *Southern Statesman*, September 1833.

Lind, Michael. "The Many David Crocketts." *The New York Times*, November 23, 1998.

"Olympic Theater." *The Morning Post*, August 11, 1979.

Thompson, Bob. "David Crockett, celebrity pioneer, went from wrestling bears to wrestling with his image." *Washington Post*. February 8, 2013.

### Books

Abernathy, Thomas P. *From Frontier to Plantation in Tennessee*. Chapel Hill: University of North Carolina Press, 1932.

Allen, Charles Fletcher. *David Crockett: Scout*. Philadelphia: J. B. Lippincott, 1911.

Arpad, Joseph, ed. "Introduction." In *A Narrative of the Life of David Crockett, by David Crockett*. New Haven, Conn.: College and University Press, 1972.

Arthur, John Preston. *Western North Carolina: A History*. Raleigh: Edwards & Broughton, 1914.

Bassham, Ben L. *Conrad Wise Chapman*. Kent, Ohio: The Kent State University Press, 1998.

Blair, Walter. *Davy Crockett, Legendary Frontier Hero: His True Life Story And the Fabulous Tall Tales Told About Him*. Springfield, Illinois: Lincoln-Herndon Press Inc., 1955.

Boylston, James and Allen Wiener. *David Crockett in Congress: the rise and fall of the poor man's friend: with collected correspondence, selected speeches and circulars*. Houston: Bright Sky Press, 2009.

Bumpers, Fuller L., Daniel F. Littlefield Jr., and Amanda L. Page. *Chickasaw Removal*. Ada, Oklahoma: Chickasaw Press, 2019.

Brooks, Van Wyck. *The World of Washington Irving*. New York: E. P. Dutton & Company, Inc., 1944.

Burke, James Wakefield. *Crockett, the Man Behind the Myth*. Burnet, Texas: Eakin Press, 1984.

Burrough, Bryan, Chris Tomlinson and Jason Stanford. *Forget the Alamo: The Rise and Fall of an American Myth*. New York: Penguin Press, 2021.

Chamberlain, Georgia Stamm. *Studies on John Gadsby Chapman, American Artist, 1808-1889*. Annandale, Virginia: The Turnpike Press, Inc., 1963.

Colyar, Arthur St. Clair., Haywood, John. *The Civil and Political History of the State of Tennessee: From Its Earliest Settlement Up to the Year 1796, Including the Boundaries of the State*. United States: Publishing House [of the] Methodist Episcopal Church, South, 1915.

Corlew, Robert. *Tennessee: A Short History*. 2nd ed. Knoxville: The University of Tennessee Press, 1990.

Cox, Mike. *Legends & Lore of the Texas Capitol*. Charleston: The History Press, 2017.

Crockett, David. A *Narrative of the Life of David Crockett of the State of Tennessee, Written by Himself*. Philadelphia: E. L. Carey and A. Hart, 1834.

———. 1786-1836. *An Account of Col. Crockett's Tour to the North And Down East: In the Year of Our Lord One Thousand Eight Hundred And Thirty-four*. Philadelphia: E. L. Carey and A. Hart, 1835.

———. *Address of Mr. Crockett, to the Voters of the Ninth Congressional District of the State of Tennessee; Together with His Remarks in the House of Representatives, January 5, 1829. Washington: Reprinted by Gales & Seaton, January 15, 1829*. Rare Books Division, Library of Congress.

———. *David Crockett's Circular*, February 28, 1831. Rare Books Division, Library of Congress.

———. *Davy Crockett and His Adventures in Texas Told Mostly by Himself*. New York: Charles Scribner's Sons, 1834.

Davis, James D. *History of Memphis: The History of the City of Memphis, Being a Compilation of the Most Important Documents And Historical Events Connected With the Purchase of Its T erritory, Laying Off of the City And Early Settlement*. Memphis, Tenn.: Hite, Crumpton & Kelly, 1873.

Davis, William. *Three Roads to the Alamo: the Lives and Fortunes of David Crockett, James Bowie, and William Barret Travis*. New York: Harper Collins Publishers, 1998.

De la Peña, José Enrique. *With Santa Anna in Texas: A Personal Narrative of the Revolution*. College Station, Texas: Texas A&M University Press, 1975.

Derr, Mark. *The Frontiersman: The Real Life and the Many Legends of Davy Crockett*. New York: William Morrow and Company, Inc., 1993.

Dorson, R. Mercer, *Davy Crockett, American Legend*. New York: Spiral Press for Rockland Editions, 1939.

Dykeman, Wilma. *Tennessee: A Bicentennial Year*. New York: A. A. Norton & Company, Inc., 1975.

Ellis, Edward Sylvester. *The Life of Colonel David Crockett: Comprising His Adventures as Backwoodsman And Hunter*. Philadelphia: Porter & Coates, 1884.

Featherstonehaugh, George William. *Excursion Through the Slave States, From Washington on the Potomac*. New York: Harper & Brothers, 1884.

Feldman, Jay. *When the Mississippi River Ran Backwards*. New York: Free Press, 2005.

Flint, Timothy, *A Condensed Geography and History of the United States*. Cincinnati: William A. Farnsworth, Printer, 1825.

Folmsbee, Stanley J. *A Narrative of the Life of David Crockett of the State of Tennessee by David Crockett, A Facsimile Edition with an Introduction and Annotations by James A. Shackford and Stanley J. Folmsbee*. Knoxville: University of Tennessee Press, 1973.

French, James Strange. *The Life and Adventures of Colonel David Crockett of West Tennessee*. New York: J. & J. Harper, 1833.

French, Janie Preston Collup and Zella Armstrong. *The Crockett Family and Connecting Lines*. Bristol, Tenn.: The King Printing Co., 1928.

Groneman, Bill. *David Crockett, Hero of the Common Man*. New York: A Tom Doherty Associates Book, 2005.

———. *Defense of a Legend, Crockett and the de la Peña Diary*. Plano, Texas: Republic of Texas Press, 1994.

Hall, Roger A. *Performing the American Frontier, 1870–1906*. New York: Cambridge University Press, 2001.

Hancock, Jonathan Todd. *Convulsed States*. Chapel Hill: The University of North Carolina Press, 2021.

Hauck, Richard Boyd. *Davy Crockett: A Handbook*. Lincoln and London: University of Nebraska Press, 1982.

Herron, Roy and L. H. Cotton Ivy. *Tennessee Political Humor*. Knoxville: The University of Tennessee Press, 2000.

Holt, Albert. *The Economic and Social Beginnings of Tennessee*. Nashville, 1923.

Hale, Duane K. and Arrell M. Gibson. *Indians of North America: The Chickasaw*. New York: Chelsea House Publishers, 1991.

Haley, James L. *Sam Houston*. Norman: University of Oklahoma Press, 2002.

Hall, Roger A. *Performing the American Frontier, 1870-1906*. New York: Cambridge University Press, 2001.

Hauck, Richard Boyd. *Crockett: A Bio-Bibliography*. Westport, Connecticut: Greenwood Press, 1982.

———. *Davy Crockett: A Handbook*. Lincoln: University of Nebraska Press, 1986.

Hayes, David G. *The Historic Reelfoot Lake Region*. Collierville, Tennessee: InstantPublisher.com, 2017.

Howe, Daniel Walker. *What Hath God Wrought: The Transformation of America, 1815-1848*. Oxford: Oxford University Press, 2007.

———. *The Political Culture of the American Whigs*. Chicago; London: University of Chicago Press, 1979.

Hutton, Lawrence. *Curiosities of the American Stage*. New York: Harper & Brothers, 1891.

Inskeep, Steve. *Jacksonland*. New York: Penguin Press, 2015.

James, Marquis. *The Life of Andrew Jackson*. Indianapolis: The Bobbs Merrell Company, 1938.

Jiji, Vera. *A Sourcebook of Interdisciplinary Materials in American Drama: J. K. Paulding, "The Lion of the West." Showcasing American Drama*. New York: City University of New York, 1983.

Jones, Kathryn E. *Crockett Cousins*. Graham, Texas: Self-published, 1984.

Karns, T. C. *Tennessee History Stories*. Atlanta: B. F. Johnson Printing Co., Inc., 1904.

Keating, John M. *History of the City of Memphis Tennessee: With Illustrations and Biographical Sketches of Some of Its Prominent Men and Pioneers*. Syracuse: D. Mason & Company, 1888.

Kilgore, Dan and James E. Crisp. *How did Davy Die? And Why Do We Care So Much?* College Station: Texas A&M University Press, 2010.

Levy, Buddy. *American Legend: The Real-Life Adventures of David Crockett*. New York: G. P. Putnam's Sons, 2005.

Lofaro, Michael A., J. B. Patterson, Timothy Flint, and Black Hawk. *Boone, Black Hawk, and Crockett in 1833: Unsettling the Mythic West*. Knoxville: The University of Tennessee Press, 2019.

———. *Crockett at Two Hundred: New Perspectives on the Man and the Myth*. Knoxville: The University of Tennessee Press, 1989.

———. ed. *Davy Crockett: The Man, the Legend, the Legacy, 1786–1986*. Knoxville: University of Tennessee Press, 1985.

Lofaro, Michael A. *The Tall Tales of Davy Crockett*. Knoxville: The University of Tennessee Press, 1987.

Lord, Walter. *A Time to Stand*. New York: Bonanza Books, 1987.

Marshall, E. H. *History of Obion County*. Union City, Tennessee: H. A. Lanzer Co. 1970.

McCormac, Eugene Irving. *James K. Polk, a Political Biography*. Berkeley: University of California Press, 1922.

Meacham, Jon. *American Lion: Andrew Jackson in the White House*. New York: Random House, 2008.

McIlwaine, Shields. *Memphis Down in Dixie*. New York: E. P. Dutton and Company, Inc., 1948.

Moore, Dr. Wayne C. "A History of Tennessee, The Land and Native People." *Tennessee Blue Book: A History of Tennessee - Student Edition*. Nashville: Tennessee State Library and Archives, 2017.

Morgan, Robert. *Lions of the West: Heroes and Villains of the Westward Expansion*. Chapel Hill: Algonquin Books of Chapel Hill, 2012.

Morphis, J. M. *History of Texas from its Discovery and Settlement*. New York: United States Publishing Company, 1875.

Opal, J. M. *Avenging the People, Andrew Jackson, the Rule of Law, and the American Nation*. New York: Oxford University Press, 2017.

Owens, Harry James, Franklin Julius Meine, and Davy Crockett. *The Crockett Almanacks*. Chicago: Caxton Club, 1955.

Parrington, Vernon Louis. *Main Currents in American Thought, The Romantic Revolution in America, 1800-1860*. New York: Harcourt, Brace, 1927.

———. *The Colonial Mind, 1620-1800*. New York: Harcourt, Brace and Company, 1927.

Parton, James. *Life of Andrew Jackson, Volume 1*. New York: Mason Brothers, 1860.

Paulding, William I. *Literary life of James K. Paulding*. New York: C. Scribner and Company. 1867.

Peña, José E, and Carmen Perry. *With Santa Anna in Texas: A Personal Narrative of the Revolution*. College Station: Texas A & M University Press, 1992.

Phelan, James. *History of Tennessee, The Making of a State*. Boston: Houghton, Mifflin and Company, 1888.

Poore, Benjamin Perley. *Perley's Reminiscences, Vol. 1-2 of Sixty Years in the National Metropolis*. Philadelphia: Hubbard Brothers Publishers, 1886.

Remini, Robert V. *Andrew Jackson*. New York: Harper Perennial, 1966.

Rickels, Milton and Patricia. *Seba Smith*. Boston: Twayne Publishers, 1977.

Roosevelt, Theodore and George Bird Grinnell. *The Book of the Boone and Crockett Club*. New York: Forest and Stream Publishing Co., 1901.

Rourke, Constance. *Davy Crockett*. New York: Harcourt Brace Jovanovich, Inc., 1934.

Schlesinger, Arthur M. Jr. *The Age of Jackson*. Boston: Little, Brown and Company, 1945.

Seale, William. *The Presidents House, A History, Vol 1.* Washington: White House Historical Association with the cooperation of the National Geographic Society, 1986.

Sealsfield, Charles. *The Americans as They Are.* London: Hurst, Chance & Co., 1828.

Seigenthaler, John. *James K. Polk.* New York: Henry Holt and Company, 2003.

Sellers, Charles Grier Jr. *The Southerner as American.* Chapel Hill: The University of North Carolina Press,1960.

———. *James K. Polk, Vol 1. Jacksonian.* London: Oxford University Press, 1957.

Shackford, James Atkins and John B. Shackford. *David Crockett: the Man and the Legend.* Chapel Hill: University of North Carolina Press, 1986.

———. and Stanley J. Folmsbee. *A Narrative of the Life of David Crockett of the State of Tennessee, Tennesseanna Editions.* Knoxville: The University of Tennessee Press, 1987.

Sloan, David W. and Lisa Mullikin Parcell, ed., *American Journalism: History, Principles, Practices.* Jefferson, North Carolina: McFarland & Company, Inc., 2002.

Smith, Jonathan Kennon. *Adam Rankin Alexander: a life sketch.* Memphis, Tenn.: J.K.T. Smith, 1992.

Sullivan, George. *Davy Crockett.* New York: Scholastic, Inc., 2001.

Thompson, Bob. *Born on a Mountaintop, on the Road with Davy Crockett and the Ghosts of the Wild Frontier.* New York: Crown Trade Group, 2012.

Thompson, Ernest T. *The Fabulous David Crockett: His Life and Times in Gibson County, Tenn. Including Tall Tales and Anecdotes of the Western Wilds.* Rutherford, Tennessee: David Crockett Memorial Association, 1956.

Tidwell, James E. *The Lion of the West, Retitled The Kentuckian, or a Trip to New York. A Farce in Two Acts by John Kirke Paulding, Revised by John Augustus Stone and William Bayle Bernard.* Stanford: Stanford University Press, 1954.

Timanus, Rod. *On the Crockett Trail.* Union City, Tennessee: Pioneer Press, 1999.

Trollope, Frances. *Domestic Manners of the Americans.* New York: Alfred A. Knopf, 1949.

Turnbow, Tony L. *Hardened to Hickory.* Nashville: Self-published, 2018.

Whisker, B. James. *The Rise and Decline of the American Militia System.* Selinsgrove, PA: Susquehanna University Press, 1999.

Wallis, Michael. *David Crockett, The Lion of the West.* New York: W. W. Norton & Company, 2011.

West, Carroll Van. *The Tennessee Encyclopedia of History and Culture.* Nashville: Tennessee Historical Society, 1998.

Wallace, Anthony F. C. *The Long Bitter Trail: Andrew Jackson and the Indians.* New York: Hill and Wang, 1993.

Ward, John William. *Andrew Jackson, Symbol for an Age.* New York: Oxford University Press, 1955.

Whisker, B. James. *The Rise and Decline of the American Militia System.* Selinsgrove, PA: Susquehanna University Press, 1999.

Williams, Samuel Cole. *Beginnings of West Tennessee, in the land of the Chickasaws, 1541-1841.* Johnson City, Tennessee: The Watauga Press, 1930.

**Periodicals**

Adkins, Nelson F. "James K. Paulding's Lion of The West." *American Literature* 3, no. 3 (1931): 249-58.

Albanese, Catherine L. "Savage, Sinner, and Saved: Davy Crockett, Camp Meetings, and the Wild Frontier." *American Quarterly* 33, no. 5 (1981): 482-501.

———. "King Crockett: Nature and Civility on the American Frontier." *Proceedings of the American Antiquarian Society* 88, pt. 2 (1979): 225-249.

———. "Citizen Crockett: Myth, History, and Nature Religion." *Soundings: An Interdisciplinary Journal* 61, no. 1 (1978): 87-104.

Axson, Stockton, 1867-1935. "Washington Irving and the Knickerbocker Group." *Rice Institute Pamphlet - Rice University Studies*, no. 2 (1933): 20.

Bederman, Gail. "Revisiting Nashoba: Slavery, Utopia, and Frances Wright in America, 1818-1826." *American Literary History*, 17, no. 3 (2005): 438-59.

Braden, Guy B. "The Colberts and the Chickasaw Nation." *Tennessee Historical Quarterly* 17, no. 3 (1958): 222-49.

Bruesch, S. R. "The Disasters and Epidemics of a River Town: Memphis, Tennessee, 1819-1879." *Bulletin of the Medical Library Association* vol. 40, 3 (1952): 288-305.

Bullock, Karen O'Dell. "Journey to Action: Exploring Davy Crockett's Baptist Family Ties." *Baptist Standard* (July 6, 2016): 56-58.

Clark, William Bedford. "Col. Crockett's Exploits and Adventures in Texas: Death and Transfiguration." *Studies in American Humor, New Series* 2, 1, no. 1 (1982): 66-76.

Crockett, David. Letters of David Crockett. *The American Historical Magazine*, 5 (1900): 41-47.

Crouthamel, James L. "Tocqueville's South." *Journal of the Early Republic* 2, no. 4 (1982): 381-401.

Davis, Curtis Carroll. "A Legend at Full-Length: Mr. Chapman Paints Colonel Crockett—and Tells About It." *Proceedings of the American Antiquarian Society* (April 1960), 155-174.

———. "Virginia's Unknown Novelist: The Career of J. S. French, a Southern Colonel of Parts." *The Virginia Magazine of History and Biography* 60, no. 4 (1952): 551-81.

Downing, Marvin. "Davy Crockett in Gibson County, Tennessee: A Century of Memories." *Tennessee Historical Quarterly*, no. 37 (1983): 54-61.

Durham, Walter T. "Noh-Noh-He-Tsu-Nageh and the Cherokee Removal." *Tennessee Historical Quarterly* 66, no. 3 (2007): 236-49.

Folmsbee, Stanley J. "David Crockett and West Tennessee." *Tennessee Historical Quarterly*, no. 5 (1974): 5-24.

Folmsbee, Stanley J. and Anna Grace Catron. "David Crockett in Texas." *The East Tennessee Historical Society's Publications* 30 (1958): 40-78.

———. and Anna Grace Catron. "The Early Career of David Crockett." *The East Tennessee Historical Society's Publications* 28 (1956): 58-85.

Gardner, John A. "Early Times in Weakley County: An Address." *The West Tennessee Historical Society Papers* 8 (1963): 69-85.

Gatell, Frank Otto. "Money and Party in Jacksonian America: A Quantitative Look at New York City's Men of Quality." *Political Science Quarterly* 82, no. 2 (1967): 235-52.

Gordon, Arthur. "Walt Disney." *LOOK*, 19.15, (July 26, 1955): 28-37.

Golden, Michael J. "The Dormant Second Amendment: Exploring the Rise, Fall, and Potential Resurrection of Independent State Militias." *William & Mary Bill of Rights Journal* 2, issue 4 (2013): 1021-1079.

Gresham, L. Paul. "The Public Career of Hugh Lawson White." *Tennessee Historical Quarterly* 3, no. 4 (1944): 291-318.

Grose, B. Donald. "Edwin Forrest, *Metamora*, and the Indian Removal Act of 1830." *Theatre Journal* 37, no. 2 (1985): 181-91.

Gunn, Brenda. "Davy Crockett is Dead, But How He Died Lives On." American Antiquarian Society (2006): 127-146.

Harlan, Louis R. "Public Career of William Berkeley Lewis." *Tennessee Historical Quarterly* 7, no. 1 (1948): 3-37.

Heale, M. J. "The Role of the Frontier in Jacksonian Politics: David Crockett and the Myth of the Self-Made Man." *The Western Historical Quarterly* 4, no. 4 (1973): 405-23.

Henry, Milton. "What Became of the Tennessee Whigs?" *Tennessee Historical Quarterly* 11, no. 1 (1952): 57-62.

Hoagland, H. E. "Early Transportation on the Mississippi." Journal of Political Economy 19, no. 2 (1911): 111-23.

Hoffman, Daniel G. "The Deaths and Three Resurrections of Davy Crockett." *The Antioch Review* 21, no. 1 (1961): 5-13.

Holladay, Robert. "Antebellum Tennessee Historiography: A Critical Appraisal." *Tennessee Historical Quarterly* 69, no. 3 (2010): 224-41.

Holmes, David and Ferris Samara. "Was the Wild Frontiersman a Prolific Penman? A Stylometric Investigation into the Works of Davy Crockett." *CHANCE*, 33:2 (2020): 7-18.

Humphreys, Cecil C., "The Formation of Reelfoot Lake and Consequent Land and Social Problems." *The West Tennessee Historical Society Papers*, no. 17 (1960): 32-73.

Hutton, Paul Andrew. "Davy Crockett, Still King of the Wild Frontier." *Texas Monthly* 14, (November 1986): 122-130, 244-248.

Hutton, Paul Andrew. "Davy Crocket, Hero or Hype?" *TexasMonthly* (November 1986).

———. Review of *How Did Davy Die? And Why Do We Care So Much?. Southwestern Historical Quarterly* 114, no. 4 (2011): 449-450.

Jarzombek, Michelle. "The Memphis-South Memphis Conflict, 1826-1850." *Tennessee Historical Quarterly* 41, no. 1 (1982): 23-36.

Jones, James P. "Audubon and the New Madrid Earthquake." *The Register of the Kentucky Historical Society* 67, no. 3 (1969): 191-96.

Jones, Jesse Aquillah. "Say It Ain't True, Davy! The Real David Crockett vs. The Backwoodsman in Us All." *Appalachian Journal* 15, no. 1 (1987): 45-51.

Jones, Thomas B. "The Public Lands of Tennessee." *Tennessee Historical Quarterly* 27, no. 1 (1968): 13-36.
Lake, Mary Daggett. "The Family of David Crockett in Texas." *Tennessee Historical Magazine* 3, no. 3 (1935): 174-78.

Lind, Michael. "The Death of David Crockett." *The Wilson Quarterly* (1976-) 22, no. 1 (1998): 50-57.

Loomis, C. Grant. "Davy Crockett Visits Boston." *The New England Quarterly* 20, no. 3 (1947): 396-400.

Mason, Melvin Rosser. "The Lion of the West: Satire on Davy Crockett and Frances Trollope." *The South Central Bulletin* 29, no. 4 (1969): 143-45.

Martin, S. "Interpreting *Metamora*: Nationalism, Theater, and Jacksonian Indian Policy." *Journal of the Early Republic*, (1999): 73-101.

McBride, Robert M. "David Crockett and His Memorials in Tennessee." *Tennessee Historical Quarterly* 26, no. 3 (1967): 219-39.

McKee, Matt. "Davy Crockett: The Man and the Legend." *Writing Ulster*, no. 5 (1998): 45-55.

Miles, Guy S. "David Crockett Evolves, 1821-1824." *American Quarterly* 8, no. 1 (1956): 53-60.

Mooney, Chase C. "The Political Career of Adam Huntsman." *Tennessee Historical Quarterly* 10, no. 2 (1951): 99-126.

Nelson, Wilbur A. "Reelfoot—An Earthquake Lake." *National Geographic* (January 1923): 94-114.

Osborn, George C. "Some Letters of William T. and Sarah Fitzgerald." *Tennessee Historical Quarterly* 6, no. 2 (1947): 179-85.

Parks, Norman L. "The Career of John Bell as Congressman from Tennessee, 1827-1841." Tennessee Historical Quarterly 1, no. 3 (1942): 229-49.

Paulsen, Barbara. "Say It Ain't So, Davy." *Texas Monthly* (November 1986): 129.

Roper, James E. "Marcus Winchester and the Earliest Years or Memphis." *Tennessee Historical Quarterly* 21, no. 4 (1962): 326-51.

———. "Marcus Winchester First Mayor of Memphis: His Later Years." *Tennessee Historical Quarterly*, no. 13 (1959): 5-37.

Rourke, Constance. "Davy Crockett: Forgotten Facts and Legends." *Southwest Review* 19, no. 2 (1934): 149-61.

Satz, Ronald N. "The Cherokee Trail of Tears: A Sesquicentennial Perspective." *The Georgia Historical Quarterly* 73, no. 3 (1989): 431-66.

Schroeder, John H. "Major Jack Downing and American Expansionism: Seba Smith's Political Satire, 1847-1856." *The New England Quarterly* 50, no. 2 (1977): 214-33.

Scruggs, Thomas E. "Davy Crockett and the Thieves of Jericho: An Analysis of the Shackford-Parrington Conspiracy Theory." *Journal of the Early Republic* 19, no. 3 (1999): 481-98.

Sellers, Charles G. "Banking and Politics in Jackson's Tennessee, 1817-1827," Mississippi Valley Historical Review, XLI, no. 1 (June, 1954), 61-84.

Sellers, Charles Grier. "Jackson Men with Feet of Clay." *The American Historical Review* 62, no. 3 (1957): 537-51.

Shackford, James Atkins. "David Crockett and North Carolina." *The North Carolina Historical Review* 28, no. 3 (1951): 298-315.

Shockley, Megan Taylor. "King of the Wild Frontier vs. King Andrew I Davy Crockett and the Election of 1831." *Tennessee Historical Quarterly* 56, no. 3 (1997): 158-69.

Smith-Rosenberg, Carroll. "Davey Crockett as Trickster: Pornography, Liminality and Symbolic Inversion in Victorian America." *Journal of Contemporary History* 17, no. 2 (1982): 325-50.

Stehle, Raymond Louis. ""Westward Ho!": The History of Leutze's Fresco in the Capitol." *Records of the Columbia Historical Society*, Washington, D.C. 60/62 (1960): 306-22.

Stiffler, Stuart A. "Davy Crockett: The Genesis of Heroic Myth." *Tennessee Historical Quarterly* 16, no. 2 (1957): 134-40.

Thruston, Gates P. "The Nashville Inn." *The American Historical Magazine and Tennessee Historical Society Quarterly* 7, no. 2 (1902): 174-77.

Turner, Frederick J. "The Colonization of the West, 1820-1830." *The American Historical \ Review*, Vol. 11, No. 2 (Jan., 1906): 303-327.

Underwood, Sharry. "Ballet Ballads." *Dance Chronicle* 9, no. 3 (1986): 279-327.

Valliere, Kenneth L. "Benjamin Currey, Tennessean Among the Cherokees: A Study of the Removal Policy of Andrew Jackson, Part I." *Tennessee Historical Quarterly* 41, no. 2 (1982): 140-58.

Van Atta, John R. ""A Lawless Rabble": Henry Clay and the Cultural Politics of Squatters' Rights, 1832-1841." *Journal of the Early Republic* 28, no. 3 (2008): 337-78.

Voss, Frederick S. "Portraying an American Original: The Likenesses of Davy Crockett." *The Southwestern Historical Quarterly* 91, no. 4 (1988): 457-82.

Vizetelly, Arthur. "Some Notable Dwarfs." The English Illustrated Magazine, v. 22 (1900): 487.

Wade, J. D. "The Authorship of David Crockett's Autobiography." *The Georgia Historical Quarterly* 6, no. 3 (1922): 265-68.

Weiss, Thomas. "Tourism in America before World War II." *The Journal of Economic History* 64, no. 2 (2004): 289-327.

Wells, Ann Harwell. "Lafayette in Nashville, 1825." *Tennessee Historical Quarterly* 34, no. 1 (1975): 19-31.

Williams, Emma Inman. "Letters of Adam Huntsman to James K. Polk." *Tennessee Historical Quarterly* 6, no. 4 (1947): 337-69.

**Online**

Baker, G. Carter. "John Patton Erwin." Nashville City Cemetery, (blog), http://the-nashvillecitycemetery.org/john_patton_erwin.pdf.

Blakemore, Eric. "Davy Crockett Was an Early PR Genius." History.com. (Aug. 7, 2017). https://www.history.com/news/davy-crockett-was-an-early-pr-genius.

Boylston, James R. "Not Yours to Give: a Fable Reexamined." Alamo Studies Forum. (April 17, 2010). https://alamostudies.proboards.com/thread/908.

Cox, Mike. "Davy's Widow Elizabeth Patton Crockett." Acton State Historic Site (blog), March 8, 2005, http://www.texasescapes.com/MikeCoxTexasTales/228-Davy-Crocketts-Widow-Elizabeth-Patton-Crockett.htm.

Falzone, Catherine. "Davy Crockett Almanacs." New York Historical Society Museum and Library, From the Stacks, (blog), June 19, 2012, https://blog.nyhistory.org/davy-crockett-almanacs/.

Hardin, Stephen L. "Lines in the Soil; Lines on the Soul: Myths, Fallacies, and Canards That Obscure the Battle of the Alamo." (blog), https://stephenlhardin.com/pdf/Archive.Lines.pdf.

Hutton, Paul Andrew. "Crockett and the Creek War: 'We Now Shot Them Like Dogs'." *HistoryNet*, (blog), December 2019, https://www.historynet.com/crockett-and-the-creek-war-we-now-shot-them-like-dogs.htm.

Matthews, Dylan. "Andrew Jackson was a slaver, ethnic cleanser, and tyrant. He deserves no place on our money." *Vox*. (April 20, 2016). https://www.vox.com/2016/4/20/11469514/andrew-jackson-indian-removal.

"Narrative of the Life of David Crockett of the State of Tennessee." American History Through Literature 1820-1870. Encyclopedia.com. (March 17, 2021). https://www.encyclopedia.com/arts/culture-magazines/narrative-life-david-crockett-state-tennessee.

Nobles, Gregory H. "Frederick Jackson Turner: Deposed King of The Wild Frontier." *Hayes Historical Journal* (blog), Winter 1993, https://www.rbhayes.org/research/hayes-historical-journal-frederick-jackson-turner-deposed-king-of-the-wild-frontier/.

Pinheiro, John C., Miller Center of Public Affairs, University of Virginia. "James K. Polk." Accessed June 24, 2021. https://millercenter.org/president/polk.

Selin, Shannon. "A Skeleton City: Washington DC in the 1820s." (blog), https://shannonselin.com/2017/03/washington-dc-1820s/.

"Walt and the King of the Wild Frontier." *The Walt Disney Family Museum* (blog). August 17, 2011, https://www.waltdisney.org/blog/walt-and-king-wild-frontier.

**Dissertations and Manuscripts**

Arpad, John Joseph. "David Crockett, An Original Eccentricity and Early American Character." PhD diss., Duke University, 1969.

Buss, M. T. Kato. "Cowboy Up: Evolution of the Frontier Hero in American Theater, 1872-1903." PhD diss., University of Oregon, 2012.

Call, Richard K. *The Journal of Governor Richard K. Call.* Call family and Brevard Family papers, State Library and Archives of Florida.

Catron, Anna Grace. "The Public Career of David Crockett." Master's thesis, The University of Tennessee, 1955.

Fieweger, Jack. "B'ars and Catamounts: A Study of Davy Crockett through Genre Medium." Honor's Thesis, University of Mississippi, 2021.

Jortner, Maura L. "Playing America on Nineteenth-Century Stages; or Jonathan in England and Jonathan at Home." PhD diss., University of Pittsburgh, 2005.

Smith, Jonathan Kennon Thompson. *The Land Holdings of Colonel David Crockett in West Tennessee*. Jackson, Tennessee: Self-published, 2003.

Smith, Aran Tyson. "The Bawdy Bluff: Prostitution in Memphis, Tennessee, 1820-1900." PhD diss., University of Mississippi, 2016.

Smith, Trevor Augustine. "Pioneers, Patriots, and Politicians: The Tennessee Militia System, 1772-1857." PhD diss., University of Tennessee – Knoxville, 2003.

Smithey, Emily Paige. "Transformation of Early Nineteenth Century Chickasaw Leadership Patterns, 1800-1845." PhD diss., University of Mississippi, 2014.

Stephens, Kyle Massey. "To the Indian Removal Act, 1814-1830." PhD diss., The University of Tennessee, Knoxville, 2013.

Tilly, Betty Baird. "Aspects of Social and Economic Life in West Tennessee Before the Civil War." PhD diss., Memphis State University, 1974.

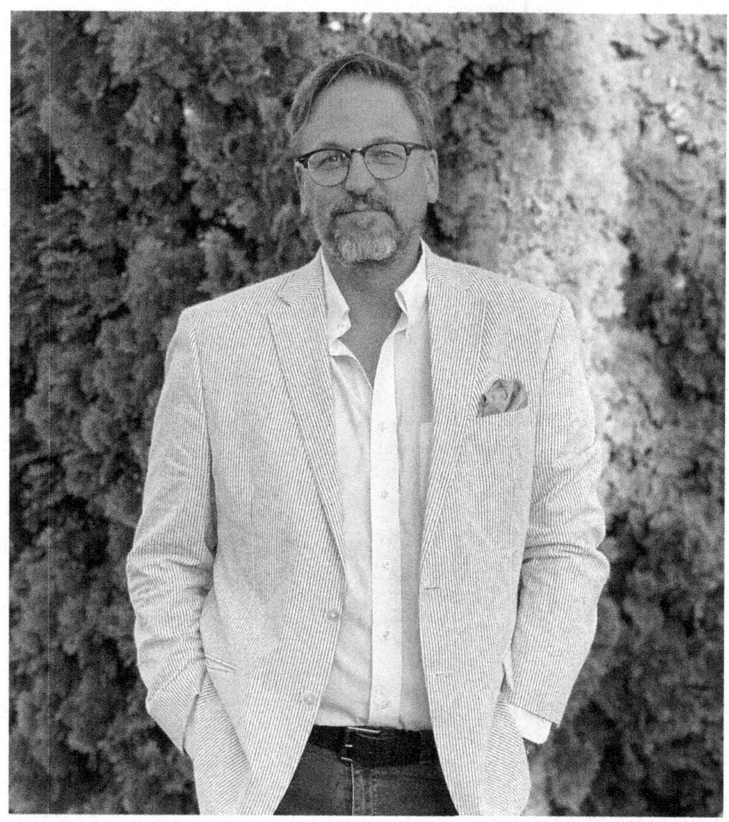

Scott Williams is the president and CEO of Discovery Park of America in Union City, Tennessee. He earned his degree in journalism from the University of Memphis, then held positions at advertising agencies and other Memphis organizations including Elvis Presley Enterprises, Inc. Before returning home to West Tennessee, he served as president and COO of the Newseum in Washington, D.C. His wife, Michelle, is a portrait artist and an art history instructor at the University of Tennessee at Martin, and they have two daughters, Alexandra and Olivia.

Every attempt was made to share this story of David Crockett's rise to fame as accurately as possible. Should you find any factual errors, please let the author know at rscottwilliamsemail@gmail.com. Corrections can be made for future printings.

If you enjoyed this book, please consider leaving a positive review on Amazon.com and, as David Crockett said, "go ahead" and share with friends and family.

TheRealDavidCrockett.com

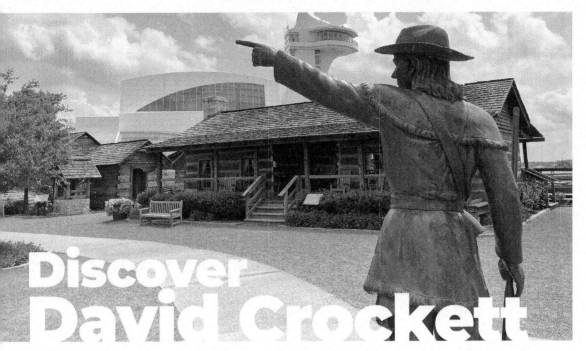

Made in the USA
Coppell, TX
21 December 2021